Capital Campaigns from the Ground Up

Capital Campaigns from the Ground Up

How Nonprofits Can Have the
Buildings of Their Dreams

STANLEY WEINSTEIN, ACFRE

WILEY

John Wiley & Sons, Inc.

For general information on our other products and services, or technical support, please contact our
Customer Care Department within the United States at 800-762-2974, outside the United States at
317-572-3993, or fax 317-572-4002.

Wiley also publishes its books in a variety of electronic formats. Some content that appears in print
may not be available in electronic books.

For more information about Wiley products, visit our web site at www.wiley.com.

Library of Congress Cataloging-in-Publication Data

Weinstein, Stanley, 1943–
  Capital campaigns from the ground up : how nonprofits can have the buildings of their dreams /
Stanley Weinstein.
      p.   cm.
  Includes index.
    ISBN 0-471-22079-5 (cloth)
  1. Nonprofit organizations—United States—Finance. 2. Public buildings—United States—
Finance. 3. Fund raising—United States. 4. Project management—United States. 5. Public-
private sector cooperation—United States. I. Title: Nonprofits can have the buildings of their
dreams. II. Title.
    HG4027.65.W45   2003
    658.15'224—dc22   2003015162

10 9 8 7 6 5 4 3 2 1

To the board members, volunteers, CEOs, executive directors, directors of development, fundraising consultants, architects, and builders who manifest their care, concern, and compassion for their neighbors and world through the buildings they create and services they provide.

Contents

Preface

Many nonprofit organizations have an urgent need for significant building projects. Yet, the process—from design through construction—seems daunting. The planning must encompass a thoughtful design phase to assure that the capital facilities truly meet the needs of the nonprofit organization and the people it serves. At the same time, the nonprofit must plan for a successful capital campaign. Prospective supporters must be identified, cultivated, and well informed about the project.

Nonprofit executives and board members want to assure that the building suits the organization's needs for years to come. They also want to be sure that the project's budget is realistic. The capital fundraising goal must be attainable. And the organization must develop the skills and resources needed to assure a successful capital campaign.

All of this takes a great deal of coordination and forethought.

Capital Campaigns from the Ground Up is based on years of experience. And for the first time, leaders in the fields of architecture and resource development have teamed together to create a book that discusses the best ways to keep the building planning and construction well synchronized and coordinated with the fundraising program.

Readers of this visionary, yet practical, book will learn how to plan and execute a successful building project and conduct a successful capital campaign. Our nation's leading experts share their experience and advice. As important, you will learn practical steps to take now to assure the success of your capital project.

Senior-level development professionals will appreciate the new approach suggested by *Capital Campaigns from the Ground Up*. These professionals will also welcome this book's holistic view, which combines project planning, strategic thinking, and resource development.

New development staff and middle-level managers will appreciate this book's practical advice concerning preparation for a capital campaign.

Nonprofit CEOs, many of whom have direct fundraising responsibilities, will find that *Capital Campaigns from the Ground Up* strengthens their general knowledge of project planning and capital campaigns.

Board leaders, community activists, and volunteers with fundraising responsibilities—especially those associated with nonprofits contemplating capital projects—will appreciate the advice to keep the fundraising potential in synch with the project costs. The book also provides them with a firm knowledge of fundraising principles and practices, facility planning, and capital fundraising. This background will enable board members to establish effective resource development policies, plan a visionary project, and evaluate strategic direction.

Architects, especially those working with, or considering working with, non-profit organizations, will gain a knowledge of fundraising principles and concerns of nonprofit institutions. Architects can help their clients and potential clients understand project costs, as well as ways of estimating the organization's fundraising potential. They will also gain practical information from across a broad spectrum of nonprofit building projects.

A central thesis of *Capital Campaigns from the Ground Up* is that, as early as possible, nonprofit leaders need to gain a firm grasp of the investment needed to design, build, and furnish their dream facilities. At the same time, they must understand their current fundraising potential and begin to take the steps needed to increase that potential to match the capital project goal.

So this is more than a how-to book. *Capital Campaigns from the Ground Up* was written to give you all the tools you need to succeed—and to inspire you to create visionary projects that respond to the most urgent community needs and human aspirations.

Stanley Weinstein, ACFRE
Albuquerque, New Mexico

Publisher's Note:
As an added bonus, there is a web site associated with this book. Readers can access the site at:

www.wiley.com/go/capitalcampaigns

The web site includes a wide variety of color photos depicting examples of the architectural styles and concepts discussed in this book.

Acknowledgments

$\mathbf{M}$ any authors begin their acknowledgments by thanking their wives. Certainly, my wife, Jan, deserves the greatest measure of my love and gratitude. Not only was she a source of personal support during the writing process, she also helped by suggesting clear language, providing expert advice concerning data management for capital campaigns, preparing the manuscript, and organizing the exhibits. Suffice to say, a great deal of this activity took place at odd hours—although any errors due to sleep deprivation are mine alone.

The reader can also appreciate how much I owe to the contributors to *Capital Campaigns from the Ground Up*. Please take the time to read about them in the Contributors section. Howard Mock of the Jaynes Corporation also helped shape a great deal of my thinking on the subjects covered in this book. His construction expertise, combined with his exemplary volunteer service to several nonprofit organizations during capital campaigns, qualifies him as one with a singular perspective. He knows how to get the greatest value for the nonprofit organization's construction investment. He also knows how to motivate others to volunteer and contribute.

Many colleagues and fellow professionals also helped shape my ideas concerning prospect research, nurturing positive relationships, and capital campaigns. Foremost among these are Lona Farr, Bruce Flessner, David Dunlop, Bobbie Strand, W.D. Broadway, and Susan Duncan Thomas. Countless presenters at AFP International Conferences also contributed immeasurably to my thinking.

Let me also express thanks to the people and institutions who graciously granted permission to use their materials and ideas. Of course, special thanks also goes to the team at John Wiley & Sons, Inc. Susan McDermott, Rose Sullivan, and Kerstin Nasdeo were a delight to work with. (They even let me end some sentences with prepositions.) I am most appreciative of their good humor, encouragement, and sound advice.

Finally, I would be remiss if I did not thank two people who continue to have an enormous impact on my life: Denkyo Kyozan Joshu Roshi, a 97-year-old Zen Master, and Seiju Bob Mammoser. Their lives embody a devotion to selfless service that can serve as a model for all who work in the nonprofit sector.

About
the Author

Stanley Weinstein, ACFRE, has spent 34 years in the nonprofit sector. He served for nine years on the AFP's National Board of Directors. Stanley received his Executive MBA from the University of New Mexico. As a distinguished consultant and founder of Stanley Weinstein & Co., he has provided services and hands-on fundraising help for more than 250 nonprofit organizations nationwide. Mr. Weinstein's capital campaigns have resulted in numerous major and lead gifts ranging from $50,000 to $50 million. His experience includes strategic planning, board development, planned giving, and capital campaigns for a broad spectrum of social welfare, healthcare, arts, religious, and educational institutions.

Contributors

Dale R. Dekker, AIA, AICP, ASID, Principal, Dekker/Perich/Sabatini in Albuquerque, New Mexico, and Las Vegas, Nevada, has served as a board member for numerous nonprofit organizations. He has also co-chaired committees in support of Albuquerque Public Schools Mill Levy and Bond Elections. Dale is a registered architect in seven states and is NCARB certified. He is also a certified planner and licensed interior designer. For three consecutive years, Dekker/Perich/Sabatini has been ranked among the 50 fastest-growing design and engineering consulting firms in the United States. Dekker/Perich/Sabatini was awarded the 2002 Firm Award for the Western Mountain Region by the American Institute of Architects (AIA). The firm combines 42 years of experience, successfully completing more than 2,000 projects valued in excess of $750 million and earning more than 75 design awards.

Mark Thaler, AIA, Principal, Einhorn Yaffee Prescott Architecture & Engineering, P.C., has focused his professional architecture career over the past 19 years on the preservation, renovation, and adaptive use of historic structures. He is the leader of the firm's Historic Preservation Group. He is experienced in existing conditions analysis, historic research, preparation of grant and national register applications, and materials conservation. Mark is a member of the National Trust of Historic Preservation, the Association for Preservation Technology, and the American Institute of Architects. His career has involved working on historic structures across the nation. Mr. Thaler's recent project to restore Montezuma Castle, in Montezuma, New Mexico, has been the recipient of numerous awards.

Charles B. Thomsen, FAIA, FCMAA, Chairman, 3D/International, Houston, Texas, has worked on hundreds of projects in most states and in 22 countries. One of Chuck's projects set the record for the world's largest lump sum bid. He has experience in nearly every form of project delivery. He is also the author of *CM: Developing, Marketing & Delivering Construction Management Services* (McGraw-Hill, 1982), and *Managing Brainpower: Organizing, Measuring Performance, and Selling in Architecture, Engineering, and Construction Management*

Companies (AIA Press, 1989). Downloadable articles concerning "Project Delivery Strategy," "Construction Project Management Controls," "Building Community Support to Fund School Construction," "CM at Risk," "Bridging," "How Much Does a Program Manager Cost?", and others are available at the 3D/International, Inc. Web site, www.3di.com. Chuck is the only person to be made a Fellow in both the American Institute of Architects (AIA) and a Fellow in the Construction Management Association of America (CMAA).

Robert D. Habiger, AIA, President of R.D. Habiger & Associates, Inc., located in Albuquerque, New Mexico, has a Masters of Architecture degree from Kansas State University. He worked on his first church project in 1969 and has specialized in the design of churches since 1981. Robert is a registered architect in Colorado, New Mexico, Texas, and Kansas. His firm specializes in ecclesiastical-related design projects as a liturgical consultant working with church communities, pastoral teams, and architects. The focus of R.D. Habiger & Associates, Inc. is how people experience liturgical spaces and how these environments affect the quality of worship and devotion. Approximately 60 percent of the firm's work is with Roman Catholic churches; the remainder is with other denominations.

Patricia Branda, MPA, is a past President of the Albuquerque Public Schools (APS) Board of Education.

Dennis Stefanacci, ACFRE, is the Founding Principal of Dennis Stefanacci and Associates, a consulting firm that specializes in developing comprehensive external relations programs for nonprofit organizations. Dennis has been in the development profession for nearly 30 years. He is known for his work in the areas of major gifts, planned gifts, and capital campaigns. In 1996 Dennis was selected as the Association of Fundraising Professionals' National Fund Raising Executive of the Year.

Capital
Campaigns
from the
Ground Up

CHAPTER 1

Coordinating Project Planning and Fundraising Planning

One of the marvels of human nature is the ability to turn an idea into something tangible. I once asked an executive with General Mills if he had been consulted on plant design prior to construction of the plant he managed. He replied, "The first time I saw this plant, it was a piece of blank paper on my desk."

Many in the nonprofit world are confronted with this same piece of blank paper. But they may not yet be aware of the challenge they face in planning and creating facilities that meet vital community needs.

What are the signs that such a challenge is arising? At first, one often senses an unarticulated need. Later, staff or board members might be heard to say, "I'm not sure this place works. We don't have enough administrative space, and the people we serve deserve better facilities." At times, a visionary leader—whether a CEO, board chair, or other strong advocate for the institution—articulates the need before it becomes apparent to others.

In other circumstances, the need for new facilities is thrust upon the nonprofit organization. Perhaps a long-term favorable lease is scheduled to expire and will not be renewed. In such a situation, board members and key staff may conclude that they have no choice other than to purchase a site and build facilities that enable the organization to carry out its mission.

In still other cases, the need for buildings and facilities might be identified during a strategic planning process. As nonprofit leaders examine their strengths and weaknesses, as well as external opportunities and threats, it is not uncommon to conclude that the organization needs dramatically expanded or enhanced capital resources—buildings, facilities, technology, and equipment—to remain responsive to pressing societal needs.

To attract and retain motivated physicians and caring staff, healthcare institutions need state-of-the-art facilities and equipment. Spiritual leaders recognize that well-designed sacred spaces are conducive to peace, worship, and celebration. Music, dance, and theater organizations call out for special facilities that invite audiences to fully experience the performing arts. To interpret the human condition, museums create appealing environments and attractive exhibits. Youth organizations as well as sports and recreation service providers create a wide range of facilities that engage the next generation of community leaders in positive, character-shaping activities. Similarly, as our population ages, many institutions work to create programs and facilities that sustain each senior's vitality, dignity, and sense of purpose.

IMPORTANCE OF EARLY PREPARATION

As soon as leaders of the nonprofit institution realize that new buildings or facilities may be required, the leaders should also begin thinking about potential sources of funding for the project. In many cases, this means preparation for a capital campaign.

You should not underestimate the amount of time and energy needed to set the stage for a successful capital campaign. For that matter, you should not underestimate the focus and wisdom needed to design and construct buildings that truly meet the needs of the organization and the people it serves.

It is easy to understand the need for timely preparation. Just contemplate the amount of time it takes to bring the board along to the point at which members feel comfortable going ahead with a capital campaign and implementing a building project. Also consider the number of steps required to translate a general sense of need into a set of architectural plans and drawings—followed by the actual construction of bricks and mortar. Are the board and staff really comfortable signing architect's agreements or building contracts before the funding is secured?

With this latter question in mind, consider the following: From the time a potential lead gift donor hears about or perceives the need for a new facility through the initial pledge or commitment to the actual first pledge payment, 19 months will have elapsed. In other words, don't think for a minute that you can have your groundbreaking and *then* secure six- or seven-figure commitments prior to building completion. Rather, individual major gift donors, foundation decision makers, and other potential supporters should be engaged and involved well before the planning is complete for the project. In this way nonprofit leaders can assure that those who will be called upon to help fund the project have been given the greatest opportunity to contemplate their role, offer advice, and attain a sense of "buy-in."

STRATEGIC THINKING: MEETING VITAL COMMUNITY NEEDS

Prior to investing the time and financial resources needed to create new or renovated facilities, it is prudent for the nonprofit organization to closely examine its strategic outlook. Key questions include:

- What are our organization's core competencies?
- What changes are taking place in our constituents' lives?
- What demographic changes are taking place?
- Whom do we serve?
- How can we better serve them?
- What will our staffing requirements be five years from now? In 10 years?
- How will our programs and services change in the years to come?
- What can we do to become known as leaders in our field?
- What facilities do we need to maximize staff effectiveness?
- Where should we be located?
- What facilities do we need to better serve our constituents?
- What should our facilities say about our organization?
- What look and feel should our facilities have to make our constituents know they are welcome and invited?

The earliest stages of facility planning are best devoted to strategic thinking. Later, you can refine your plans and address more tactical issues.

From the earliest stages, it is most helpful to begin getting a handle on the size and nature of the building or buildings contemplated. This will help nonprofit leaders to develop useful ballpark estimates of the potential costs. Chapter 4 will help you refine these expense estimates.

STRATEGIC THINKING: MEETING DONOR NEEDS

It is not enough to confine your early planning to facility needs. Rather, it makes sense to begin thinking about what motivates donors and prospective donors. A small number of people don't seem to have a philanthropic bone in their bodies. However, there are countless individuals, corporate decision makers, and foundation officers who gladly donate generously when asked to make a positive difference in people's lives. There are times when they donate out of respect for the volunteer requesting the commitment. There are also occasions when donors give out of a sense of enlightened self-interest—as when a book publisher donates to a literacy program. Often the rationale for the pledge or contribution is a profound belief that the donor has been blessed in some way and feels a deep need to "give something back." Some donate due to strong philanthropic beliefs. All want to give to organizations they trust to use their resources wisely.

From the earliest stages of capital project planning, the organization's leaders must begin to identify those specific decision makers and affluent individuals most likely to develop an interest in the project. The organization must also begin to think about ways of approaching and engaging each prospective pace-setting supporter. In most campaigns one-third to one-half of all the funds donated to a capital campaign will come from the top 10 donors. With this in mind, you can readily see how important it is to nurture positive relationships with your best prospects as soon as possible.

PREREQUISITES FOR CAPITAL FUNDRAISING SUCCESS

The twenty-first century continues to be a period of intense competition for philanthropic support. To conduct a successful capital campaign, the nonprofit organization must convince its constituents that the project is worthy of support. The plan must be visionary. Donors must also have confidence that the budget is realistic.

Experienced fundraising professionals focus on seven prerequisites for a successful capital campaign:

1. The nonprofit must have a positive image. The organization should be recognized as a leader in providing valuable programs and services to its constituents. Potential supporters must have *confidence* in the institution.

2. The need for the capital project must be well articulated. The *case for support* for the campaign must be *understood and accepted*—especially by potential pacesetting donors.

3. The organization must have identified and nurtured positive relationships with potential donors who have the *capability and willingness* to support the campaign at pacesetting levels.

4. The nonprofit must attract *strong volunteer leadership.* The campaign organization will require enthusiastic and generous leaders and volunteers—people who have peer relationships with potential top donors.

5. The philanthropic *environment and timing* must be right.

6. The campaign must be well organized and staffed with individuals *capable of undertaking* and supporting a major project initiative and fundraising campaign.

7. The board of directors must have a sufficient number of members who are influential in the community. Additionally, advisory and governing board members *must be enthusiastic supporters* of the organization's capital campaign aspirations.

Often, organizations begin their capital project planning prior to having the seven prerequisites well established. It is helpful to remind yourself of these key success factors as early as possible. Stephen R. Covey in his book, *Seven Habits of Highly Effective People* (Simon and Schuster, 1989), reminds us to "Be proactive" and "Begin with the end in mind."

Be honest. How does your organization rate? Is your organization well respected? Is the need for new facilities well established and understood? Have you begun to identify and involve your top prospects? Have you begun to nurture relationships with potential affluent and influential volunteers? Are you aware of your region's economic conditions and competing campaigns? Do you have strong development staff, record-keeping, and fundraising systems in place? Is your board composed of a sufficient number of well-established community leaders who are committed to the project?

With these questions in mind, begin to think about and implement the steps you can take to strengthen your organization. This book will give you lots of ideas about the specific ways you can pave the way for a successful building project and capital campaign.

PREREQUISITES FOR FACILITY PLANNING SUCCESS

When contemplating your organization's facility and building needs—and later when interviewing architects—keep the following seven points in mind:

The building and facilities must be sufficient for years to come. The organization must understand the space requirements related to its current and projected services. The organization must also project the space, equipment, and technology needs of current and future staff.

Later, we will take a more in-depth look at facility planning. Even if the organization is planning to build in phases, wisdom dictates that planners take a broad look at the organization's evolving facility needs. Some needs are obvious. Healthcare institutions need adequate research and clinical space. Churches, synagogues, and mosques must create sacred spaces adequate for the congregation. Educational institutions need adequate sports and recreation facilities, as well as classrooms, research facilities, and community buildings. Arts institutions need studio and performance spaces. Museums need exhibit and interpretive facilities.

Some space requirements are easier to underestimate. Entrances and public gathering spaces add to the facility's aesthetics and usefulness. When less-experienced planners make their preliminary estimates of total square footage, they sometimes fail to allow enough space for the building's hallways and infrastructure. Thought should be given to growth of staff and future administrative needs. And one should not underestimate the value of flexible multiuse rooms and meeting spaces.

The organization must have a firm grasp of the total capital project budget. Once the organization gains a sense of its total needs and related square footage, planners can begin getting rough estimates of project costs. Begin this process as soon as possible. Confer with architects, builders, real estate developers, and others to refine your projections. Total projected costs may include any or all of the following: strategic planning, facility planning, architectural designs, legal fees, traffic assessments, engineering drawings and schematics, fundraising preparation and precampaign planning study, capital campaign support, land purchase, building purchase, renovation, site preparation, new construction, moving costs, lease adjustments, furnishing and interiors, insurance, interest and other carrying costs, and other expenses unique to each organization's circumstances.

Aesthetics matter. The interplay of space and light must be well planned and well executed. This may not be your earliest concern. However, when choosing an architect, look carefully at the individual or firm's body of work. During interviews, listen carefully for a well-articulated philosophy. Choose wisely.

The building must be consistent with the organization's image and mission. Organizations that present themselves as "world-class" institutions often have first-rate facilities that reinforce their message. Organizations that serve the poor strive to have attractive—but more modest—facilities that indicate their concern for their clients. All strive for a sense of appropriateness. All deserve well-designed, safe, comfortable, and functional facilities. Many planners, architects, and builders believe that special care and attention must be given to entrances, lobbies, and public spaces.

The facilities must fit or complement the surrounding space and environment. Again, this might not be one of your organization's earliest concerns. Still, these are most important considerations when choosing architects and when dealing with neighbors or community representatives. Early planning for traffic control, environmental impact, parking, and communication with neighborhood groups pays huge dividends. Suitable materials, landscaping, engineering, orientation, as well as interaction with surrounding buildings and the environment are all vital concerns that help create truly great buildings and facilities.

The architect must understand and share the values of the organization. Representatives of the nonprofit best understand how the organization interacts with the people it serves. For example, an agency that provides counseling or support services for grieving children might want to create a warm homelike setting. The organization can save time and energy—and avoid a great deal of vexation of spirit—by engaging the services of an architect who is interested in creating an inviting and familiar setting. To be sure, the organization does not want to be presented with one, let alone 10 sets of "institutional" drawings.

The architect must develop a strong and positive relationship with the builder. Everything seems to go smoother when the nonprofit organization works with an experienced architect who has a good relationship with the construction company.

WHAT TO KNOW FROM THE "GET GO"

In addition to the points just delineated, you also need to be aware of the issues described in the following sections.

Building and Facility Planning Options

Your organization has many building and facility planning options. Nonprofits have many choices to make relative to their facility needs. The organization can choose to "make do" in its current facilities. The organization might decide to renovate and even expand its current home. The institution might determine that acquiring land and building new facilities is the best way to assure its future. The nonprofit might choose to look for existing facilities to purchase and renovate. Or the organization might want to examine several locations. On top of all that, nonprofit leaders will want to explore different options concerning the fundraising goal relative to the amount of long-term debt, if any, the organization is willing to assume.

To thoughtfully study these complex options, a nonprofit board can establish a facility planning committee. The sample job description (see Exhibit 1.1) will give you a good sense of this committee's responsibilities.

The Importance of Lead Gifts

Capital campaigns need pacesetting lead gifts to succeed. Old hands at capital campaigns recognize what they call the "Rule of Thirds." One-third of all the funds

EXHIBIT 1.1   FACILITY PLANNING COMMITTEE
JOB DESCRIPTION

XYZ NONPROFIT ORGANIZATION

Facility Planning Committee
Job Description

Overview:
The Facility Planning Committee will study XYZ Nonprofit Organization's short and long-term facility needs and make recommendations to the Board of Directors concerning each potential facility solution, estimated costs, potential sources of funding, pros and cons of each potential solution, and a recommended course of action.

Time Commitment:
The committee will meet once a month for six months. Each meeting will last approximately $1\frac{1}{2}$ hours.

Committee Composition:
Approximately seven members total, composed of members of the Board of Directors together with other community leaders. This Facility Planning Committee is composed of people who have experience and knowledge of facility planning, real estate, finance, and related topics. Experience with government funding and/or capital fundraising not necessary but a plus. The Committee will be supported by XYZ Nonprofit's staff.

**Facility Planning Committee
Responsibilities:**

✓ Seek to understand strengths and weaknesses of XYZ's current facilities. Estimate the amount of space and facility requirements needed to accommodate XYZ's staff and constituent services in future years. Understand XYZ's strategic long-term facility requirements.

✓ Identify facility solution options. Make at least a preliminary assessment of each of the following options: reconfigure, renovate, enhance, and/or expand current facilities; evaluate possibility of purchasing and renovating existing facilities in the region to be served—examine at least three sites that might best meet XYZ's needs; purchase land and construct new facilities—obtain preliminary total project cost estimates; if needed, examine accomplishing work with phases or staggered elements of a master site plan; and any combination of the first four options.

✓ Seek pro bono preliminary advice from architects, facility planners, and construction company executives concerning XYZ Nonprofit's needs and options. Seek preliminary advice from staff, consultants, community leaders, and others concerning potential sources of funding.

✓ Make periodic reports to the Board of Directors concerning options under consideration. Recommend a specific course of action to the Board—including when to engage architectural and capital campaign support services.

raised will come from the top 10 donors. One-third comes from the next 100 donors. And the remaining third comes from all the other donors combined.

In recent years however, capital campaign results have been even more skewed toward top donors. Frequently, the top 10 contributors donate one-half or more of the campaign total. The next 100 donors might pledge and contribute one-third of the total. Thus, the remaining 10 percent to 20 percent might come from the rest of the capital campaign prospect pool.

At times, it is even wise to look for what has been called the "special distribution capital campaign." In such cases, the organization may not have a large number of affluent supporters but does have several of extraordinary wealth. By engaging these special supporters, the final results of the capital campaign might reveal that one or two individuals donated well over half of the total raised.

In most capital campaigns, the largest single commitment accounts for at least 10 percent to 20 percent of the total raised. Church and synagogue campaigns may not be as top-heavy. In those campaigns, we frequently see 50 percent of the campaign total coming from the top 10 percent to 15 percent of the participating households—rather than the top 10 individual gifts or pledges. Exhibits 1.2 through 1.10 will give you a good sense of the level of contributions needed for success. Look at each gift pyramid carefully; each has variations based on the size of the prospect pool and the level of lead gift available. Exhibit 1.11, from Marilyn Bancel's book, *Preparing Your Capital Campaign* (Jossey-Bass, 2000), is a useful tool for creating a gift pyramid for your organization and relating that pyramid to the number of prospects needed to succeed. Bancel's "Campaign Gift Table (Pyramid)" is an illustration of a traditional campaign model.

EXHIBIT 1.2   SMALL CONSTITUENCY, $1 MILLION GIFT PYRAMID

STANDARD OF INVESTMENTS NECESSARY TO ACHIEVE $1 MILLION GOAL

Number of Gifts Required	Investment Level Three-Year Pledge Period	Annual Amount	Value
1	$150,000	$50,000	$150,000
2	75,000	25,000	150,000
3	50,000	16,667	150,000
4	30,000	10,000	120,000
8	15,000	5,000	120,000
14	7,500	2,500	105,000
17	5,000	1,667	85,000
25	3,000	1,000	75,000
30	1,500	500	45,000
104			**$1,000,000**

EXHIBIT 1.3   SMALL CONSTITUENCY,
$ 2 MILLION GIFT PYRAMID

STANDARD OF INVESTMENTS NECESSARY TO ACHIEVE $2 MILLION GOAL

Number of Gifts Required	Investment Level Three-Year Pledge Period	Annual Amount	Value
1	$300,000	$100,000	$300,000
2	150,000	50,000	300,000
3	75,000	25,000	225,000
5	50,000	16,667	250,000
9	30,000	10,000	270,000
15	15,000	5,000	225,000
20	7,500	2,500	150,000
26	5,000	1,667	130,000
30	3,000	1,000	90,000
40	1,500	500	60,000
151			**$2,000,000**

EXHIBIT 1.4   SMALL CONSTITUENCY,
$ 3 MILLION GIFT PYRAMID

STANDARD OF INVESTMENTS NECESSARY TO ACHIEVE $3 MILLION GOAL

Number of Gifts Required	Investment Level Three-Year Pledge Period	Annual Amount	Value
1	$500,000	$166,667	$500,000
1	300,000	100,000	300,000
2	150,000	50,000	300,000
3	75,000	25,000	225,000
6	50,000	16,667	300,000
10	30,000	10,000	300,000
20	15,000	5,000	300,000
30	7,500	2,500	225,000
50	5,000	1,667	250,000
60	3,000	1,000	180,000
80	1,500	500	120,000
263			**$3,000,000**

EXHIBIT 1.5   MODEST CONSTITUENCY,
$2.5 MILLION GIFT PYRAMID

STANDARD OF INVESTMENTS NECESSARY TO ACHIEVE $2.5 MILLION GOAL

Number of Gifts Required	Investment Level Three-Year Pledge Period	Annual Amount	Value
1	300,000	100,000	300,000
2	150,000	50,000	300,000
3	75,000	25,000	225,000
3	50,000	16,667	150,000
5	30,000	10,000	150,000
20	15,000	5,000	300,000
30	7,500	2,500	225,000
50	5,000	1,667	250,000
100	3,000	1,000	300,000
200	1,500	500	300,000
414			$2,500,000

EXHIBIT 1.6   LARGE CONSTITUENCY,
$5 MILLION GIFT PYRAMID

STANDARD OF INVESTMENTS NECESSARY TO ACHIEVE $5 MILLION GOAL

Number of Gifts Required	Investment Level Three-Year Pledge Period	Annual Amount	Value
1	1,000,000	333,334	1,000,000
1	500,000	166,667	500,000
1	300,000	100,000	300,000
2	150,000	50,000	300,000
3	75,000	25,000	225,000
4	50,000	16,667	200,000
10	30,000	10,000	300,000
25	15,000	5,000	375,000
40	7,500	2,500	300,000
60	5,000	1,667	300,000
200	3,000	1,000	600,000
400	1,500	500	600,000
747			$5,000,000

EXHIBIT 1.7   SMALL CONSTITUENCY, STRONG LEAD GIFTS, $15 MILLION GIFT PYRAMID

STANDARD OF INVESTMENTS NECESSARY TO ACHIEVE $15 MILLION GOAL

Number of Gifts Required	Investment Level Three-Year Pledge Period	Annual Amount	Value
1	$3,000,000	$1,000,000	$3,000,000
1	1,500,000	500,000	1,500,000
3	1,000,000	333,333	3,000,000
3	500,000	166,666	1,500,000
6	300,000	100,000	1,800,000
9	150,000	50,000	1,350,000
11	75,000	25,000	825,000
15	50,000	16,666	750,000
25	30,000	10,000	750,000
35	15,000	5,000	525,000
109			$15,000,000

EXHIBIT 1.8   LARGE CONSTITUENCY, $10 MILLION GIFT PYRAMID

STANDARD OF INVESTMENTS NECESSARY TO ACHIEVE $10 MILLION GOAL

Number of Gifts Required	Investment Level Three-Year Pledge Period	Annual Amount	Value
1	$1,500,000	$500,000	$1,500,000
1	1,000,000	333,333	1,000,000
2	500,000	333,333	1,000,000
3	250,000	83,333	750,000
10	100,000	33,333	1,000,000
13	50,000	16,666	650,000
24	25,000	8,333	600,000
50	15,000	5,000	750,000
100	10,000	3,333	1,000,000
200	5,000	1,666	1,000,000
750	1,000	333	750,000
1,154			$10,000,000

EXHIBIT 1.9   SPECIAL DISTRIBUTION, $6 MILLION GIFT PYRAMID

SPECIAL DISTRIBUTION STANDARD OF INVESTMENTS NECESSARY TO ACHIEVE $6 MILLION GOAL

Number of Gifts Required	Investment Level Three-Year Pledge Period	Annual Amount	Value
1	$3,000,000	$1,000,000	$3,000,000
1	500,000	166,666	500,000
2	300,000	100,000	600,000
3	150,000	50,000	450,000
4	75,000	25,000	300,000
6	50,000	16,666	300,000
10	30,000	10,000	300,000
15	15,000	5,000	225,000
20	7,500	2,500	150,000
25	5,000	1,666	125,000
50	1,000	333	50,000
137			**$6,000,000**

EXHIBIT 1.10   LARGE AND AFFLUENT CONSTITUENCY, 200 MILLION GIFT PYRAMID

STANDARD OF INVESTMENTS NECESSARY TO ACHIEVE $200 MILLION GOAL

Number of Gifts Required	Investment Level Three-Year Pledge Period	Annual Amount	Value
1	$30,000,000	$10,000,000	$30,000,000
1	20,000,000	6,666,666	20,000,000
2	10,000,000	3,333,333	20,000,000
4	5,000,000	1,666,666	20,000,000
8	2,500,000	833,333	20,000,000
15	1,000,000	333,333	15,000,000
30	500,000	166,666	15,000,000
40	250,000	83,333	10,000,000
80	150,000	50,000	12,000,000
100	100,000	33,333	10,000,000
200	50,000	16,666	10,000,000
360	25,000	8,333	9,000,000
500	10,000	3,333	5,000,000
800+	5,000	1,666	4,000,000
2,141			**$200,000,000**

EXHIBIT 1.11   CAMPAIGN GIFT TABLE (PYRAMID)

Proposed Campaign Goal: $_____

Number of Gifts Needed	Gift Range	Total Percentage	Number of Prospects Needed
1	10%–20% of goal = $_____	10%–20%	4–5
2	5%–10% of goal = $_____	15%	6–8
4	2.5% of goal = $_____	10%	16
8	1% of goal = $_____	10%	30
16	00.6% of goal = $_____	10%	50
32	00.3% of goal = $_____	10%	100
64	00.15% of goal = $_____	10%	200
A great many smaller gifts	_____	5%–15%	
		100%	

Source: Marilyn Bancel, *Preparing Your Capital Campaign,* Jossey-Bass, © 2000. This material is used by permission of John Wiley & Sons, Inc.

Multiyear Pledges

Capital campaigns are based on multiyear pledges. All donors are capable of giving more over a multiyear period than they can in any one year. Typical pledge payment periods span three or five years.

The Problems of Average Gift Plans

Never seek the average gift. A closely related point to that raised in the previous section is the one counterintuitive fundraising mistake many people make. They naturally simplify the fundraising task with a statement such as, "We need to raise $1.5 million. Why don't we ask our top 100 donors to give $15,000 each?" As simple as this idea sounds, it rarely, if ever, works. And even when an organization succeeds with this type of plan, be assured that the nonprofit has barely approached its true fundraising potential.

There are three reasons the average gift plan doesn't work. First, some prospects decide not to donate; hence, the organization needs more prospects than it realizes. Second, some prospects may wish to donate an amount less than that requested. Finally, some prospects may have the capacity and interest to donate a great deal more than the amount requested.

As attractive as the "same gift amount from top prospects" idea might sound, anyone in a position to exert influence over the organization's decision-making processes should find a gracious way to thank the presenter for the input, but bring the focus back to the importance of pacesetting contributions. Another way of stating the principle is: "Not equal giving, but equal sacrifice." This thought recognizes that each individual has his or her own giving capacity and interest level.

An even more egregious error is to attempt a campaign based on the notion of "many small gifts." Such a campaign may, indeed, attract many small gifts, but will also fall far short of the goal.

Continue Ongoing Support

Well-executed capital campaigns don't diminish ongoing support. Nonprofit leaders often express the concern that a capital campaign will "rob Peter to pay Paul." They ask, "Won't our best donors simply donate to the capital campaign instead of our annual appeal?" The answer is simple. A main message of every capital campaign is, "We need your ongoing support. Your capital pledge should be in *addition* to your annual contributions."

Please remember that capital campaigns are based on face-to-face conversations. Your top donors and best prospects will understand the importance of their continued support. And some capital campaign grants and donations will come from individuals, foundations, or corporations that had not been regular donors to your organization.

Manage your appeals and messages wisely. Speak to your development staff and capital campaign consultant about a comprehensive and integrated approach to the organization's total need for contributions. With such an approach, your ongoing support should remain steady or increase modestly during your capital campaign solicitation and pledge period.

Expect one more benefit: Frequently, donors who were making large pledge payments for the capital campaign do not drop all the way back to their pre-campaign annual support levels; rather, they become more generous annual donors following the capital campaign.

Add Endowment Goals

Many capital campaigns include endowment goals. Just as capital campaigns should be designed and executed so as not to diminish annual support, so too can they be designed and executed so as to increase the organization's endowment funds. The endowment funds are often integral to the campaign for a number of reasons. First, the endowment funds can help maintain the newly built or renovated facilities. Second, the endowment funds can help support the programs and services that are central to the organization's mission and to the facility's purpose.

Board Member Responsibility

Those closest to the organization must set the pace. Leadership begins with the board. When board members lead in giving, others follow. One reliable old capital campaign guideline states that the board of directors should contribute approximately 15 percent or more of the capital campaign goal. If those closest are not committed to the cause, how can we expect others to give generously? This rhetorical question is so important that grant officers and experienced philanthropists frequently ask quite specifically about board giving. They want to know that 100 percent of the board has made a financial commitment, and that many board members donated at generous levels.

Two Important Early Steps

Your two most important early steps are to develop reliable ballpark estimates of total project expenses and to begin identifying prospects capable of supporting the organization at the required levels. Architects and builders can furnish preliminary estimates of project costs. These ballpark estimates are usually expressed as an expected range. Surprisingly, many of these early estimates are remarkably close to final actual costs. You can help refine the early projections by reminding planners and advisors about the total project costs to be estimated. The information and forms in Chapter 4 should help with this process.

Once the organization has a sense of the magnitude of the campaign needed, it becomes easier to focus on the gift levels needed—and the specific prospects capable of commitments at these levels.

For example, an organization contemplating a $6,670,000 campaign might determine that it needs a $1 million lead gift. Philanthropists with a net worth of $25 million or more might be in a position to consider such a gift. Some foundations, such as The Kresge Foundation, fund capital projects at that level. Some corporations might consider such a gift under extraordinary circumstances. The point is, organization leaders must identify realistic potential sources of leadership gifts. As important, the best time to begin nurturing positive relationships with these decision makers is now. Clearly, inviting your best prospect to the groundbreaking ceremony is probably too little too late.

Focus on Support for People

The case for support focuses on the people you serve, not on institutional needs. James Gregory Lord, in *The Raising of Money* (Third Sector Press, 1985), states that, "Organizations have no needs." He points out that communities have needs to satisfy. People have needs and challenges. For an organization to succeed, it must have answers and solutions.

When creating your case for support and campaign materials, focus on the people you serve. Stress your organization's achievements and competencies. Let potential donors know how their investments in facilities will help the nonprofit better serve the people looking to the organization for vital programs and services.

The Phases of Capital Campaigns

Capital campaigns have distinct phases, each of which takes time. Many authorities (Bancel, *Preparing Your Capital Campaign,* Kent E. Dove, *Conducting a Successful Capital Campaign,* Jossey-Bass, 2000, and others) describe "typical" capital campaign phases and timelines. Exhibit 1.12 shows the phases in a graphic presentation. In general, most nonprofits should anticipate the following campaign stages:

1. *Preparation phase (6 months to 3 years or more).* This time is devoted to project planning and strengthening the organization's fundraising capacity.

   Success is determined by how well the project meets the needs of the external constituencies, how well the organization has identified and cultivated relationships with top donors, and how well the organization has understood and reconciled project costs with fundraising potential.

2. *Prospect identification and cultivation (early and ongoing).* This is not really a phase of the campaign. However, I included it in the Capital Project and Campaign Timelines, Exhibit 1.12, to indicate the importance of beginning this work as early as possible and continuing it at least through the intermediate phase of the campaign.

   Success is determined by the quality of the prospects identified, the thoughtfulness in designing meaningful cultivation activities, and the organization's ability to nurture genuine and warm relationships with potential major donors.

3. *Precampaign planning study phase (3 to 6 months).* This time is devoted to selecting the fundraising consulting firm, developing a test case for support, securing appointments with potential top donors, conducting confidential interviews (by the fundraising consultant), and delivering the report. It is important to consider the interviews and study as an important part of the cultivation process and an integral part of the campaign.

   Success is determined by the choice of firm, the quality and objectivity of the study, the quality of the interviewee list, and the board's response to the study recommendations.

4. *Quiet phase (6 to 12 months).* This time is devoted to recruiting campaign leaders and soliciting their commitments. Campaign leaders rate the giving capacity of their best prospects and match that capability to named gift opportunities. This phase, which is also called the *advancement phase* is characterized by gracious approaches to potential pacesetting lead gift donors.

   Success is determined by the selection of the appropriate volunteer and staff person to dialogue with the prospective donor. Of course, the graciousness of the approach and solicitation is crucial. And it is most important to make a clear request based on the prospective donor's max-

EXHIBIT 1.12 CAPITAL PROJECT AND CAMPAIGN TIMELINES

ACTIVITY	2004						2005												2006						
	Jul	Aug	Sep	Oct	Nov	Dec	Jan	Feb	Mar	Apr	May	Jun	Jul	Aug	Sep	Oct	Nov	Dec	Jan	Feb	Mar	Apr	May	Jun	Jul
Capital Campaign																									
Preparation	XXXXXX	XXXXXX	XXXXXX	XXXXXX	XXXXXX	XX																			
Prospect ID and Cultivation		XXXXXX	XXXXXX	XXXXXX	XXXXXX	XXXXXX		XXXXXX	XXXXXX	XXXXXX	XXXXXX		XXXXXX	XXXXXX											
Precampaign Planning Study							XXXXXX	XXXXXX	XXXXXX																
Board Campaign and Quiet Phase										XXXXXX	XXXXXX	XXXXXX	XXXXXX	XXXXXX	XXXXXX										
Intermediate Phase													XXXXXX	XXXXXX	XXXXXX	XXXXXX	XXXXXX								
Public Phase															XXXXXX	XXXXXX	XXXXXX	XXXXXX	XXXXXX	XXXXXX	XXXXXX				
Victory Celebration																				XXXXXX	XXXXXX				
Dedication Ceremony																									XXXXXX
Design and Construction																									
Study Options	XXXXXX	XXXXXX																							
Predesign and Program		XXXXXX	XXXXXX	XXXXXX	XXXXXX																				
Schematics					XXXXXX	XXXXXX	XXXXXX																		
Design Development							XXXXXX				(Pause for Fundraising)				XXXXXX	XXXXXX	XXXXXX								
Construction Documents																	XXXXXX	XXXXXX							
Bid																		XXXXXX	XXXXXX						
Preconstruction																				XXXXXX	XXXXXX				
Construction																						XXXXXX	XXXXXX	XXXXXX	XXXXXX

imum capacity, rather than on a safe or "expected" donation level. This is also the phase during which 100 percent of the board members can be expected to make their commitments.

The quiet, or advancement, phase often encompasses first-tier (lead gift) solicitations and second-tier (major gift) solicitations.

5. *Intermediate phase (3 to 6 months).* This phase is devoted to follow-up visits and conversations with lead gift and major gift prospects who have not yet made their commitments. Campaign volunteers and staff also call upon third-tier (special gift) prospects. The important point is that the campaign leadership must secure pledges of at least 50 percent of the campaign goal prior to any public announcement. During the intermediate phase, campaign leaders recruit additional volunteers and provide training and orientation prior to "going public."

   Success is determined by the quality of volunteer training, continued cultivation activities, the peer relations established with top prospects, and by the graciousness of the personal appeal. These same qualities make the volunteer recruitment process more fruitful.

6. *Public phase (6 to 12 months).* This phase often begins with a highly visible kick-off event. The organization announces the campaign and reveals that more than 50 percent of the goal has already been committed. Public relations activities are increased, and the largest number of campaign volunteers are kept busy meeting face-to-face with prospective supporters. Late in the campaign, the organization may wish to include phone and mail appeals to the broader base of capital campaign prospects. Still, the focus should remain on the personal contacts.

7. *Victory celebration (2 to 4 months preparation).* Once the organization has reached or gone over its capital campaign goal, it should stage a victory celebration. The event should be imaginative. Invitations should be warm and effusive. Donors and volunteers need to be thanked for a job well done. They all have participated in something larger than themselves. Each should share in a sense of pride.

   Be enthusiastic. Don't bore your guests. Be generous and gracious with the organization's acknowledgments. Reveal attractive naming plaques. Give acknowledgment gifts inscribed with volunteer and donors' names. Have fun. Visit those who couldn't attend the event and personally express the organization's gratitude.

8. *Conclusion and pledge payout.* Recruit your best volunteers and donors for additional involvement activities—being careful not to burn out those who worked the hardest. Continue to maintain records and relationships. If the construction is completed well after the campaign victory celebra-

tion, be sure to invite donors and volunteers to an opening celebration. Create many opportunities for supporters to tour the facilities, and continue to have pride in their participation with the project.

Provide summations of pledge payment history and gracious pledge reminders. Stay in touch in the most personal manner possible.

Facility Planning and Construction Projects

Facility planning and construction projects have distinct phases, each of which takes time. Many authorities (Andy Pressman, AIA, *Professional Practice 101,* John Wiley & Sons, Inc., 1997) describe facility planning and construction phases and timelines. Exhibit 1.12 shows the design and construction process in a graphic format together with the fundraising timeline. In general, most nonprofits should anticipate the following facility planning stages:

1. *Early exploration of options (3 to 18 months).* During these early months, the nonprofit looks at many planning options. Tasks include: determining whether the perceived need is real (e.g., ask: Does the organization need more space, rather than a reorganization of existing space?); determining whether new or enhanced facilities are needed; discovering, which, if any, existing buildings are available for purchase and renovation; obtaining preliminary estimates of purchase and renovation costs; exploring sites that might be suitable for purchase; obtaining preliminary estimates of potential design and construction costs; getting early input and buy-in from board members, potential key supporters, and other stakeholders; obtaining early estimates of sources and amounts of funding available (funds available from organization's surplus, government grants, loans, sale of assets, contributed income potential); and making a decision to proceed with the project.

   During this stage, organizations often receive informal or pro bono support from architects, builders, resource development consultants, real estate professionals, and developers. More complex project planning might dictate that the organization hire consultants and project planners to furnish additional information and help facilitate the decision-making process.

2. *Predesign phase (2 to 6 months).* When a nonprofit organization engages the services of an architect or other space-planning professional, the organization is considered to be in the predesign phase. The broadest facility challenges and solutions are well articulated. Now the planning goes into high gear.

   Working with professionals, the organization resolves issues dealing with remaining planning options, environmental analysis, architectural programming (determining the organization's facility needs, design considerations, and space requirements), architectural services and responsibilities, site analysis, site design, and a host of other early planning issues.

3. *Schematic design (1 to 2 months preparation).* Toward the end of the pre-design phase, the architect prepares the schematic drawings. These are the first drawings and proposals that describe the architect's conceptual framework for approaching the design. These schematics also include preliminary floor plans and give the nonprofit organization an under-standing of the look and feel of the proposed new buildings and/or ren-ovations. Prior to moving to the design development phase, the organization may pause to assure that the funding is in place.

4. *Design development (1 to 5 months or more).* During this intense period, issues dealing with design refinement, mechanical, electrical, plumbing, lighting, and acoustic engineering are addressed. Of course, the profes-sionals also address critical issues dealing with structural design for wind and seismic forces. Finally, the architects deal with what they refer to as "materials and methods."

5. *Construction documents (1 to 3 months).* Once the issues above are resolved, the architect prepares the construction documents.

6. *Bid phase (1 to 3 months).* If the organization has not already negotiated a "design and build" contract with one company that provides both design and construction, the nonprofit now prepares requests for proposals and receives bids from construction companies. (In Chapter 5, we will discuss various project delivery methods). If the organization has not done so already, now would be a good time to get a general sense of expected pay-ment schedules for the construction phase. Cash flow planning is critical.

7. *Preconstruction (2 to 4 months).* Remember that construction cannot start the day after the contract is signed. Materials must be ordered. Contrac-tors must schedule labor and equipment. Everything takes time.

8. *Construction administration (3 to 24 months).* Simple renovations and even new construction can be accomplished in as little as three months. Most projects take longer. Your architect and builder will be able to estimate the construction time. Again, from the earliest points on, the organiza-tion should be able to project and monitor income, expenses, and cash flow.

The Importance of Volunteers

Volunteers are crucial to the success of your project. They play two vital roles in suc-cessful capital projects. Professionals who provide pro bono services bring a depth of knowledge to the organization's earliest planning phases. Affluent and influential volunteers with peer relationships to community leaders make it pos-sible for the organization to develop realistic prospects for pacesetting lead gifts. Volunteers help plan stronger projects. And they are crucial to the capital campaign's success. With these points in mind, every nonprofit should view recruiting and retaining volunteers as one of its highest priorities.

Many of the main messages conveyed in this book are first articulated in the section "What to Know from the Get Go" you just read. If you skimmed this section, consider reading it again with a highlighter in hand. Or make notes. It is especially important for people reporting to the board of directors to convey accurate and realistic information about the nature of capital campaigns. As one wag said, "It ain't what you don't know that makes you a fool. It's what you know that ain't so."

CHAPTER 2

Confidence and Communications

Imagine this: You meet with a community leader and philanthropist to discuss your organization's capital campaign. You ask, "What do you think of our case for support?" The philanthropist replies, "I didn't have to read your material. As soon as I saw that it was from your organization, that was as much as I needed to know. If you say the organization needs $3 million for facilities, I know you *do* need it and will use the funds wisely. Just looking at the letterhead was enough for me."

That's the kind of response we all like to hear from our supporters. But how many nonprofits inspire such confidence? The vast majority of people working with nonprofit organizations wish that their organizations were better known. Even the people working for large national nonprofits often feel that they have a public relations challenge. I have heard people from local Red Cross chapters say, "Everyone seems to know about our work for large disasters, but few know the valuable work we do day in and day out. We need to do a better job of letting the world know of the scope and depth of our services."

Recall the first prerequisite for success: "The organization must have a positive image. . . . Potential supporters must have *confidence* in the institution." In this regard, two issues must be addressed. To be well prepared for a capital campaign, the nonprofit organization first must be a leader in providing vital services; the organization's services and programs must be strong and relevant to the community. Second, potential supporters must know about these strong programs. In the words of one wise wag, "He who tooteth not his own horn, his horn goeth untooteth."

In other words, the organization must be worthy of support. And the organization must effectively communicate its achievements and aspirations.

Building confidence is the lifelong responsibility of every institution. The organization must have a strong sense of mission and purpose. The services and programs must be well administered, cost-effective, responsive to societal needs, and aligned with community values. The organization must have earned a reputation for fiscal responsibility. The staff and board must be well respected. And the organization must have strong internal and external communication programs.

Perhaps your organization is strong in all these arenas. More likely, the non-profit needs improvement in one or more of these confidence-building factors. As it happens, these issues are so important that organization development professionals refer to them as "key success factors." Let's look at each to assess your organization's strengths and make suggestions for improvement.

MISSION AND PURPOSE

Strong organizations have a clear and unified sense of mission. In *The Complete Guide to Fundraising Management* (John Wiley and Sons, Inc., 2002), I suggested that organizations try this experiment: In separate confidential interviews, ask organization leaders to describe the organization's mission. Some organizations convey a clear sense of mission, purpose, and focus. Others don't. Often, the organization's top people cannot clearly articulate the institution's mission and purpose. In some cases, you may even find very different views of the organization. I have often told the story of a West Coast historical society whose marketing director said, "To increase our income, we should behave more like the museum we are. We can increase attendance, open a gift shop, and dramatically increase our income." The director of the institution's programs said, "The important thing to remember about our institution is that we are *not* a museum. Our mission is to preserve the artifacts entrusted to us and make them available to scholars."

One might think that such divergent views of the organization's mission are rare. They most definitely are not. The case just cited might be somewhat more extreme than most. But innumerable nonprofit leaders differ from their colleagues in their view of the organization's mission. Even with churches and religious institutions, where the mission would be presumed to be understood, differences arise. At times these differences are simply ones of emphasis—as in cases where some members of the congregation feel strongly about the importance of charitable outreach programs, whereas other members of the congregation stress the church's internal needs. At times the differences are much greater and schisms arise.

In situations where the organization's leaders cannot articulate a unified view of the mission, one or two mechanisms might be at work. In the first case, the organization might really have unresolved issues concerning its mission. In the second case, the organization has done a poor job of communicating its mission and purpose to the organization's leaders and key constituencies.

The prescription for the first ailment is straightforward. The organization must engage its key staff and board members in meaningful conversations concerning the nonprofit's mission, values, and vision of the future. A facilitated strategic planning process might be just what the doctor ordered.

The second ailment—situations where the mission was clearly defined but key leaders now seem unable to articulate this agreed-upon view—can be frustrating. Perhaps the issues were resolved by appropriate board and staff discussions and votes in the past, but new board members or staff have not bought in to the past decisions. Perhaps the world has changed so much that the old mission statement is no longer valid. Or perhaps the mission wasn't so clearly defined after all.

Great care must be taken not to endlessly dredge up old issues. Mission statements, once adopted, should be changed infrequently and only with great thought. At the beginning of most consulting assignments, I ask to review organization marketing materials and internal documents. In well over half the cases, I find multiple versions of the mission statement. Sometimes the variations are minor; other times, the mission statements are so different they could have come from separate organizations.

No wonder the organization's leaders can't articulate a unified view of the institution's mission. It is incumbent upon the nonprofit's CEO and board president to see that the board-approved mission statement is well communicated. Begin by assuring that all communications use the same version. Beyond that, work to see that every board and staff member, as well as the key volunteers, can recite an "elevator speech" that states what the organization does, for whom, and why that should matter to the community.

Board, staff, and volunteers reaffirm their understanding and commitment at retreats, planning sessions, committee meetings, fundraising orientation sessions, and a host of other formal and informal gatherings. Key messages should be repeated often. The organization's leaders can work to create buy-in. As important, they must convey the organization's mission, purpose, and vision of the future so clearly—and so often—that constituents can restate these central messages in their own words.

Some years ago, I was working for a regional symphony orchestra. One of the main messages I wrote and urged to be used in multiple communication channels was, "The New Mexico Symphony Orchestra is crucial to our region's economic and cultural life." That was a message that seemed to resonate well among our state's business leaders. Later, I was representing a regional theater company and spoke to a business leader about sponsorship of one of the plays. He agreed, but then stated, "I can help you with this sponsorship. But do understand that the New Mexico Symphony Orchestra will continue to be one of my company's major commitments. After all, the New Mexico Symphony Orchestra is crucial to our region's economic and cultural life."

I stifled my urge to jump across his desk and kiss him on the cheek as he quoted the tag line *verbatim*. Key messages are like that. You find words that resonate. You repeat them. And after some time, community leaders begin to repeat them back to you. Here is another example. When Red Cross volunteers are asked about their organization's mission, without hesitation they respond in their own words that the organization's purpose is to "Prevent, prepare for and respond to disasters and emergencies." Please work to see that representatives of your organization can state your mission and purpose with such clarity.

SERVICES AND PROGRAMS

The sine qua non of any nonprofit organization is its services and programs. What would the social/service agency be without its case management, job training, counseling, treatment, and charitable programs? Can you imagine a symphony orchestra without its performances? Of what value would your church, mosque, or synagogue be without its daily or weekly prayer and worship services? Can you imagine an effective advocacy organization that did not attempt to change societal values and laws? Is there a conservation or preservation organization that does not work to preserve our nation and world's natural and man-made treasures? How about a museum without exhibits? Would anyone support a healthcare institution that did not conduct research, prevent illness, or heal the sick? What support could an education institution expect if it did not inculcate a lifetime desire for learning or did not prepare its students to respond to an ever-changing complex world?

Board and Staff Responsibilities

Staff and board members of nonprofit organizations have a responsibility to assure that the programs and services offered are of the highest quality possible. Staff members implement the programs and services. They serve on the front line of service delivery. Board members establish the strategic direction and policies needed to grow a strong organization. The board members also hire and evaluate the effectiveness of the CEO or executive director. Moreover, board members approve and monitor the budget, working to assure the organization's fiscal strength. And the board and staff share responsibility for raising the funds needed to assure strong programs and adequate facilities.

And yet, if you ever attend a large number of board meetings, you might notice that a great deal of time is devoted to relatively small-scale special event fundraisers, perfunctory financial reports, standing committee reports, the executive director's report, and a host of sometimes gossipy side issues. Rarely will you hear meaningful discussions about how the organization can strengthen its services and programs. Indeed it is an unusually strong board that works closely with staff to understand the strategic issues related to service delivery. And only very strong administrative leaders know how to engage the board in focusing on the strategies and resources the organization needs to excel in its programs and services.

Here are some questions nonprofit leaders might ask:

- Whom do we serve?
- Are there others we are not yet serving who need our services?
- Are our referral network and marketing efforts strong enough to assure that all who could benefit from our programs and services feel invited to participate?
- Are our services effective?
- What vital societal needs are we serving and do our services reflect community values?
- What can we do to strengthen our performance standards and services offered?
- Are we providing the services in the most cost-effective manner?
- Are there other services we should provide that we are not providing yet?
- Are there others working on the same problem with whom we can collaborate?
- What are others who provide services similar to ours doing that we should be doing?
- What mistakes have they made that we should avoid?
- Are we taking the steps necessary to attract, train, and retain the best service providers possible?
- What resources and facilities are needed for the staff to excel?
- What steps can we take to be perceived as leaders in our field?

Consider setting up an ad hoc board and staff committee to study issues such as these and others unique to your organization. The ad hoc committee should also make recommendations concerning ways in which the organization can strengthen its services. Such discussions could also be integral to a strategic planning process.

It is not enough to have strong programs. You must also communicate your program effectiveness and successes to constituents, stakeholders, and supporters. Your success in fundraising has a direct relationship to the quality of services your organization provides. Your fundraising success is also tied to your ability to let the world know of your achievements. When preparing for capital campaigns, the "world" to focus on is made up of potential supporters of the campaign—especially those capable of pacesetting leadership-level pledges and contributions.

When communicating with these most important prospects, stay focused on the people you serve—not your institution's needs. We will come back to this point in Chapter 6 when we discuss the case for support and capital campaign materials.

FISCAL RESPONSIBILITY

A discussion about ways to inspire confidence in the organization would not be complete without a look at the institution's approach to financial management. Some organizations have garnered well-deserved reputations for fiscal responsibility. They have surpluses and balanced budgets almost every year. Deficits are not tolerated. Other organizations seem to limp along from year to year. These organizations are well known for their recurring crises and emergency appeals. In between these two extremes are myriad agencies and nonprofits that always just get by. They don't seem to grow. They often lack vision. Few of these groups achieve their full potential as service providers.

So what accounts for these differences?

Some organizations—often, private schools, universities, and some hospitals—are naturally strong. They have excellent earned income, healthy endowment funds, strong boards, and long histories. At the opposite end of the spectrum are organizations that appear to be addicted to crisis management. Growing deficits, "save our organization" appeals, board and staff turnover, and doubt about the integrity of the financial reports characterize these institutions. Some social service agencies operate in this manner. Regretfully, many arts organizations also fall into this category.

In between the two extremes, organization administrators remain so distracted by day-to-day operations that they never make time to address strategic issues or ways of strengthening the organization's finances.

So what is to be done?

First, it is imperative to recognize that the board of directors is responsible for strategic decision making and for the fiscal health of the organization. But to be effective, the board needs a strong staff. If the current CEO or executive director is not capable of giving the board the support it needs to fulfill its obligations, the board has the responsibility to replace the CEO or executive director with someone in whom they do have confidence. To establish strategic direction and realistic budget performance, the board should be clear about the quality of financial reports it expects, the quality of information it needs, and the staff support it requires.

In other words, the board must set the tone. The board president, working with the executive director, should begin with the idea that deficits—even small deficits—are not to be expected, let alone tolerated. Perhaps expenses have to be cut. Spending should always be controlled to the extent possible. Or, organization leaders might ask fellow board members to "step up to the bat" and increase personal contributions and fundraising efforts. Even more basic is the concept that budget projections need to be realistic and well formulated. The board has every reason to expect the staff to make detailed, good-faith, and accurate projections.

The board of directors should be composed of people who possess superb business acumen. It is axiomatic that every organization wants to recruit good team players. Let's also recruit people who will help the staff sharpen its financial management skills. Begin with a thoughtful process for preparing and approving the organization's annual budget. Follow up with monthly reports comparing the actual results to the plan. Expect the staff and board treasurer to recognize any significant variance. Expect the board and staff to act in a timely manner to avoid crises.

See that your organization plans and achieves surpluses in most years. Maximize your earned income. Deliver cost-effective—yet high-impact—services while maintaining a reputation for fiscal responsibility.

BOARD AND STAFF RELATIONSHIPS

If you want your organization to be well respected in the community, begin by developing an atmosphere of mutual respect between your board and staff. If the board and staff aren't functioning smoothly together, be assured that their differences will become known to the organization's constituents and supporters.

Encourage open communications. Air issues. Hallways and parking lots after board meetings are most assuredly not the places to discuss differences. These should be aired during board meetings. Mature managers bring people of differing views together. Thoughtful board officers understand the importance of addressing issues, not people. Wise leaders understand the value of uniting everyone in pursuit of a cause larger than any individual. Focus on the mission and vision of the future.

One of the board's most important responsibilities is to assure that the organization is led by a competent and well-respected CEO or executive director. The chief executive often serves as the public face of the institution. He or she should be more than a good manager; the organization is most respected when it is headed by a visionary—yet practical—leader. Moreover, strong chief executives surround themselves with strong staff. Programs are strengthened. Financial reporting is timely and reliable. Board and staff relations are positive as well as productive.

Another hallmark of this strong partnership is the mutually supportive relationship of the board chair and nonprofit chief executive. They confer with each other on a regular basis. They work to assure that board members are well informed concerning major issues facing the institution. They focus on strategic opportunities and are not distracted by peripheral issues. They create an optimistic culture in which there are few, if any, unpleasant surprises. They work together to assure that the organization runs smoothly. They understand the appropriate roles of the board and of the staff. They help communicate a united view of the organization's mission and vision of the future.

Board committee members work closely with the staff. In fact, experienced staffers know that they are most effective when they support and work with board members who bring expertise and resources to the organization.

Beyond the working relationships, successful organizations create a wide variety of opportunities for social interaction. Retreats, open houses, joint attendance at conferences, holiday season parties, cultivation gatherings, victory celebrations, and a host of other happenings are times when board members can get to know each other better and bond with staff.

COMMUNICATIONS

Now that we have addressed some of the main elements that strengthen the organization and make it worthy of support, we can turn our attention to communications. The nonprofit institution preparing for a capital campaign works to concentrate all of its public relations, marketing, and communication programs on five key messages: (1) the organization's position statement; (2) the organization's achievements and reputation; (3) the organization's vision; (4) the organization's invitation to participate; (5) the organization's campaign theme.

Position Statement

Take the time to discover and articulate your organization's unique position in the philanthropic marketplace. Some nonprofits have developed a "tag line" or "position statement." They focus on their age, experience, size, geographic scope, service offering, values, or other singular organization characteristics. Examples include: "Brooklyn's oldest—but most forward-looking hospital," "Arizona's only professional theater," "Compassionate services for women and children experiencing homelessness," "Education you can use," "America's foremost cancer research and treatment center," "The largest museum in the South," "The oldest zoological hospital in the world," "Excellence in patient care, medical education, and clinical research," "The world's only accredited liberal arts college for deaf students," "The country's oldest and largest organization for girls."

In actual practice, these tag lines, or organization identifiers, are not always presented with the organization's logo or on the letterhead. Still, the phrases are frequently repeated in letters, news releases, press kits, annual reports, and other communication pieces. It pays to develop such simple statements and refine them. Repetition is central to your success in defining your organization.

The Organization's Reputation

Through perseverance, hard work, and a bit of luck, many organizations have already established a reputation for strong programs combined with fiscal integrity. However, in more cases, even people close to the institution know too little about the organization's achievements. To refine the nonprofit's message, answer the following questions.

- When was the organization founded?
- What awards has the organization received?
- What programs and services does the organization offer?
- How many people does the organization serve each year?
- In addition to statistics, which stories and testimonials can leaders share that indicate program success and have emotional appeal?
- What data do you have indicating the cost-effectiveness of your programs and financial integrity?

Once you have gathered this information, be sure that it is integrated into briefing documents, fundraising appeals, case statements, institutional brochures, fact sheets, board orientation books, volunteer training materials, and other forms of communication.

Vision

C.P. Snow in his Godkin lectures at Harvard said, "Being right or wrong is not enough, but it is cardinal that you should be positive." This brings us to the next main message that your organization must project. Let the philanthropic community know that your organization has a positive vision of the future. Most organizations can develop a vision statement that is similar to the following:

> In three to five years, XYZ Nonprofit will be known for its leadership in providing quality programs for the people we serve. Moreover, our organization will be well respected for its strong board and staff, its reputation for fiscal responsibility, and for its exemplary marketing and public relations programs. Our infrastructure and facilities will make it possible for XYZ Nonprofit to better serve our constituents.

When you write your vision statement, be specific about the services your organization offers and the people you serve. Emphasize the positive elements of your plan. Remember, too, that you will need to find a way to package your information and make it irresistible. Malcolm Gladwell in his book, *The Tipping Point* (Little, Brown and Company, 2002), calls this the "Stickiness Factor." Another truism is that messages don't "stick" unless they are repeated frequently enough.

Invitation to Participate

Harold J. "Si" Seymour wrote one of the true classics dealing with philanthropic fundraising, *Designs for Fund-Raising* (Fund-Raising Institute, 1988). In it he describes "Two Universal Aspirations." People want to know that someone wants them, cares about them, and will listen to what they have to say. With this in mind, we see that the first aspiration of all people is "to be sought." Every individual also needs to feel that he or she is "a worthwhile member of a worthwhile group."

There is a transcendent quality to being immersed in a cause larger than oneself. Leaders of nonprofit organizations have a responsibility to invite volunteers and financial supporters to partner with the organization. Over the years, I have observed that organizations generally fit into one of three models regarding how they relate to their "external constituencies." In Exhibit 2.1 you will see the *inward-focused organization,* the *external-focused organization,* and the *partnership model* organization.

People working in the inward-focused organization seem to neglect their service recipients, donors, and volunteers. All the attention flows inward. You know these organizations well by their bureaucratic attitudes, political infighting, and their nonresponsive way of dealing with external constituencies. Peter F. Drucker in his book, *Managing for Results* (Harper & Row, Publishers, 1964), reminds us that, "Neither results nor resources exist inside the business. Both exist outside. There are no profit centers within the business; there are only cost centers." Nonprofit organizations also suffer if they fail to concentrate on external constituencies: the donors, volunteers, and community leaders who can unlock the resources needed for success.

The external-focused organization pays attention to the world outside. Perhaps the organization conducts occasional surveys. Often the staff will meet to discuss what it thinks service recipients, donors, and volunteers want or need. The organization becomes less bureaucratic and more responsive to its external constituents. Still, the organization retains a bit of an "us and them" viewpoint.

The partnership model organization nurtures consistent, ongoing, and meaningful dialogue with its service recipients, board members, volunteers, donors, and community opinion leaders. Buy-in is the natural outcome of these intensely genuine partnerships. The organization forms such strong bonds that it no longer views the philanthropic community as an "external constituency."

EXHIBIT 2.1   THREE ORGANIZATION BEHAVIORS
(RELATIONSHIP TO STAKEHOLDERS)

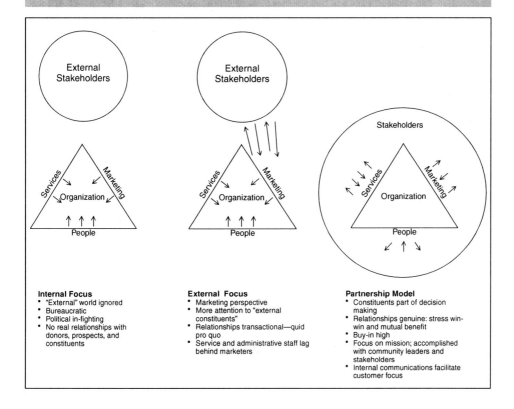

Internal Focus
* "External" world ignored
* Bureaucratic
* Political in-fighting
* No real relationships with donors, prospects, and constituents

External Focus
* Marketing perspective
* More attention to "external constituents"
* Relationships transactional—quid pro quo
* Service and administrative staff lag behind marketers

Partnership Model
* Constituents part of decision making
* Relationships genuine: stress win-win and mutual benefit
* Buy-in high
* Focus on mission; accomplished with community leaders and stakeholders
* Internal communications facilitate customer focus

Rather, the board, staff, volunteers, and community leaders work together to define problems and develop solutions.

Think of the times you worked closely with an attorney, tax advisor, or consultant. Wasn't the relationship most productive when your thoughts and concerns were paramount? Don't you think that people interacting with nonprofit organizations would appreciate this same sense of alliance?

With this in mind, one of your main messages should be, "XYZ Nonprofit offers an opportunity for donors and volunteers to play an important part in a cause larger than themselves." But that is not enough. You must actually engage your board members, volunteers, donors, and community leaders.

Communications experts often state, "What you do speaks one thousand times more than what you say you do." So, invite stakeholders and potential donors to planning sessions, briefings that include real question-and-answer periods, open houses, and breakfast or lunch meetings with organization leaders. Encourage dialogue. Listen. Seriously consider the advice offered. And when your campaign gets underway, offer opportunities for people to participate as donors and volunteers.

Campaign Theme

As you get closer to organizing your capital campaign, it becomes imperative to give sufficient attention to the campaign theme. To stimulate discussion and to generate buy-in, the organization's leaders and representatives of the philanthropic community might wish to consider ideas from four main approaches to campaign themes: the nonprofit's tagline, the building name, a variation on generic campaign themes, and a theme that uniquely captures your supporters' values.

In the first case, the organization might have developed a strong identifying message—a tagline that works as well for the campaign as it does for the organization. The Barrett Foundation had used the phrase "Building Futures for Women and Children" in its general communications, so when the organization began its capital campaign to build a new home for homeless women and children, the theme was already in place. And there was the added advantage that campaign communications reinforced the organization's main message.

If community leaders understand the need for the facility you are raising funds for, and the facility's proposed name tells the story, the simple use of the building name may be sufficient to convey the campaign's value to the community. For example, the Greater Albuquerque Hispano Chamber of Commerce was preparing for a capital campaign to raise the funds needed for a new headquarters and services building. The draft case statement was titled "Barelas Job Training Center." Upon seeing the draft case statement cover, one committee member exclaimed, "I was wondering how we would present the rationale for contributing to a new headquarters building. This makes so much sense. We will focus on the main benefit of the facility—our program focus—job training for the people coming to this historic neighborhood." The case statement naturally led to discussions concerning the importance of job training and the importance of the project to the Barelas neighborhood. That was as much of a theme as this successful campaign ever needed.

Many campaigns use one of numerous generic themes: Campaign for Excellence; Vision for the Future; Twenty-first Century Fund; Second-Century Fund; Vision, Commitment, Victory! These or variations of these tried-and-true messages might work for your nonprofit.

Finally, your organization leaders may wish to consider a theme unique to your circumstances. Some years ago, I conducted the planning study and provided campaign support for the New Mexico State Bar. The steering committee, recognizing the constituents' singular relationship to the profession and to the Bar Association, chose the theme, "For Pride and Profession." The alliteration and simplicity of the message, combined with some extremely dedicated staff and volunteer leadership, helped lead the campaign for the new Bar Center to victory.

This brief discussion will help you develop your organization's campaign theme. Just one cautionary note: The process by which you determine your theme is even more important than the actual decision you make. If key people—especially potential campaign leaders or pacesetting donors—discuss the campaign theme and make the final decision, your organization will be better off than if the theme were written by even the most gifted copywriter. (The reader is probably getting the point that one main message of this book is the importance of Buy-in! Buy-in! Buy-in!)

Take a copy of Exhibit 2.2, "Choosing a Campaign Theme," to a meeting of key stakeholders. (An additional list of church capital campaign themes is presented in Chapter 12.) Let the ideas serve as a point of departure for discussion.

EXHIBIT 2.2   CHOOSING A CAMPAIGN THEME

Consider four sources of ideas for campaign themes: your organization's tagline, the building name, a variation on generic campaign themes, and a theme that uniquely captures your supporters' values. All ideas are valid. Make every effort to reach consensus among all capital campaign committee members.

1. Does this nonprofit organization have a tagline that might also work for the capital campaign?

   Other organizations have used themes such as "Building Futures for Women and Children"; "Compassionate Services for People in Need"; "Prevent, Prepare, Respond"; and other themes that worked as well for the capital campaign as for the organization's ongoing fundraising efforts.

2. Does the building name tell the whole story? Is the name sufficient for a campaign theme?

   Building names such as "Barelas Job Training Center" and "Campaign for the Santa Fe Children's Hospital" convey meaning to potential donors.

3. Do any of the following campaign themes work for your organization? Do any ideas flow from these?

   Bridge to the Future
   Campaign for Excellence
   Vision for the Future
   Compassion and Service
   Twenty-first Century Fund
   Vision, Commitment, Victory!
   Fiftieth Anniversary Campaign
   Arise and Build
   Building for Tomorrow
   Hope for the Future
   Rooted in Tradition . . . *Building for the Future*

4. What values motivate your nonprofit organization's supporters? Can these be combined into a punchy campaign theme?

   A state bar used the theme "Pride and Profession." The Telluride Historic Museum used the theme "Celebrating Telluride's Colorful History and Rich Heritage." The Albuquerque Jewish Community Center used the theme "Heritage! Vision! Values!"

   What theme works best for *this* nonprofit organization's capital campaign?

Encourage free and open discussion of all ideas. Reach consensus on a theme that appeals to all key stakeholders. In all probability, it will serve you well throughout the campaign.

COMMUNICATIONS PLAN

To inform, educate, and inspire potential donors to support your organization's campaign, a thoughtfully targeted and vigorous public relations effort has to be implemented. The nonprofit institution will benefit from compelling printed materials, frequent and positive mention in key regional publications, and a carefully designed cultivation program. Promoting the goals of the campaign in every appropriate media will build awareness and generate buy-in.

Every nonprofit organization can benefit from a three-part public relations campaign:

1. *A broad-based public relations campaign that focuses on the organization's achievements and aspirations.* Focus on free media to the extent possible. Radio and TV interviews reach broad-based audiences and help achieve credibility for the organization. Learn the art of getting your news releases placed. Speak to service clubs. Develop a comprehensive marketing and public relations program. Smaller nonprofits can benefit from pro bono services and simple-to-administer basic plans. In any case, it pays to recruit a board member with marketing and public relations experience.

2. *An education and relationship nurturing program targeted to the universe of potential supporters for the organization.* Begin by developing a comprehensive list of potential supporters. Chapter 6 will tell you more about prospect identification and segmentation. Among those targeted will be the nonprofit's natural constituencies—that is, alumni for educational institutions, subscribers and ticket purchasers for performing arts groups, all members of religious congregations, members, volunteers, current and past board members, board member contacts, community leaders, other people who may have some reason to support the organization, as well as past, current, and potential donors at all economic levels.

   At a minimum, all of these potential supporters should begin to receive periodic communications from the organization. Three newsletters a year constitute a reasonable minimal expectation. Invitations to special event fundraisers will keep the organization's name in mind—and raise ongoing operating funds. Many organizations find it helpful to issue periodic (but not too frequent) e-newsletters. Make these attractive, and give recipients an easy way to opt out, if that is their desire.

Your organization may also consider inviting the universe of potential supporters to open houses and other large, free gatherings. The small percentage who actually come will have identified themselves as supporters with a high degree of interest.

Be creative. Stay in touch with all potential supporters.

3. *A highly personalized program for those people identified as prospective pacesetting contributors to the campaign.* Your top 50 to 125 prospects deserve very special treatment. Larger institutions may wish to extend highly personalized communications and invitations to as many as 300 top prospects.

In addition to the communications that the organization's universe of prospects receives, very top prospects for pacesetting leadership gifts receive invitations to breakfast, lunch, or dinner with the organization's CEO and/or board president. These prospective supporters also receive warm and personal follow-up calls tied to invitations to small-scale gatherings of community leaders. Briefings at cultivation gatherings are well planned and carefully executed. Many of the top prospects are also included in the organization's confidential interviews for the precampaign planning study. Suffice to say, 50 percent to 85 percent of all the funds that will be donated will come from these prospects. Be sure that no top prospects are neglected and that all are made to feel important and appreciated.

When formulating your organization's communication plan, begin with the premise that your most important tasks focus on making the organization worthy of support. Public Relations experts remind us that who we are accounts for 1,000 times more than who we say we are. When the organization has been strengthened and its messages honed, a broad-based communication plan can be implemented. But remember that highly targeted communications and personal contact with top prospects are the keys to capital campaign success.

CHAPTER 3

Building a Strong and Committed Board

Every nonprofit CEO dreams of the possibility of working with a strong and involved board of directors, yet few organizations realize their full potential. They find it difficult to recruit people of affluence and influence and get them engaged in the institution's mission. Here's why this is one of the most important challenges facing the nonprofit organization preparing for a capital campaign:

- Board member giving generally totals at least 15 percent of the campaign goal.

- Board members are expected to have the business acumen needed to make thoughtful decisions concerning the organization's strategic direction and facility plans.

- Board members are expected to have peer relationships with other community leaders—relationships that are central to the organization's ability to attract financial and volunteer support. Board members play a leading role in identifying prospects, nurturing relationships, and securing contributions.

- Mature and thoughtful board members are a source of wisdom. They remind us that when the going gets tough, the tough get going—in the right direction.

Clearly, a new and fresh approach is needed when discussing board development. Too many myths and near myths surround the subject. But before examining the myths and realities related to board development, let's review basic principles that may not be "fresh," but still hold up as guides for our actions. As John Locke said, "Truth, like gold, is not less so for being newly brought out of the mine."

TWO OLD SAWS

We have all heard that nonprofit agencies should look to the "three Ws": wealth, work, and wisdom. The adage has it that each board member should provide at least two of the "three Ws"; however, experience tells us that one of the Ws—wisdom—had better be one of the criteria for board membership. At times, wealthy or hard-working board members, who happen to lack common sense, cause great grief for their institutions. So look for wealthy people, hard workers, and people with a solid reputation for sound judgment.

Another point of view has been repeated so often it has become a cliche: "The board's responsibilities are the 'three Gs'—give, get, or get off." This saying is a bit crude. Many agree that the "three Gs" are close to the mark, but fail to recognize that some people on the board can play an important role even if they were not recruited for their fundraising ability. Still, when planning for your capital campaign, give great preference to affluence and influence. Recruit potential pacesetting contributors and people who can bring the organization closer to other potential lead donors.

If you are associated with a grassroots organization, and the idea of seeking wealthy people to serve as board members offends you, please reconsider. Perhaps you have subtle or unarticulated prejudices concerning wealth. Perhaps your thought processes discriminate against the affluent. If so, please remind yourself that people rely on your organization for first-rate programs and services. These are not possible without adequate financial resources and facilities. And your campaign needs large gifts to succeed.

Simply put, we want to recruit people who will use their influence to help the nonprofit organization achieve its aspirations and garner the resources it needs to better serve its constituents.

Recruit such people and know that you are recruiting a board that will lead your campaign to success and will raise the level of all your organization's achievements.

RECRUITING BOARD MEMBERS

It is best to think strategically about potential board members. First, determine the attributes needed from the board as a whole and from each potential board member. This thought process should take place without regard to any notions about whom your organization can recruit. Don't decide that a key person will say no even before you ask him or her to serve.

To think and act strategically; observe the guidelines in the following subsections.

Determine Your Board Needs

A few board members should have *program knowledge* and *experience*. To meet these needs, look to your service volunteers, affluent constituents, and respected authorities in the field. Other board members will need to have *specialized skills* and *knowledge*. For example, at least one board member should be an attorney. Another should have a strong accounting background. Marketing and public relations skills are helpful, as are experience with banking and financial institutions. Organizations planning for capital projects might wish to recruit a board member with real estate development knowledge. Exhibit 3.1, "Board Nominations Grid," lists the usual attributes, professions, and diversity attributes needed for a well-balanced and effective board of directors.

Clout is a must. Board members should have a strong community presence, many business contacts, and prestige. Recruit people of affluence and influence.

Potential pacesetting contributors are vital to your board's credibility and effectiveness. Recruit generous people. If you have already developed a list of potential top donors for the capital campaign, consider recruiting one or more of these prospects for the board. Also, look to your own donor records. Too often, nominating committees recruit people they hope will become top donors to the organization but overlook the obvious step of considering the organization's current top donors as potential board members. Be sure that your staff brings the organization's top donor list and top prospect list to the nominating committee's attention.

Consider Desirable Personal Qualities

Integrity is a must. Only consider "principle-centered" people—men and women who avoid even the appearance of conflict of interest. Also, look to a *record of community service* and a willingness to get involved. Again, your best prospects for capital campaign lead gifts, as well as your own top donors, should be considered.

Strong board members are mature individuals who *understand the value of teamwork*. Above all, they are *enthusiastic* and have a record for making good things happen.

Broaden Your Sources of Names and Expand Your Selection Process

Do not consider only friends and acquaintances of nominating committee members. Think strategically.

If you wish to have generous people on your board, examine your donor records and public acknowledgments from other nonprofit institutions. At

EXHIBIT 3.1   BOARD NOMINATIONS GRID

																									Actual Number	Minimum Desired
SUPPORT	Other Community Involvement																										
	Contributes Annually																										
	Board Meeting Attendance																										
RELATIONSHIPS	Political Influence																										
	Personal Affluence																										
	Access to People with Money																										
	Personal Fundraising																										
	Volunteer Organizer																										
PROFESSION	Other Business																										
	Educator																										
	Manufacturing																										
	Public Relations/Media																										
	Medical																										
	Banking																										
	Retail																										
	Lawyer																										
	Accountant																										
ETHNICITY	Other																										
	Hispanic																										
	Anglo																										
AGE	56+																										
	36–55																										
	20–35																										
SEX	F																										
	M																										
NAME																											

times, you will find a person who is generous to your organization who no one seems to know. At times, you will uncover people who give modestly to your organization, but very generously to some other nonprofit. In either case, you have unearthed a potential board member you might have overlooked.

Also, ask each board member and key staff member to suggest names. Look for people who meet multiple selection criteria. If, for example, you believe that your board needs more minority representation, more wealth, and has no attorney currently serving, ask, "Can anyone suggest a wealthy minority attorney who might be asked to serve?" Such questions often lead to people who might not have been considered. (This particular example came from an actual situation where a new person who met the criteria was suggested and recruited. Moreover, he became a generous board chair within three years of being recruited.)

Develop a List of Potential Board Members

This list should be larger than the number of known openings. For one reason or another, some people simply say no, but you can greatly increase your success rate by assigning the right volunteer and staff member to go on the recruitment visit. Enthusiastic recruiters with peer relationships and strong presentation skills do very well indeed. Still, 30 percent to 60 percent of the people you attempt to recruit—especially if you are going for high visibility community leaders—will say no.

Some people turn out to be overcommitted. They know that they can only be effective if they focus their attention on a few organizations. Still, they should be asked to serve. The invitation to become a member of the board of directors will serve as an important relationship-building step. And at times the community leader might surprise you by saying yes. Perhaps he or she found the work on another board frustrating and looks forward to an opportunity to serve elsewhere. For that matter, he or she might decide not to serve on your board but would agree to make a few key introductions or even solicitations on behalf of your nonprofit.

In conclusion, nonprofit organizations should attempt to recruit at least two times the number of people they hope will serve. All the names should be quality people. If more agree to serve than you expected, your organization will end up with a large, powerful board. As my mother used to say, "My prayer for you is that you should have such problems."

Use Care When Recruiting Board Members

Take the same care when recruiting board members that you do when asking for a major donation. Involve a respected volunteer—often the board chair. Ask in person. Be gracious and thorough in explaining opportunities and responsibilities. Believe in your organization. Be bold. Be charming. Be truthful. Offer the prospective board member an opportunity to serve on a dynamic board.

One final cautionary note: Do not ask community leaders if they are willing to serve on your board if you are not prepared to accept them if they say yes. Some organizations adopt the backward policy of finding out whether someone is willing to serve and then taking the name to the nominating committee or board for consideration. Imagine how you would feel when asked by a board member if you were willing to become a board member, and you indicated your willingness to do so, and then you were not invited to join the board. That is not the way to nurture positive relationships. Yet, it is surprising how often this happens. Sometimes the board member didn't have the authority to recruit new members. Sometimes the process is too convoluted. And sometimes the volunteer forgets to bring up the name for consideration. Whatever the reason, see that it doesn't happen in your organization. Simplify your nominating process so that people who say they are willing to serve are preapproved.

MYTHS, NEAR MYTHS, AND REALITIES

Now that we have explored some of the underpinnings of successful board development, let's turn our attention to some of the common notions—the myths and near myths—that lead nonprofit organizations astray.

Myth: Only large, well-established organizations can recruit movers and shakers.

Truth: Passionate and articulate people can recruit highly effective board members—including community leaders—even for new or small nonprofit organizations. Later, in the section "More on Recruitment," you'll find more advice about ways to increase your recruitment success rate.

Myth: Small boards are most effective; if the board gets too large, it's nearly impossible to keep board members involved.

Truth: If you are serious about fundraising, you simply must recruit a larger number of board members. Not all board members will be effective fundraisers. Therefore, the larger board membership assures that an adequate number of volunteer leaders will be available for resource development. The board membership should also be strategic and designed to maximize networking with the community's decision makers.

Near Myth: The main purpose of the board is resource development. When we recruit members, we must be very explicit about each board member's fundraising responsibilities.

Truth: The main purpose of the board is to develop policies and a unified vision for the organization. Resource development is an equally important responsibility. And if, when recruiting, we say, "Ours is a fundraising board; each of our board members is expected to participate in personal solicitations," it is likely that the board prospect will find a reason not to serve.

A more successful strategy is to say something like this: "We would be most grateful if you would help us by making three to five introductions for fundraising purposes." Often, the potential board member will respond by saying, "I'm not quite sure what you mean by that." This gives the recruiter an opportunity to respond, "Each board member has his or her own fundraising comfort level. Some allow us to use their names to get appointments. Some help us get appointments and go with a staff member on the visit; the staff person is the one who discusses gift opportunities. Still others are comfortable getting appointments and asking for contributions. The most important point to us is that each board member helps in a way that is most comfortable to him or her." With this conversational approach, the number of people saying yes to recruitment increases, and more board members find a way in which they can help with fundraising.

Myth: Past board chairs know the organization best. They make ideal chairs for the nominating committee.

Truth: The past chair is often burned out, sometimes bitter, and occasionally the reason the organization didn't recruit the right people in the first case. Be cautious about establishing the "past board chair heads the nominating committee" policy. Be sure your nominating committee is composed of positive people who know the community well, think big, think strategically, and are willing to visit potential board members personally.

Myth: Boards must manifest their sensitivity to constituent needs by assuring that the people served are represented on the board.

Truth: Some constituencies—the downtrodden, the disenfranchised, the homeless, and others—are not necessarily likely to be effective board members. Recruiting people you serve may provide valuable input; however, such recruitments probably will not fill your board with the clout needed to bring additional resources to the organization. Another approach would be to fill your governing board with community leaders, then establish constituent advisory committees that can provide input for board and staff members.

Myth: If the nominating committee is composed of people who know the community well, they can get together once or twice a year to generate a list of well-known people who can add prestige to the board of directors.

Truth: Nearly everyone knows that the nominating committee is the most important committee of the board. That said, nominating committees usually meet briefly, kick around a few names, and make too many decisions based on personal acquaintances. Rather, their decisions should be based on the strategic needs of the organization. The nominating committee must meet frequently enough to understand the organization's strategic needs, research a broad list of potential board members, and develop effective recruitment strategies. Moreover, the nominating committee should give serious thought to leadership development and succession. Finally, nominating committees can have broader responsibilities—including making recommendations concerning a wide range of issues dealing with board effectiveness.

Myth: Everyone knows the short list of the community's most prestigious movers and shakers. Unfortunately, they are always asked and nearly impossible to get to serve.

Truth: The total list of highly effective people is larger than most people realize. Moreover, even movers and shakers on the short list can be recruited. And even if they turn down the opportunity to serve now, the recruitment was a valuable cultivation activity, and the leader may be available for service later.

Myth: The real work of the board is done at the committee level. We need to run the most efficient meeting possible and not waste board members' time with unneeded discussion.

Truth: Very efficient meetings—those in which committee recommendations are rubber-stamped without discussion—are boring and are not effective. Time should be allocated at each board meeting for discussion of strategic issues and major decisions. After discussion, the matter can then be referred to committee. Such a practice creates buy-in.

Near Myth: Board members have the prime responsibility for fundraising. They must be willing to set up appointments with their peers. The reason so many fund drives fail is that too many board members simply don't make their calls.

Truth: Board members share responsibility for fundraising. If the staff does not play a leadership role in setting up appointments, too few cultivation and solicitation visits will take place.

Myth: It is helpful to establish a "floor" for board giving. For example, some boards require a $2,500 a year minimum contribution; others may require donations of $10,000, $100,000, or even more annually.

Truth: The suggested floor often becomes a "ceiling." Some people choose not to serve. Others who can afford a great deal more give only the suggested amount.

True, but Not the Whole Story: The main concern of every organization is to develop a unified and visionary view of the future. The not-for-profit institution needs to have everyone understand how the organization will best meet the needs of those people being served.

Truth: The preceding statement is correct. However, every organization undergoes times when the vision of the future is not yet developed nor universally understood. Moreover, if a main concern of the board becomes how to best nurture positive relationships among its own members and with people who can make a difference, the organization will survive its challenges and go on to develop and achieve its visionary destiny.

MORE ON RECRUITMENT

Often, small or grassroots nonprofit organizations have boards of directors composed of strong and committed people who don't happen to be well connected with the community's power structure. When the idea of recruiting affluent movers and shakers for the board is introduced, there is a great deal of resistance to the concept. Some board members say that no one on the board knows such people, so they can't recruit them. Others worry that the character of the organization will change if the board is enlarged with preference given to people of affluence and influence.

As stated when we examined the myths and truths, many small and new organizations have had good fortune recruiting strong community leaders. I recall one performing arts organization that was able to recruit a board composed of generous donors. Before the institution even had its first organizing meeting, the founding artistic director—a person new to the state—called on community leaders and enthusiastically described his vision for a major regional theater company. Soon he and a small group of supporters had recruited an exceptionally strong board, one composed of individuals, each of whom donated several thousand dollars to hundreds of thousands annually.

How is it possible for a new, small, or grassroots organization to develop a strong board? How can a nonprofit agency expand and enhance its board? What works? Here are some ideas that have worked well for my clients.

Have an Adequate List of Strategic Selections for Your Board of Directors

Recall that you are developing a list of community leaders who can strengthen your board. These are people of affluence and influence. In some cases they have special skills you need for your board. They are selected because of the human and financial resources they can bring to your organization. They are not selected merely because someone on the nominating committee knows them and thinks they will say yes. That can help; but organizations preparing for capital campaigns often need to look beyond their current network. Moreover, the organization will need to develop a large enough list of potential strong board members to assure a sufficient number of committed, involved, and effective board members.

Find Several Key People Willing to Make Introductions

Perhaps some of your current board members know community leaders well enough to make introductions and secure appointments. These vital connections are best uncovered when the organization's executive director, consultant, or director of development meets one-on-one with each board member. Board members do a better job of recalling who they know when they are comfortable in their own homes or offices—near their lists and databases.

Be sure to have conversations with each board member concerning what it takes to build a strong board and the qualities you are looking for in potential new board members. Find out who your board members know. Explain that you would like the board member to help with the recruitment.

When seeking people to make introductions, go beyond your current board members. Old friends, business associates, past board members, executive staff, fellow members of service clubs, and others can also be called upon to make introductions. In the example of the founding of the new theater company, the founding artistic director called upon an old friend, a professor in the local university's theater department. The artistic director asked his friend which community leaders seemed most interested in the arts. He also asked the theater professor to introduce him to the community leaders. In some cases, the professor introduced the wannabe artistic director directly to selected community leaders. In other cases, the professor gave permission to use his name when calling for appointments. Both approaches worked well.

Secure Appointments

Use all your graciousness and social skills to secure eyeball-to-eyeball meetings with potential board members. Don't tell them that you would like to meet to discuss board membership. Rather, explain that you would like to discuss the organization and seek their advice on a range of issues. (If you did limit your request for a meeting to the subject of board membership, prospective members can too easily dismiss the idea before they have heard about the organization's vision.)

Words such as "The XYZ Organization is doing some very valuable work and is refining its vision of the future. I'd like to meet with you to bring you up to date on the organization and get your input and advice on a broad range of issues." If the community leader asks what kind of advice you are looking for, you can reply, "It's important that we get input concerning our plans and community needs. We'd also appreciate your help in discussing future volunteer and board recruitment. We'd love to know who you see as potential leaders who get things done."

When suggesting an appointment, be positive. Expect the person to say yes. If a mutually respected friend or associate gave permission to use his or her name, you might say something such as, "Peggy Atterberry suggested we get together. She thought you would enjoy hearing about the XYZ Organization. She also thought that you would be able to offer advice concerning the organization's future."

Also, promise to keep the meeting short, and offer a number of alternative dates. Positive, specific suggestions work well. When seeking appointments, get used to using language such as, "I'm free all of Thursday afternoon, and I'm open for breakfast Tuesday, Wednesday, and Thursday the 22nd, 23rd, and 24th of this month." Choices and specific suggestions are very positive. Even if the person with whom you are trying to meet can't make any of the dates you suggest, it is easy enough to turn the situation around and ask, "What dates do you have open?"

One final point: If at all possible, see that the person calling for an appointment with the community leader has an established relationship. Friendly, respectful peer relationships make these introductions evolve quite naturally. But if you don't have such ties to the potential board member, fear not. Recall that our friend the theater company artistic director was new in the state when he called upon the community leaders.

Learn the Language of Recruitment

When we discuss the structure of a major gift solicitation, we think in terms of seven steps to the conversation:

1. Building rapport.
2. Stating the case.
3. Asking questions.
4. Listening to advice and perhaps objections.
5. Responding appropriately.
6. Closing by asking for the commitment.
7. Tying down follow-up steps.

These same seven steps work well for recruitment purposes. In fact, when "closing" by asking someone to consider coming on your board, you are also asking that person to become a financial supporter. After all, potential board members should be informed of their duties and responsibilities. And the people you are recruiting probably already know that board members are expected to be generous to the institution. So one can readily see how closely analogous board recruitment is to major gift solicitation.

Recall that all gracious meetings begin with brief introductory pleasantries. Being respectful of the prospect's time, you will want to move directly into your brief overview of the organization and its future. Ask questions. Seek advice. Once you have heard the prospective board member say something positive about your organization, speak about the role of the board in the organization's future. Explain responsibilities, time commitments, and why you believe the person you are speaking to can help. Listen. Listen. Listen. Respond appropriately.

If you secured the appointment with the help of an intermediary, you might say, "Ivan Connection spoke highly of you and thought you would enjoy the opportunity to serve."

If the prospective board member points out that the organization currently has a weak board, or has not yet established a strong community presence, the recruiter might say, "We know we have a long way to go. We also know that people of your stature and position in the community have a history of overcoming obstacles. I hope you agree that our plan and vision are inspiring. If so, please *adopt us* and help us put together the ideal team to achieve our most important goals. Once you join our board, I feel confident that we'll have great success in recruiting additional well-respected community leaders." The key phrases here are "adopt us" and "help us put together the ideal team." Experiment. Speak out loud. Find your own ways of expressing these most powerful messages.

If you are meeting with a community leader together with his or her spouse, you might say, "I know that both of you are busy, and you know your schedules and commitments best; that's why I wanted to meet with you together. You both understand why the work we are doing at XYZ Organization is important. So I thought you could decide which, or both, of you would be able to serve on our board of directors."

Another variation on the "recruit the spouse" strategy begins by recognizing that, often, the spouse has more time and nearly the same clout as the well-known community leader. In such cases, you can do very well indeed by securing appointments with the community leader's spouse and asking him or her to serve. This is an often-overlooked strategy for recruiting effective board members while increasing the prestige of the board.

If you are speaking with a corporate leader who simply will not consider another board membership, you might ask the corporate leader if he or she would be willing to "make one or two introductions—for fundraising or board recruitment purposes." Often you will receive a positive reply, and those two introductions might make a huge difference in your organization's future. Another approach is to ask, "Do you have a leader in your organization who feels passionately about this issue?" If you are successful in recruiting a high-level corporate executive, your chances of receiving generous annual support and a larger capital campaign commitment increase dramatically. Moreover, some marketing directors, finance directors, COOs, and other executives—especially folks committed to your cause—make marvelous board members.

Learn How to Handle Recruitment Objections

Street-smart leaders anticipate the most common reasons people give for not being able to serve and develop responses to these objections. Example objections and possible alternative responses include:

Objection: "I'm overcommitted. I'm simply too busy."

Response: "One of the reasons we wanted to speak with you is your commitment to our community. When you get involved with a project, people know that good things will happen. Do you see a way of making some time to work with us? What support can we give to make board service easier?"

Response: "Everyone we speak to says that we need you on our team. We have a strong staff and a great consultant who will help guide our capital campaign. We can give you the kind of support you need to be effective. Please be assured that we will never waste your time. On the contrary, I know that you will be proud of your association with us and what we will accomplish together."

Response: "Tell me a bit about some of the boards you're serving on. Is it possible that your term might be up soon on one of them? We'd love to reapproach you when your schedule clears a bit."

Objection: "My favorite charity is ABC Nonprofit Agency. I feel very committed to them and serve on their board."

Response: Any of the preceding; or, "I know how committed you are to ABC Nonprofit. The leaders of our organization hope that you will find it in your heart to join our board of directors or capital campaign committee for the next two years. That's a critical time in our organization's history and I know you can play an important role. Also know that we have a strong staff that will support you so your time commitment can be well controlled."

Objection: "I don't know enough about your organization. And I have my doubts that this is a cause with which I want to be involved."

Response: "Please don't decide today. Let me send you more information. I won't take any of your time now, but I'll send you updates on our progress. If it's okay with you, I'll get back to you in six months or so. Let's talk about your involvement and level of commitment then." (Only use this type of language if you are able to follow up with additional positive news. Be sure to keep a tickler file of follow-up steps required.)

Objection: "Our corporation is facing a number of critical challenges right now. I've cut back entirely on my community projects. I don't believe I can become involved for quite some time."

Response: "I understand; your first responsibility is to your employees and stockholders. Would you feel comfortable if we spoke to your spouse about service on our board? You are both so well respected, I feel confident that Pat would make a marvelous board member."

Response: "Well I certainly understand. Perhaps you can help in another way. Do you have a leader in your organization who feels passionately about this issue? If you could ask around, we'd be very pleased to have one of your senior executives on our board—especially if he or she has a personal passion for our work."

BOARD SIZE

Some organization development experts express concern that "large boards are unwieldy and unmanageable." This is an idea that you will rarely hear from an experienced fundraising professional. The reason is simple: The main concern of fundraising professionals is that old saw, "Successful fundraising is the right person asking the right prospect for the right amount for the right project at the right time in the right way." There are six "rights" in the preceding sentence, the first of which is "the right person asking." To be assured that the institution has a strong board member with a peer relationship to each prospective donor, it helps to have a somewhat large board. The more board members, the more potential volunteer fundraisers.

When asked, "How large should our board be?" some experts might be tempted to reply, "How long is a piece of string?" The implication is that the original question has no answer. Let me attempt a less cynical and more definitive answer. A board of 7 to 11 members has the potential advantage of cohesiveness. With such boards, administration and governance should not be a burden to the staff. However, as the organization's need for contributed income increases, so too does its need for more board members. A board composed of 12 to 24 active and committed community leaders can accomplish wonders. At times, large arts institutions and other organizations that need to raise substantial funds each year recruit boards with approximately 30 members. Boards with more than 30 or so members rapidly lose their effectiveness.

STAFF SUPPORT

The advice to increase board size should not be taken without the understanding that the staff may need to grow. Certainly, a board of any size cannot be effective without adequate staff support. High-quality staff work involves scheduling meetings, sending reminders, conducting proactive consultations with board members, providing committee members with briefing and option papers, answering questions and providing information requested, and a whole host of time-consuming—but critical—support functions.

This care and feeding (literally) of board members pays off. A somewhat large—but well-supported—board can work miracles. This is especially true if the organization takes care to see that there are many social opportunities for board members to bond with each other. Feelings of friendship, when mixed with a deep sense of accomplishment, become an irresistible force.

FREQUENCY OF MEETINGS

"How often should the board meet?" may be the wrong question. Meeting monthly but getting little done annoys busy people who must use their time wisely. Meeting once a quarter makes it difficult to keep the board informed and engaged. The board that meets once a year has probably abrogated its responsibilities. While there may be no right or wrong answer, let's examine some guiding principles:

- *Board meetings should be interesting, action-oriented, well run, and offer opportunities to discuss strategic issues.* Let's start with "interesting." If you find your meetings taken up with boring recitations of routine financial reports, meaningless small committee updates, and attention to peripheral issues, board members begin to daydream about obtaining a cease-and-desist order. Expect attendance to decline while resignations increase.

  Matters improve when the focus becomes action-oriented. People begin to pay attention. Some even volunteer for important assignments. You know you are on the right track when your board meeting minutes are filled with notes about who is doing what by when.

  Quality people expect meetings to start and end on time. The meetings must deal with substantive issues. And board members do not want to merely sit back and listen to committee reports.

  The full board should air all important issues prior to referring those strategic concerns to the appropriate committee. The preliminary but thoughtful discussions inform the committee as to which issues should be addressed. This allows the committee to do a better job. As important, board members know that their attendance at the meetings is meaningful. Each board member is given an opportunity for input into strategic decision making. This creates a greater sense of buy-in.

- *Boards composed of people living within driving distance of each other should meet 6 to 12 times per year.* Presuming the organization's mission and purpose is important, meeting at least once every two months should not be a burden. And a growing nonprofit organization dealing with facility planning needs the support and attention of its board. Board members need time together to arrive at thoughtful decisions. Meaningful and timely meetings allow each board member to maximize his or her contribution to the project.

- *Organizations that meet only quarterly need to take extraordinary steps to keep board members engaged.* Often, nonprofit organizations with a regional, national, or international scope find it difficult to meet more than four times a year. In such cases, the board and staff will want to use a variety of techniques to keep the board members informed and engaged. Consider forming an executive committee that meets more frequently. Schedule conference calls of key committees. Assure that board members involved with facility planning or with the capital campaign communicate frequently with each other and with staff.

- *Organizations engaged in facility planning and capital campaigns should consider increasing the number of board meetings.* Extraordinary times call for extraordinary measures. A fully engaged board will want to continue making progress on a broad spectrum of strategic issues. The world will not stop just because the organization is engaged in a capital and endowment project. Other important issues will arise. These must be addressed. And facility planning and capital campaigns require a great deal of time and attention. Additional meetings can add to the sense of urgency. Moreover, professionals with fundraising responsibilities appreciate the opportunity to catch up with board members. Development staff and capital campaign consultants can use this "face time" to encourage each board member to stay on track and complete his or her contacts. Activities that keep project planning, donor cultivation, and solicitation processes moving forward are not always agenda items. Progress often occurs when board, staff, and consultants have brief motivating reminder chats during breaks and just before or after the meetings. Some board members will never attend a meeting solely devoted to fundraising, but they will come to regularly scheduled meetings. Just plan on speaking with them informally, gently encouraging each to "set up one or two team visits."

BOARD MEMBER RETENTION

If your board of directors has a problem with retention, take the time needed to diagnose and correct the problem. Exit interviews can help. These can be conducted by a well-respected board member. Exhibit 3.2, "Board Member Exit Interview," covers most of the questions you might wish to ask. Nonprofit organizations can use this when someone leaves before his or her term has expired (especially important) or when the board member has reached his or her term limit.

Usually the answer becomes clear after speaking frankly to current and departing board members. The organization might be spending too much time on petty matters. The nonprofit might have slipped into an "all talk-no action" mentality. Perhaps the meetings are poorly run or boring. At times there can

EXHIBIT 3.2   BOARD MEMBER EXIT INTERVIEW

1. Please describe your recollections of the recruitment process. Who recruited you? Were the board member responsibilities explained clearly? Did actual board service match your expectations?

2. Do you have any recommendations concerning board recruitment?

3. How would you describe your service on the board? Was your board membership fulfilling and rewarding? Was your board membership in any way disappointing?

4. As a board member, how would you rate the support you received from the organization's staff?

5. Do you have any suggestions for improving staff support?

6. Do you believe that board meetings were well run and an effective use of your time?

7. What suggestions would you make to improve board meetings?

8. Do you believe the organization provides board members with enjoyable and meaningful social opportunities? Yes____ No____

9. Does the organization offer too few, too many, or just the right number of social opportunities?

10. What factors led you to leave the board? Term expired? Time constraints? Commitment to another nonprofit organization? Other? (Please explain.)

11. What suggestions would you make concerning improving board effectiveness?

Note: Interviews should be conducted by a fellow board member. Comments and suggestions may be given confidentially—with the understanding that thoughts might be shared with members of the nominating committee or on a selective basis according to the interviewee's wishes. The interviewer should also take this opportunity to thank the board member for his or her service, as well as for the time and advice offered at the exit interview.

even be an approach to board meetings that can only be described as "too efficient." I once attended a board meeting that lasted precisely one hour. During that meeting, committees reported, and the board approved the following: a major purchase of a costly new information system; the approval of a strategic plan; the acceptance of a support contract for a major gift initiative; an award given to a key volunteer; and approval of several routine committee reports. Maybe you think that sounds like a good and productive meeting, a well-organized effort that ran smoothly because "the real work was done in committee." Sound familiar? Well, there was a problem. This organization had a terrible history of attrition of its board members. In an interview, one board member who was planning to depart said, "They do good work. The committees seem to function well; but there is no real reason to go to the board meetings. All the work is done beforehand. It doesn't matter if I'm there or not." Fortunately, this story has a happy ending. The organization changed the way it ran meetings and encouraged open discussion before matters were referred to committee. The dissatisfied board member stayed on and later made a six-figure contribution to the institution.

When the organization faces difficulties, be sure to stay focused on solutions. Some boards respond appropriately to financial problems. They approve realistic budgets in the first place. They hold themselves and the staff accountable. They offer realistic alternatives to solve the problem. Nonprofit leaders have to work through these difficulties while remaining as positive as possible. Even strong, well-intentioned people are unlikely to stay on board in the face of continual crises and pleas to "help save the organization." That gets old real fast.

So, care for your board. Ask them what they need to be more effective. Maintain fiscal discipline. Encourage lots of social opportunities. Conduct meaningful meetings. Dream big dreams. And make board membership a positive experience.

BUY-IN FOR THE CAPITAL CAMPAIGN

To assure success of your visionary plans, board members must be committed to the capital project and campaign. By following the advice in this chapter, this critical success factor should develop naturally. Board members will gain buy-in through multiple opportunities for involvement: service on a strategic planning committee; service on a facilities planning committee; serious board discussions throughout the process; service on an architect selection committee; service on a capital campaign consultant selection committee; service on a precampaign planning study committee; service on a construction company selection committee; and service as a capital campaign volunteer. If staff makes key decisions without board input, the campaign can get into trouble before you even get started. The board is responsible for the institution's policies, budget, strategic direction, and faithfulness to mission. Do everything possible to keep board members engaged in these most important responsibilities. The rewards for doing so are, as Arnold Schwarzenegger would say, "HUGE!"

CHAPTER 4

Project Planning*

DALE R. DEKKER, AIA, AICP, ASID

The interaction and exchange of ideas between the nonprofit organization and the architect is where true problem solving is achieved. The design team is led by mature designers who see themselves as expert "toolmakers," making the tools (the drawings, studies, models, and other relevant information) used to aid in the decision-making process of representatives of the nonprofit institution.

Any responsible design effort must respond to an overall vision. The nonprofit's vision is expressed through its values and goals. The facilities designed for each institution must ultimately augment and reinforce the goals and values of the nonprofit and assist the board and management in achieving them.

Each institution must develop its own set of values. Nonprofit organizations commonly express the following *values:*

- Concern for the community and the people served
- Safety
- Integrity
- Innovation
- Concern for the environment
- Employee relations
- Long-term outlook—a commitment to the future
- Adaptability, flexibility, and timely response to change

The nonprofit organization's facility *goals* might include:

*Printed with permission from Dale R. Dekker, Dekker/Perich/Sabatini.

- To improve the nonprofit organization's ability to fulfill its mission, enhance its programs and services, and operate in the most cost-effective manner possible.
- To enhance the organization's ability to attract and retain motivated, well-trained, and top-quality employees.
- To increase staff productivity and efficiency.

Great care must be given to the nature of the nonprofit institution and its facility needs. Healthcare institutions require environments that promote healing. Faith-based organizations build sacred spaces—places for worship and praise. Performing arts institutions inspire their audiences with their performance spaces, as well as with the performances given in them. Educational institutions create spaces that are conducive to learning. Conservation and preservation institutions reflect their values through their architecture and concern for their history and environment.

To be successful, administrative facilities must responsibly and creatively address unique functional and aesthetic issues. Nonprofit facilities require sensitivity and attention to each organization's unique circumstances and concerns. Common issues include:

- Creating an easily identified and accessible "front door," or main entrance, that presents the right image to the public while providing appropriate security to the facility. Also, creating a conveniently located "back door" for proper servicing of the facility.
- Proper storage, protection, and preservation of the nonprofit organization's records.
- Easy "wayfinding" and functional staff flow for efficient, effective operations.
- Cost-effective, efficient, and appropriate environmental, fire protection, building finishes, and code-compliance systems.
- An appropriate response to visual context and an image that speaks appropriately to function, place, and time.
- A well-thought-out construction phasing and move strategy.
- An appropriate urban design solution that responds to the unique character of the community in which the facilities are built.

Architects experienced with designing projects for nonprofit institutions develop problem-solving methodologies that are well suited to each client's needs. Function and efficient operation are always essential. Solving problems and finding optimal solutions for the nonprofit organization require the architect to remain focused on the client's concerns throughout the entire process, from predesign through construction and warranty.

PRELIMINARY THOUGHTS
AND COST ESTIMATES

Prior to engaging the services of an architect, the nonprofit organization should make some very preliminary decisions and cost estimates. The organization can determine if it wishes to expand or renovate current facilities. Perhaps the organization can determine that its strategic needs can be met only with new facilities.

The organization can examine potential locations. With donated services available to well-respected nonprofit institutions, the organization can also begin to sketch its space requirements. Experienced advisors can help the organization develop its first rough estimates of the total project costs. Exhibit 4.1 shows a number of building types and the related construction costs. Note that these construction costs *do not include* site acquisition, soft costs (design fees, soil testing, environmental inspections, fees to specialty firms), financing costs, fundraising costs, and furnishings.

To help estimate total capital expenses, consider the following:

- Site acquisition typically accounts for 15 percent to 20 percent of the total project cost. Real estate agents can provide up-to-date information concerning available land and the price for each actual site. Alternatively, they can also provide general information concerning price per acre in the areas being considered.

- Construction costs typically account for 60 percent to 70 percent of the total project expenses. Examine Exhibit 4.1 again. Determine what type of facilities the nonprofit is building. Refine estimates with advice from local builders and architects.

- Soft costs, such as architectural and engineering fees, account for 10 percent to 20 percent of the total project.

- Fundraising expenses can range from 5 percent to 15 percent of the campaign total.

- Furnishings can account for 5 percent to 10 percent of the total project.

- Financing costs can vary greatly. In a campaign with a three- to five-year pledge period, financial institutions may provide favorable rates for the pledge period. Projects that are planned to raise less than the entire amount needed require longer-term notes to finance the unfunded balance. The organization's lending institution can help project these costs.

- Every organization should add a 5 percent contingency fund to its total project cost estimates.

Adding up all the low-percentage estimates, you arrive at 100 percent of the total project costs. And that's before considering any financing that may be

EXHIBIT 4.1   BUILDINGS AND THEIR RELATED
CONSTRUCTION COSTS

Office Building
$75–$95/sq. ft.

Educational
$85–$105/sq. ft.

Senior Assisted Housing
$65–$80/sq. ft.

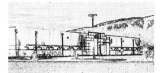

Office Shell
$60–$85/sq. ft.

Religious Remodel
$55–$110/sq. ft.

Specialty Educational
$100–$150/sq. ft.

Religious
$85–$120/sq. ft.

Auditorium/Concert Halls
$150–$200/sq. ft.

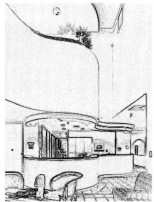

Medical Office
$90–$110/sq. ft.

Visitor Center
$100–$150/sq. ft.

Higher Education
$115–$155/sq. ft.

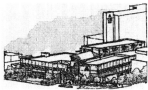

Medical
$125–$155/sq. ft.

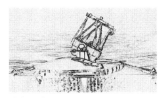

High Tech
$150–$1,000/sq. ft.

Multiple Family Housing
$60–$75/sq. ft.

EXHIBIT 4.1   (CONTINUED)

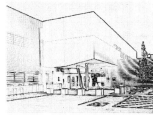

Research Center
$150–$175/sq. ft.

Museum/Exhibit Space
$90–$135/sq. ft.

Laboratory
$140–$200/sq. ft.

Printed with permission from Dale R. Dekker, Dekker/Perich/Sabatini.

needed. But do not be too concerned about percentages of the total attributed to each element in the plan: The *total* project costs—by definition—will always equal 100 percent. The percentages are helpful for keeping project elements relatively in line with each other. The more important work is making realistic projections concerning each of the planning dimensions, as these cost estimates will continue to be refined throughout the entire process. The point is, careful early work will produce good estimates that will hold up well.

Exhibit 4.2 from Marilyn Bancel's book, *Preparing Your Capital Campaign* (Jossey-Bass, 2000), provides a very detailed worksheet for estimating total project costs.

SELECTING AN ARCHITECT

Nonprofit organizations want to select architectural firms that have the experience and qualifications needed to create workable solutions to the institution's facility needs. Nonprofits also want to work with firms that share their values and aspirations.

Often, the selection process is informal. Board members and key staff may know well-established architects with the experience needed. At times, key decision makers have had direct experience working with the firm. On other occasions, a prominent architect might be a member or long-term supporter of the nonprofit institution. Even in these cases, preliminary meetings help clarify expectations and processes. And in every case, organization leaders need to observe due diligence and take care in preparing contracts.

Often, the nonprofit organization may be obligated to follow formal procurement practices. Public institutions and organizations that have established procurement policies requiring formal bidding are familiar with their legal obligations. Moreover, institutions contemplating complex and visionary facility plans may wish to adopt a formal bidding process. The usual process involves the following phases.

EXHIBIT 4.2   COST CATEGORIES FOR THE BRICKS-
AND-MORTAR CAPITAL CAMPAIGN

	A	B	C	D
1		Year 1	Year 2	Year 3
2	**BEFORE THE CAMPAIGN**			
3				
4	**Plans**			
5	Institutional strategic plan			
6	Design and development of new programs and initiatives			
7	Institutional operating postconstruction budget			
8	Facilities plan			
9	Planning workshops			
10	Board retreats: hosting, facilitator, travel, and so on			
11	Communications plan			
12	Financial plan for entire project and campaign			
13	Allocated staff time			
14	Other			
15	**SUBTOTAL: PLANS**			
16				
17	**Capital Project Preparation**			
18	Architectural designs			
19	Realtor, site search			
20	Legal fees			
21	Environmental impact reports			
22	Neighborhood education, polling, meetings			
23	Traffic and parking assessments			
24	Engineering drawings, schematics			
25	Architectural models			
26	Allocated staff time			
27	Other			
28	**SUBTOTAL: PROJECT PREPARATION**			
29				
30	**Campaign Preparation**			
31	Seed fund development, consultant fees			
32	Donor and prospect cultivation and communications			
33	Feasibility study			
34	Advance or down-payment fund			
35	Allocated staff time			
36	Other			
37	**SUBTOTAL: CAMPAIGN PREPARATION**			
38				
39	**TOTAL PRECAMPAIGN COSTS**			

EXHIBIT 4.2   (CONTINUED)

40	**DURING CONSTRUCTION AND CAMPAIGN**			
41				
42	**Acquisition Costs***			
43	Land			
44	Structures			
45	Occupancy or air rights			
46	Other			
47	(*less advance fund, line 34)			
48	Other			
49				
50	**Construction Costs**			
51	Capital project management plan			
52	Contractor estimate or bid			
53	Additional materials			
54	Contract or construction manager			
55	Insurance			
56	Other			
57	**SUBTOTAL: CONSTRUCTION**			
58				
59	**Carrying Costs**			
60	Construction loan and loan fees			
61	Loan carrying costs			
62	Interest income lost			
63	Other interest payments on loans			
64	Other			
65	**SUBTOTAL: CARRYING COSTS**			
66				
67	**Operating and Logistical Costs**			
68	Rental costs during displacement			
69	Lost revenues during closure or displacement			
70	Long-term storage			
71	Other			
72	**SUBTOTAL: OPERATING COSTS**			
73				
74	**Endowment Funds**			
75	**Reserve Funds**			
76				
77	**Fundraising Costs**			
78	New equipment			
79	Additional staff positions			
80	Consultant fees			

EXHIBIT 4.2 (CONTINUED)

81	Case and marketing materials			
82	Cultivation, host expenses, events			
83	Communications			
84	Travel			
85	Pledge attrition			
86	Allocated staff time			
87	Other			
88	**SUBTOTAL: FUNDRAISING COSTS**			
89				
90	**Other Institutional Costs**			
91	Administrative staff time allocated to the project			
92	Other new staff positions			
93	Overhead additions			
94	**SUBTOTAL: INSTITUTIONAL COSTS**			
95				
96	**TOTAL PROJECT AND CAMPAIGN COSTS**			

Source: Marilyn Bancel, *Preparing Your Capital Campaign*, Jossey-Bass, © 2000. This material is used by permission of John Wiley & Sons, Inc.

Request for Proposal

The request for proposal (RFP) contains the following:

- A statement of the project scope
- The contact person
- The basis for selection, that is, qualifications of the firm submitting, including a request for a preliminary fee or a description of how the fee will be calculated
- Selection process, including how the submittals will be reviewed and whether an interview will be conducted
- Calendar of events, including presubmittal meeting, if applicable, proposal due date, selection committee review date, and interview of short list date

Before issuing the RFP, the nonprofit organization should have it reviewed by its attorney.

Develop a Short List

Typically, instead of selecting a firm based *solely* on the submitted proposals, the selection committee will review the proposals with the aim of selecting from three to five well-qualified firms to interview. The selection is based on experience with similar projects, approach to problem-solving and project planning, and the firm's responsiveness to the RFP requirements.

While the committee is meeting to select the short list, members can also prepare for the interviews. They should decide on the format of the interview process, the questions to ask, who is going to ask the questions, and the selection criteria.

Interview Architects

Allow 30 minutes to an hour for each interview. If at all possible, hold all interviews on the same day. Make every effort to have the identical interview team present for all interviews. Stick to the predetermined questions and format. Allow time for a question-and-answer period during which both the architect and the selection committee can ask questions.

Consider asking whether the architect has any experience with aiding in fundraising. Perhaps one or more of the candidates will have knowledge of funding resources. Others might have experience making presentations to potential funders. Still others might have actual experience in grant preparation or securing government funding.

Always ask the architect to describe the firm's relevant experience. Ask involvement questions that encourage the architect to fully describe how the firm handled difficult situations or circumstances such as those faced by your nonprofit organization.

Also include these questions:

• Who will do the work?
• What are the qualifications of the key design team members?
• How will the chemistry and partner arrangement work with these key people?

Ask the first two questions directly to the representatives of each firm. Listen carefully. Some firms have strong salespeople, but assign junior people to do the actual work. The last question concerning chemistry and partnering is one of the keys to selecting the right architect for your project. This is the question committee members ask themselves. Select a well-qualified firm that lets you know who will do the work and that you are sure can work in a positive manner with the nonprofit organization's staff and volunteers.

Check References

In the RFP and during the interview, request references. Have one person check references for all final candidates. This assures that fairness and a unified approach will be applied to each firm. Make sure that the firm has a good track record. Ask questions concerning overall satisfaction. Ask specific questions concerning working relationships and problem-solving skills.

Prepare Contract

The architect that the nonprofit organization selects must be registered to do business in the nonprofit organization's state. Often the contract is based on AIA Form B141. The contract describes the responsibilities of the parties involved and the terms.

The cost can be on a fixed-fee basis, a percentage of project cost basis (a method often used with public institutions), or a fee-for-basic-services basis. The fixed-fee contract lists all deliverables and their related fees. Common elements include the kick-off meeting, programming phase, schematic phase, design development, construction documents, bidding, and construction administration services.

Architects describe what is included in their basic fees. Clients can expect to pay more for special models, grant applications, and other specialized work related to the capital campaign. However, many architects gladly provide pro bono support for the capital campaign by making presentations to potential donors. Of course, these presentations are scheduled in the location where the architect does business. Nonprofit organizations can expect to pay extra fees if the architect has to travel for the presentation.

PREDESIGN PHASE

From the architect's point of view, an early question is, "Who is the client?" In the broadest sense, the nonprofit institution is the client. But that doesn't answer a number of closely related questions. Who speaks for the organization? Is there a facilities planning committee? Is there one person—perhaps the executive director or board chair—who is pushing the project forward? Is there a foundation or outside funder motivating the project? Who can make the decision to move forward? Who is authorized to sign contracts and commit the organization's financial resources?

The nonprofit institution's board and administrative staff need to clarify these issues. The organization's leaders must understand the institution's human dynamics as well as its formal decision-making processes.

Once these issues are addressed, the organization can begin to articulate its vision. Architects may well be the people who solve problems and design the facilities, but the nonprofit representatives remain the "backseat drivers." They know their wants and needs best.

In preliminary conversations with the architect, the client should be able to describe the rationale for the facilities. Many questions are sure to be unanswered; however, most "broad-brush" issues might be resolved. These include the following:

- What facilities are contemplated? How will the building or buildings be used? What is their function?
- Which people and how many people will use the facilities?
- Where will the facilities be located?
- What kind of environment and level of quality are expected?
- What are the organization's aesthetic considerations? What statement to the community does the nonprofit organization wish to make?
- What is the organization's preliminary total project budget? What "back of envelope" calculations has the organization made?
- When will the facilities need to open? How much timing flexibility does the organization have?

When organization leaders can answer these questions, meaningful conversations can be had, not only with architects but also with potential donors. The preliminary questions just listed are at the heart of quiet conversations with the organization's best prospects.

Management Team Formation

Effective project leadership is essential, in conjunction with clear definitions of roles and responsibilities. Clear lines of communication and authority are necessary to make timely decisions. At the outset of the project, the architect will request that either an individual project manager or a management team from the nonprofit organization be established as the point of contact for the duration of the project. Working with the architect's design team personnel, this team will facilitate the decision-making process regarding all aspects of the project.

An early and important gathering is the kick-off meeting. During this meeting, team members are introduced to each other. The team reviews the goals for the project and discusses major issues. As important, the team identifies lines of communications. Finally, the management team reviews the project planning approach. The meeting is also useful in clarifying expectations regarding budget, schedule, and a host of related issues. All decisions, including those concerning process and decision-making authority, are documented.

The architect's design team meets regularly with the nonprofit's team. Nonprofit organizations with departments or functional divisions should assign one person the responsibility for collecting surveys and scheduling interviews.

Facility Programming

The architect will prepare a program document that will be used as the basis of the design for the project. This document will include space requirements, with a graphic inventory of spaces, adjacencies, goals, and objectives for the project. Information gathering is the first and perhaps the most critical part of the project. The design team listens to the nonprofit organization's staff and volunteers to determine the space needs and organizational requirements that will shape the interior of the new facility. At the same time, the architectural team investigates the site and code requirements for the project. The architect then prepares a draft planning document for the client's review and comment. Any revisions will be incorporated into the final program document.

Space Requirements

The architect starts this process by creating a custom *space requirement survey* that can be distributed to key staff at the nonprofit institution. This survey will ask questions about personnel and staffing projections, shared support spaces, storage and equipment, adjacencies and information flow, security, public access requirements, and hours of operation. At Dekker/Perich/Sabatini, we recommend that the department representatives distribute the survey approximately one week prior to our interviews with key personnel from each department. Department managers or the management team will determine the number of interviews.

Frequently, interviews can be scheduled during a one-week period. Typically, design team members and the architect's staff meet with key personnel to review the completed survey and discuss the goals and objectives for the project. After each departmental interview, design team members tour the department to observe the existing conditions and to discuss workflow. Members of the nonprofit organization's management team may attend these meetings. In any case, the architect's design team meets with the appropriate representatives of the nonprofit organization upon the completion of the interviews to review the information collected.

At the end of the staff interviews, the design team will interview or meet again with the institution's executives and other key stakeholders. The purpose of these conversations is to establish the big picture for the project, including the goals and objectives that will shape the entire project. The success of the completed project will be measured against these goals.

Space Standards

During the architect's interviews, the design team looks at the way people work and how the existing environment either does or does not support that work.

This is the first step in determining how each space should be configured and how much square footage should be allotted. Space standards will be established for all workplaces, both enclosed and open, and for all support spaces such as conference rooms and workrooms. The management team will approve the standards for each space. The architect's goal is to create consistent space standards in order to provide a flexible facility. Each required space in the building would be assigned a space standard.

Square Footage Totals

Each department will have its required spaces listed, including any projected growth to create a department area. The architect also documents the requirements for all unique spaces—auditoriums, worship space, exhibit space, classrooms, laboratories, surgery units, and so on. A circulation factor is added to each department area to account for corridors and hallways, to create a department gross area. All department gross areas are totaled and a building tare factor will be added to accommodate the building structure and vertical circulation such as elevators and stairs and restrooms. The sum will be the basis for the size of the new building.

Adjacencies

The architect documents the requested departmental adjacencies in a matrix and a graphic format. These diagrams allow the architect to locate departments and functional units throughout the building and within the nonprofit organization's existing facilities.

Conceptual Design

The conceptual design phase of a project answers the major question, "How should the facility work?" The thrust of conceptual design activity is to prepare multiple options that investigate the functional organization of the project components. These options are often illustrated in the form of two-dimensional space, massing, and functional organization diagrams. The integration of the building with the site and the existing buildings is a major consideration. Service access, pedestrian access, vehicular access, and connections to existing circulation and related facilities are also considerations in this phase.

Blocking and Stacking

During this phase of the project, the design team reviews the departmental space and adjacency requirements and prepares options of how to configure the interior of the facility to meet those requirements. A key objective is to determine how many floors the nonprofit organization needs to meet its total square footage requirements.

The architect can present a number of options by "blocking" departments onto floor plates, and then "stacking" them onto different floors. The space available, along with the adjacency requirements, determines where a department is *best* located. The floor plans during this phase do not contain actual room and workstation layouts. Rather, the plans show the arrangement of the building shell's components, such as stairs, restrooms, elevators and lobbies, and other key functional components. Detailed space plans will be prepared during the space planning phase.

Space Planning

Once the building configuration is roughly established the actual layouts, or space plans, can be prepared. The layouts are prepared based on the established space standards and internal adjacencies. These plans show the location of all enclosed spaces, including offices, support spaces, and spaces unique to the nonprofit organization and its mission. Open office area layouts will show systems furniture or low-height partitions. The space planning works hand in glove with the building shell configuration. The shell should allow for flexibility and multiple configurations of the space plans.

At this stage, the nonprofit organization may wish to request that the architect label some of the key offices. Rather than simply showing office space, the layouts can label spaces as, for example, "Job Placement Director," "Computer Training Center," "Youth Ministry," or "Director of Pediatric Oncology." In this way, nonprofit leaders can use even these preliminary layouts when speaking with potential donors. People considering pacesetting lead gifts are less inspired by generic office space than they are in providing the resources needed to fulfill the nonprofit organization's mission. This is an important principle: Early on, nonprofit leaders and the design team should work to see that all design work, layouts, and drawings are labeled for maximum fundraising effectiveness.

The architects and the interiors staff work together to establish structural column placement and the overall shape of the building that is compatible with office layouts and special space requirements. On the building perimeter, the architect typically works with a module that allows for flexibility in the future. For example, a 5-foot window module will allow a 10-foot by 15-foot office (150 square feet) or a 15-foot by 15-foot office (225 square feet). Window heights are coordinated to avoid conflict with office furnishings. This information feeds into the schematic phase where more detail is developed.

The predesign work, facility programming, and space planning efforts account for approximately 10 percent of the architect's time devoted to the total project, from predesign through construction administration. The nonprofit organization can expect to pay 10 percent of the total architect's fees for this work.

SCHEMATIC DESIGN PHASE

The schematic phase attempts to answer two basic questions: "How should the facility work?" and "How should the facility look?" This phase will further refine the project. With the information gathered, the architect can now prepare a site plan, floor plan(s), building elevations, building sections, and preliminary building systems selections.

The specific methodology utilized during this phase can be described by the often-used, but nevertheless accurate phrase, "designing from the inside out." This simply means paying attention to the detailed facility requirements so that the "real" problems are solved—that is:

- Functional adjacencies are accommodated.
- Floor loading is adequate for the activity to occur there.
- Door sizes are functional for what passes through them.
- People—especially visitors—staff, and material flows are accounted for.
- Security is considered in the functional layout.

Paying attention to all of the details of the project during the schematic phase eliminates the need to rethink the organizational approach later or force something to work inappropriately.

Approximately 15 percent of the architect's time is devoted to the schematic phase. By the end of the schematic phase, the nonprofit organization will have paid approximately 25 percent of the architect's fees.

At this point, many nonprofit organizations pause in the facility planning process and concentrate on fundraising. At the conclusion of the schematic phase, the nonprofit organization will have the drawings, preliminary cost estimates, and models it needs to effectively conduct a precampaign planning study and capital campaign. The nonprofit organization need not proceed directly into the design development phase. Many choose to secure a large percentage of the capital campaign goal prior to committing financial resources for design development and construction.

DESIGN DEVELOPMENT PHASE

The thrust of this phase is to research, evaluate, and, finally, select the building systems for the facility. Architects consider the availability and appropriateness of materials, equipment and labor, construction sequencing and scheduling, economic analysis of construction and operations, user safety, maintenance requirements, energy conservation, special systems, and life safety code analysis.

The architect's team selects, documents, and fully integrates all systems, including architectural, civil, structural, mechanical, electrical, and any special systems. Communication among the various technical disciplines during this phase is absolutely essential. Experienced and qualified architects know that it is their responsibility to make this crucial communication happen.

Approximately 15 percent of the architect's total time is devoted to design development. At this stage, the nonprofit organization will have refined cost estimates, computer renderings, and a proposed project completion schedule.

INTERIOR SPACE DEVELOPMENT PHASE

The interior design aspects of the space are developed during the design development phase. Themes established by the building design are incorporated into the interior details to create a consistent design, both inside and out. Specialty lighting is selected and interior features are developed. Interior finish options are selected and presented to the management team.

At this time, architects work with the nonprofit organization's information systems representatives to develop a data/telephone cabling and wireless strategy for the facility. This information is necessary to insure the long-term flexibility of the facility. Future internal moves will be seamless, with a forward-thinking plan for technology in place.

CONSTRUCTION DOCUMENTS PHASE

This phase implements the detailed decisions made in the design development phase. The key here is thoroughness. Well-qualified architectural firms make sure that every aspect of the project is covered down to the smallest detail. The work produced in this phase ensures that no aspect of the project is left to the imagination or whim of a contractor—a very expensive practice. The architect prepares contract documents, including bidding requirements, contract forms, contract conditions, specifications, and construction drawings.

Coordination of disciplines will be the responsibility of each discipline manager, not just the architectural project manager. This occurs through regular meetings during which the architects, contractors, and subcontractors exchange information and review specific checklists. This process assures adequate follow-up to all action items.

Preparation of construction documents requires approximately 35 percent of the architect's time. At this stage, the nonprofit organization has selected its finishes and colors. The technical specifications will be complete. And all bid and construction documents for all phases of work will be in place. Final cost estimates are also established.

FURNISHINGS PHASE

Once the project moves into the construction document phase, the design team focuses on the furnishings. The objective is to provide a consistent look throughout the facility.

To determine the extent of furnishings required, the architect's first step is to prepare furniture layouts for all spaces. Workplace layouts are designed to maximize the space and respond to the nature of the nonprofit organization's work. A well-designed workplace is one that supports the way a user works; it accommodates current and future technology, and is easily modified for future occupants. This approach can result in increased productivity, improved employee retention, and decreased workplace injuries.

The design team will inventory the existing furnishings to determine which items should be refurbished and/or relocated. Once the extent of new furnishings is established, architects can prepare a preliminary budget and select options for the new furnishings.

A complete furniture package is then prepared and issued for negotiated pricing. Many architects coordinate installation and prepare a "punch list" upon completion.

ARTWORK, ACCESSORIES, AND PLANTS PHASE

Architects work with the nonprofit organization to create an art program consisting of fine art, prints, and poster art as required to create a consistent theme for the new facility. The process begins with an inventory of the organization's existing artwork. Then the design specialists work with representatives of the nonprofit organization to create a budget for new items. Once the artwork is selected, the design team will coordinate matting, framing, and installation of the new and existing pieces.

The architect will also select accessories for the facility and work with a local interior plant design and maintenance company to select plants and containers.

MOVE PHASE

In response to each nonprofit organization's specific facility plans, there may be a number of staff moves both prior to construction and afterward. Prior to renovations, key staff will need to be housed in temporary facilities. Nonprofits that are building new facilities have to continue operations even as they leave their old site and move to their visionary new spaces. The architect might be called upon to provide space planning services and to work with the management team to develop a comprehensive move-phasing plan.

CONSTRUCTION CONTRACT ADMINISTRATION PHASE

The decisions reached during the design phase must be implemented. Plans must become a reality. To do this, architects must first develop an understanding with the contractor. Experienced architects and contractors know that they are part of a larger team with one goal in mind: to construct facilities that meet the requirements of the contract documents, implementing the nonprofit organization's desires—within an acceptable cost.

Successful architects know that this cooperative arrangement is far better than an adversarial one. The architectural firm must perform its primary duty—looking out for the interest of the nonprofit institution—in a fair and responsible manner. But most important, this activity is a test of whether the architects, as representatives of the nonprofit organization, are going to back down or hold to the plans that the design team and the nonprofit's management team just spent a lot of time and money developing.

During construction, the architect's key team members visit the site weekly, or more often as necessary. The project manager and project architect, the two individuals most familiar with all aspects of the project, will coordinate this activity.

Architects devote approximately 5 percent of their time to the construction bidding process and another 20 percent of their time to the construction administration process.

ELEVEN-MONTH WARRANTY INSPECTION

An important aspect of the architect's responsibilities to the nonprofit institution is the 11-month warranty inspection. Organization leaders should not overlook this crucial opportunity to resolve any remaining issues. The architect reviews work quality, contractual obligations, and construction performance as it relates to the construction documents. Contractors have an obligation to fix what isn't right.

CONCLUSION: ACHIEVING DESIGN EXCELLENCE

Dedicated and well-qualified architects want to create facilities for nonprofit institutions that are truly responsive to community needs and lasting in quality. This means they must go the extra mile. No task can be undertaken without understanding its importance and implication in the entire scheme of the project. No task should be completed without a recheck of its results.

Dekker/Perich/Sabatini recommends that nonprofit organizations work with firms that use an approach that includes a quality assurance team to review all work. This formal mechanism, led by experienced principals within the collective team, will ensure that all of the right questions get asked and that all of the firm's work is fully checked and rechecked. By choosing firms that accomplish tasks right the first time, you will reduce costs, minimize stress, and have the maximum impact on overall quality control.

CHAPTER 5

Project Delivery Strategies*

CHARLES B. THOMSEN, FAIA, FCMAA

Early in a project, a client must select a process for design and construction. The process will affect the financing, the selection of the project team, the schedule, and the cost.

A client usually has a wide range of options. In addition to the traditional process, a client can choose *design-build, fast-track,* or *bridging.* Pricing options include guaranteed maximum price (GMP), cost-plus, target-price, and fixed-price contracts.

All these processes are flawed but they can all be made to work. The best choice is governed by the exigencies of the project. Pressures on schedule, budget, the symbolic role or practical functionality of the design, the experience of the client's management, the project's corporate or government oversight, or the regulation of procurement policy will influence strategy.

DESIGN AND CONSTRUCTION PHASES

Design and construction can be divided into three distinct phases: project definition (PD), design, and construction (see Exhibit 5.1).

These phases (and their subphases) can be overlapped, subdivided, or regrouped, but none can be eliminated. If one phase is done poorly, the following phases are usually impaired.

1. *Project definition.* At 3D/International, we subdivide this phase into two activities:
   - *Discovery.* The identification and analysis of project requirements and constraints.

*Printed with permission from Charles B. Thomsen, 3D/International.

EXHIBIT 5.1   THE THREE PHASES OF DESIGN
AND CONSTRUCTION

Project Definition	Design	Construction

Printed with permission from Charles B. Thomsen, 3D/International.

- *Integration.* The description of the project and the plan (including an estimate of cost and time for delivering it).

2. *Design.* Typically, design is divided into three phases:
   - *Schematic design.* The basic appearance and plans.
   - *Design development.* An evolution of design that defines the functional and aesthetic aspects of the project and the building systems that satisfy them.
   - *Construction drawings and specification.* The details of assembly and construction technology.

3. *Construction.* Construction can also be divided into several basic activities:
   - *Procurement.* The purchasing, negotiation or bid, and award of contracts to construct the project. This activity occurs at many levels. The way the client buys construction affects the methods that may be used by construction managers, general contractors, subcontractors, and suppliers.
   - *Shop drawings.* The final fabrication drawings for building systems. One could easily argue that shop drawings are really the last phase of design. They are included in the construction phase only because they are done by contractors after they have been selected.
   - *Fabrication, delivery, and assembly.* The manufacture and installation of the building components.
   - *Site construction.* The labor-intensive field construction and the installation of systems and equipment.

WHEN TO CONTRACT FOR CONSTRUCTION

The nonprofit organization's decision as to when to contract for construction is an important one. Choices include: traditional process, design-build, bridging, and fast-track. Let's briefly examine each.

Traditional Process

Traditional process is the term used for projects that are bid or negotiated *after* an architect/engineer (AE) completes construction drawings. However, shop drawings are done by contractors, so it's correct to argue that in all processes some design is done by the contractor.

Design-Build

Design-build contracts are typically negotiated before project definition, or just after. The design-build contractor does all design (including construction drawings) and then administers the construction process.

Bridging

Bridging is a hybrid of design-build and the traditional process. The contract documents are prepared by the nonprofit organization's architect/engineer. He or she specifies the project's functional and aesthetic requirements, but the details of construction technology are described with performance specification. The construction contract is awarded halfway through design. Construction drawings are done by a design-build contractor or a general contractor (GC) with an AE, who is also the "architect of record," as a subcontractor.

Exhibit 5.2, "Traditional, Bridging, and Design-Build Processes," illustrates the differences among these three choices of when to award the construction contract. The dollar sign ($) indicates when the construction contract is awarded.

Fast-Track

Fast-track is jargon for overlapping design and construction to accelerate completion. It may be done with the traditional process, bridging, design-build, or any other process.

There is no technical reason not to overlap design and construction. The problem is cost control. Construction begins before the design is complete, so the final scope and, therefore, the final price may be disputed.

There are two ways to fast-track a project. A single contract can be awarded to a general contractor or construction manager (CM) who builds the project under a cost-plus contract with a guaranteed maximum price (GMP). Or the nonprofit institution may retain a construction manager who may bid the project in stages with complete contract documents for each stage. The contracts for each stage are typically bid to trade contractors. The general contractor is eliminated. The fast-track process is illustrated in Exhibit 5.3.

EXHIBIT 5.2   TRADITIONAL, BRIDGING,
              AND DESIGN-BUILD PROCESSES

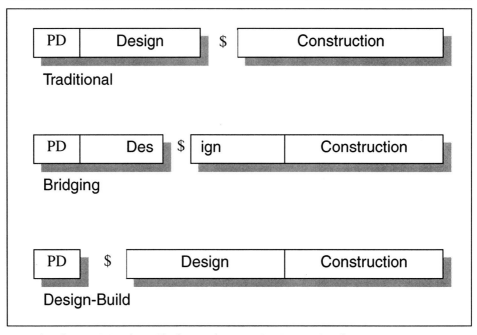

Printed with permission from Charles B. Thomsen, 3D/International.

EXHIBIT 5.3   THE FAST-TRACK PROCESS

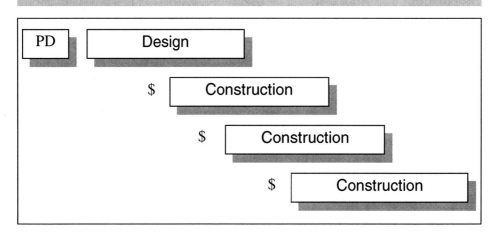

Printed with permission from Charles B. Thomsen, 3D/International.

CONTRACT DOCUMENTS

There are three classic ways to specify something: by product, by prescription, or by performance. For example, if the nonprofit organization wanted heating/ventilation/air conditioning (HVAC) equipment, documents could specify the manufacturer's *product* that would do the job and say "or equal," or they could *prescribe* what it's made of and how it's made (e.g., the horsepower, duct size, metal thickness, and so on), or the documents could specify the *performance* (the air changes, temperature, and humidity results that are required). The latter method provides latitude to contractors to meet the nonprofit organization's requirements.

A construction contract that includes a fixed price, a target price, or a GMP requires a description of the result that the contractor must produce. Let's examine some documents that accomplish this aim.

Construction Drawings and Specifications

Construction documents show how the building is made and what it's made of. The drawings show details such as the size and location of reinforcing rods, wiring runs, and duct sizes. The specifications typically define the construction by product or by prescription. In the United States, most AEs believe that these detailed construction drawings and specifications are the proper way to define the required result and to enforce a contract.

Bill of Quantities

In countries influenced by the British, licensed quantity surveyors measure drawings, calculate the amount of each required material, and prepare a bill of quantities. Construction contractors bid on the unit cost of each building material. These unit-price contracts are common for tenant fit-out in office buildings in the United States.

Design Development and Performance Specifications

In many countries, projects are bid with what we would call design development drawings (35 to 50 percent of the level of detail that is contained in a full set of construction drawings and specifications). Performance specifications describe what systems must do, rather than how they will do it. Construction drawings are completed by design-build contractors who maintain a staff of architects and engineers.

KEY DECISIONS

There are infinite variations in project delivery strategy, but there are four basic decisions. They are: (1) number of contracts, (2) selection criteria, (3) relationship of owner to contractor, and (4) terms of payment. These decisions aren't either/or; there are shades of gray.

Number of Contracts

A project may be awarded to one contractor, as in design-build. In the traditional process, there are two contracts: one with an AE and one with a construction contractor. If the nonprofit organization also engages the services of a project manager (PM), there are three main contracts. With a construction manager (CM), the nonprofit may have contracts with 40 prime subcontractors, or it may purchase building materials and equipment, and arrange multiple labor contracts. There may be thousands of contracts.

With multiple contracts, the nonprofit can fast-track a project (overlap design and construction). Direct purchase of labor and materials eliminates overhead markups. Unbundling design allows selection of specialists, and unbundling construction allows careful selection of specific manufacturers and trade contractors. As the number of contracts increases, the opportunities to save time, money, and improve quality also increase.

So does risk. Nonprofit organizations that choose to manage multiple contracts must manage the contracts well or take the responsibility for management failures. Consequently, most nonprofits package contracts under a general contractor (GC) or choose a CM to help them if they use multiple contracts.

The term "construction manager" is frequently used synonymously with "project manager." Often, the term "project manager" is used with the traditional process, and "construction manager" is used with multiple-contract fast-track. A general contractor may take the title of construction manager with a guaranteed minimum price (GMP) contract. The same company may provide all three kinds of services for different clients.

Selection Criteria

A contractor may be selected on the basis of price or qualifications. Nonprofit organizations often consider both and require a proposal (which could be a management plan or a design) *and* a price.

Typically, AEs are selected with an emphasis on qualifications, and construction contractors are selected on the basis of price. But there are nonprofits that select AEs on price and those that select GCs on qualifications. The selection criteria are influenced by what is to be bought. If it's a common product, easily defined and easily evaluated, there is little reason *not* to choose on the basis of price. But if the product is unusual or proprietary, or if service is required, or if intellectual qualities (talent, creativity, wisdom, judgment, or experience) are required, selection is usually based on qualifications.

Contractual Relationship

You may view contractors in one of two ways: as an agent or as a vendor. An agent represents the client's interest and has a fiduciary responsibility; a vendor delivers a specified product for a price. Agents tend to work for a fee and are usually selected on the basis of qualifications, whereas vendors sell a product for a price and are usually selected on the basis of cost.

Typically, AEs are viewed at the agency end of the spectrum, and contractors are at the vendor end. But there are exceptions. Some nonprofits ask contractors to act as their agents in procuring and managing construction, and treat AEs as vendors of plans and specifications.

When nonprofit institutions need guidance or advice, they typically choose an agent (a fiduciary) relationship. Nonprofits that know exactly what is required typically form vendor relationships.

There can be a conflict of interest if a contractor is both agent and vendor, or if a contractor changes from agent to vendor in the course of a project. For instance, an AE who designs a building for a fee is usually precluded from bidding on construction. Some decision makers don't worry about the conflict of interest and instead look for good reputations and continuity.

Terms of Payment

A contractor may be paid based on the contractor's costs. At the other end of the spectrum is a fixed-price. Contracts tend to be on a cost-plus basis when the scope is unknown, and on a fixed-price basis when the requirements are well defined. There are variations between cost-plus and fixed-price. The common arrangements are:

- *Cost-plus contract.* The contractor is paid actual costs plus a fixed or a percentage fee.

- *Cost-plus contract with target price.* The contractor is paid actual costs plus a fee. However, a target price is set, and the contractor shares in the savings or the overrun. The target price is modified by change orders as the project progresses.

- *Cost-plus contract with a guaranteed maximum price.* The contractor is paid actual costs plus a fee. However, a maximum price is set, and the contractor will share in the savings but will pay all of the overrun. The GMP is modified by change orders. (Note: Many people use the term GMP synonymously with fixed-price. That is incorrect. A GMP is a lid on a cost-plus contract with a defined scope. It is one of the most difficult of all contracts to manage. It has the problems of both lump-sum and cost-plus contracts. It is more susceptible to change orders than a lump-sum contract because it is typically given before construction drawings are complete. There will also be many issues over the definition of "cost"; for example, rental rules on contractor-owned equipment, or ownership of workman's compensation refunds or penalties.)

- *Unit-price contract.* The contractor is paid a predetermined amount for each unit of material put in place (or removed).
- *Fixed-price contract.* The contractor is paid a fixed sum for the work.

These payment terms may be combined in one contract. For instance, many contracts are fixed-price lump-sum with unit-price provisions for rock removal during excavation or tenant work during lease-up. Change orders may be based on a cost-plus arrangement.

TYPICAL PROJECT DELIVERY METHODS

Variations are infinite. Examples of the most common follow.

Traditional Process

Most projects are design, bid, build. An AE defines the nonprofit's needs, designs the building, prepares construction drawings and specifications, and administers construction. Drawings and specifications serve two purposes: They are guidelines for construction, and they comprise the contractual definition of what the contractor is to build. Contractors are prequalified and short-listed. They usually provide a bond. Typically, the low bidder is awarded the work. The AE is at the agent end of the spectrum; the contractor is at the vendor end. The traditional process is illustrated in Exhibit 5.4.

> **Pros.** The process is easy to manage. Roles are clear; the process is universally understood. Since the nonprofit has a defined requirement and a fixed-price, it appears prudent.

> **Cons.** Construction can't start until design is complete. There is no fixed-price for construction until much work has been done. If bids are over the budget, more time and money are lost to redesign. Design suffers from a lack of input from contractors and subcontractors. Procurement of subcontractors by the general contractor during the bid period is typically unbusinesslike.

Traditional Process with a Project Manager

Nonprofit organizations can add project or construction management companies to the traditional process to mitigate the traditional flaws (see Exhibit 5.5, the Traditional Process with PM).

EXHIBIT 5.4   THE TRADITIONAL PROCESS

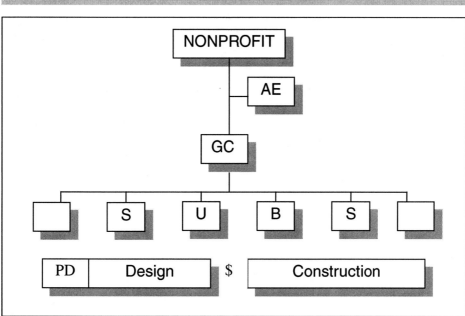

Printed with permission from Charles B. Thomsen, 3D/International.

The idea is to select an organization with experience in construction to: improve cost, schedule, and quality control; improve the constructibility of the design; develop risk management and claims protection programs; improve other management controls to smooth the process; and improve field management. Although it is not yet common in the industry, some firms have also emphasized the project definition phase as an important project management service.

Often, project managers unbundle design and construction contracts. Instead of a single AE, projects may have a planner, a design architect, a production architect, and separate architects for different aspects of the interiors. These firms may be selected by the nonprofit organization and PM, and assigned to the lead architect. The PM may also negotiate major items of manufactured equipment and subcontracts, and assign them to the eventual general contractor. That maintains a single, bonded price for construction, but allows direct negotiation (and useful collaboration) with specialty subcontractors and manufacturers. Procurement of subcontracts also provides cost feedback. That reduces the possibility of a bust on bid day.

Fast-Track

At times, a nonprofit organization may need to look for ways to accelerate schedules. Fast-track—starting construction before finishing design—is a common technique. Fast-track can be used with the traditional process, with bridging, or with design-build; however, it is most common with CM.

EXHIBIT 5.5   TRADITIONAL PROCESS WITH PM

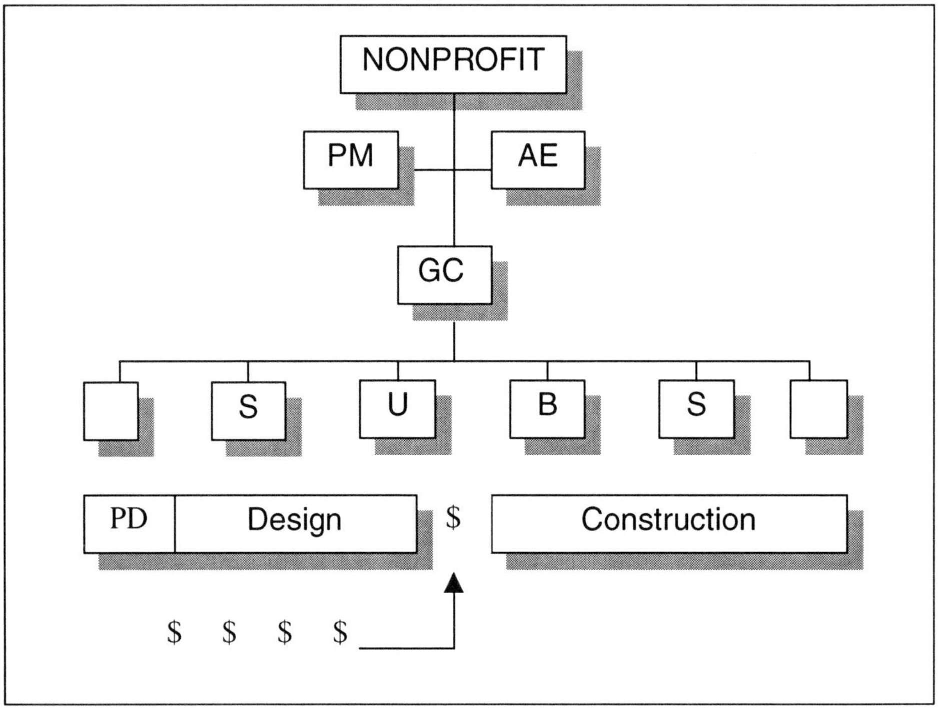

Printed with permission from Charles B. Thomsen, 3D/International.

Pros. The process saves time.

Cons. The problem with fast-track is inherent in its advantage. Since construction is started before design is complete, the nonprofit organization lacks the security of a fixed-price based on complete construction documents. There is no contractual assurance that the project will be completed within the budget. There are two common approaches to this problem: construction management at risk and construction manager as agent.

CM at Risk

People in the construction industry have different ways of referring to CM at risk. All begin with the idea that construction management is central to this process. Some focus on a "Negotiated Cost-Plus General Construction Contract with a Guaranteed Maximum Price (GMP)." Others use shorthand, such as "CM/GC." In any case, the argument is simple. Since the project isn't fully designed when construction begins, the contract should be cost-plus. But to give the nonprofit organization security that the project will be built within the budget, the contractor provides a GMP. The CM agrees to pay for costs that exceed the GMP and are not the result of changes in the contract documents (see Exhibit 5.6).

Pros. The process works for nonprofit organizations that can select contractors on the basis of qualifications and integrity. CM at risk centralizes responsibility for construction under a single contract. The CM/GC becomes a collaborative member of the project team and provides valuable input, value engineering, and advice during the design phase.

Cons. The contract can be hard to enforce. The guaranteed maximum price is given before contract documents are complete, so the GMP is essentially a defined price for an undefined product. Conflicts may arise over what was logically implied by incomplete documents. Also, a CM can't get enforceable subcontracts with incomplete drawings.

Nonprofit organizations and institutional clients with complex buildings should be circumspect about a cost-plus contract with a GMP. First, it is difficult for some institutions to award and administer cost-plus contracts. Second, nonprofit institutions are vulnerable to claims and change orders.

EXHIBIT 5.6   CM AT RISK

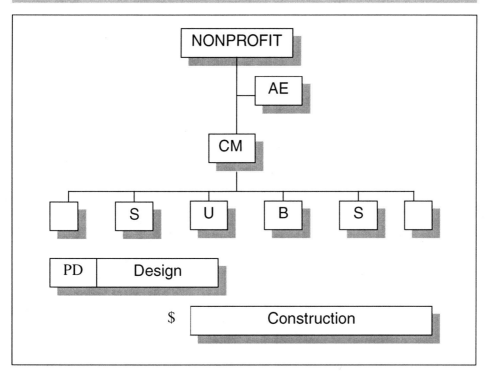

Printed with permission from Charles B. Thomsen, 3D/International.

Awarding a contract on the basis of incomplete documents increases vulnerability to claims and litigation. To avoid this problem, a GMP should be given only for those documents that are complete. A CM can then add an appropriate contingency for the unbid portion of the work.

CM as Agent

The general contractor is eliminated and replaced with a construction manager who manages the project in an agency (fiduciary) capacity (see Exhibit 5.7).

The CM bids construction to trade contractors just as a GC would, beginning with items critical to the schedule. One common strategy to avoid downstream overruns is to award only the shop drawing phase of the first trade contracts. The CM delays final notice to proceed with construction until most of the work is bid and the project cost is certain. On government work, the sub-

EXHIBIT 5.7   CM AS AGENT

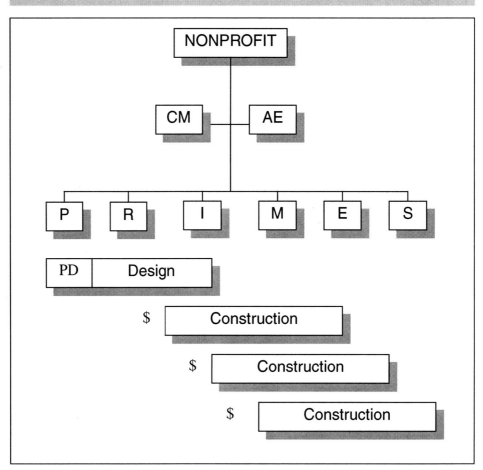

Printed with permission from Charles B. Thomsen, 3D/International.

contracts are directly with the owner. In the private or nonprofit sectors, the CM may hold the subcontracts as agent of the owner.

Pros. Nonprofit organizations have a professional construction manager on their side of the table. The multiple trade construction contracts are fixed-price, based on complete documents with little room for change orders.

Cons. Multiple contracts can be difficult to administer. If one prime trade contractor damages another by delay, the nonprofit can get caught up in the fight.

Design-Build

With design-build, one company provides both design and construction. Some nonprofits like the design-build idea, but they want to cherry-pick specialized designers. In these cases, the AE is a subcontractor to a GC or a design-build contractor (see Exhibit 5.8). It is not uncommon for GCs and AEs to form strategic alliances and present joint design-build proposals.

Pros. There is a single point of responsibility for both design and construction. Design-build contractors add construction practicality to design imag-

EXHIBIT 5.8   DESIGN-BUILD

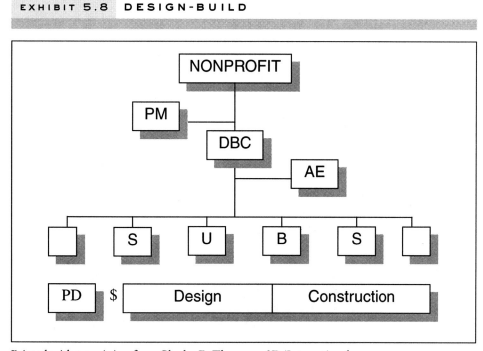

Printed with permission from Charles B. Thomsen, 3D/International.

ination. Nonprofit organizations get an enforceable price sooner for construction and can fast-track the project, if needed. The earlier enforceable price provides valuable information for fundraising purposes. The contractor can negotiate subcontracts methodically so the nonprofit can benefit from good prices, reliable subcontractors, better technology, and tighter contracts.

Cons. More projects would be design-build if they could be bid, but it's difficult to formulate an enforceable price before design begins. The paradox: It's hard to define the work to be done for an agreed-upon price without design; but if design is done, then it's not design-build.

Some design-build companies work under an AE fee with a target price until the design is set, then they negotiate a final price for construction. They agree that the nonprofit may obtain prices from other contractors as well. The design-build contractor begins in an agent role and changes to a vendor role. Many do so with integrity. But nonprofits may feel that it is unwise to hire a contractor to define a product as an agent that the contractor will then sell as a vendor.

Bridging

Bridging is the American name for a design-build process common in Europe and Japan and in the petrochemical industry. In the bridging process, there are two AEs. The first AE is under contract to the nonprofit organization. Bid documents define the functional and aesthetic characteristics of the project. They include drawings similar to design development in the traditional process. There is a combination of performance and traditional specifications. These documents define the parts of the building that the nonprofit wants to control, typically the functional and aesthetic aspects. But the documents leave considerable latitude for contractors to look for economies in construction technology.

The project is bid (or negotiated) by design-build contractors or by a GC with an AE as a subcontractor (see Exhibit 5.9). The contractor's AE (the second AE) does the final construction drawings and specifications, and is the architect of record. Typically, construction doesn't begin until the final construction drawings are complete and it is clear that there are no misunderstandings about what is intended by the bid documents. If there is disagreement, the nonprofit owns the plans and may use them to take competitive bids.

Pros. Bridging has the beneficial attributes of the traditional process: a bonded, enforceable lump-sum contract and complete contractual documentation before construction starts. It also has the beneficial attributes of design-build: centralization of responsibility, integration of practical con-

EXHIBIT 5.9   BRIDGING (WITH PM)

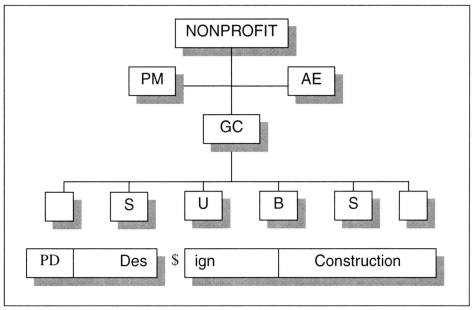

Printed with permission from Charles B. Thomsen, 3D/International.

struction knowledge into final design, and reduction of the time and cost required to obtain an enforceable lump-sum price for construction.

By centralizing responsibilities during construction, bridging minimizes the opportunity for contractor claims based on errors or omissions in the drawings or specifications. It also centralizes the responsibility for correction of postconstruction faults in the design or construction.

Cons. The major problem with bridging is that it's new in the United States. The construction industry is large, and replete with many contractors, AEs, consultants, subcontractors, manufacturers, and suppliers. Tradition is the great facilitator. These organizations don't all understand bridging and may not perform well without careful management.

CONCLUSION

As noted at the beginning of this chapter, all the processes described here are flawed, but they can all be made to work. The best choice for each nonprofit organization is governed by the exigencies of the project. The primary issue is the quality of the people. Simply, the best way to get a good project is to get good people to do it, set the environment for collaboration, and make sure responsibilities are clear.

CHAPTER 6

Prospect Identification and Cultivation

Often, when nonprofit leaders gain a sense of the total cost of the capital and endowment project, a feeling of panic soon follows. Where will such investments come from? To whom shall we turn? Who are our best prospects? How can the organization inspire the generous contributions that will make a campaign succeed?

When asked such questions, executive directors, board chairs, and directors of development often point out that they can seek support from the following seven broad classifications of donors and grantors:

1. Individuals
2. Businesses/corporations
3. Foundations
4. Government agencies
5. Associations (professional associations and unions)
6. Service clubs (e.g., Rotary, Kiwanis, Lions, Civitan, etc.)
7. Churches and synagogues

However, knowing the broad donor categories is just a beginning. Organization leaders must first establish a database of all current and potential supporters. The master database includes the names, addresses, phone numbers of opinion leaders, stakeholders, and constituents. In other words, the master list is a database that contains everyone with whom the organization communicates. Once this is established, staff can begin a process that realistically identifies potential capital campaign donors and nurtures positive relationships with these specific decision makers. Simply put, your staff and board must put together a real prospect list, then begin to get these potential donors involved with your organization.

YOUR BEST PROSPECTS

Your best prospects share your organization's values, are philanthropic, have the capacity to provide support at generous levels, and have some identifiable reason to support your organization. To find these folks, look to the following:

- *Constituents.* Universities garner support from their alumni. Hospitals seek support from former patients. Symphonies raise funds from season subscribers. Churches receive contributions from members of the congregation. Wildlife refuges receive donations from conservationists. Be sure to record the names, addresses, and phone numbers of your constituents—the people who use your organization's services. Nonprofit organizations that serve the poor look to other constituencies for major support.

- *Current and former board members.* The people who make policy and guide the nonprofit organization are often the organization's best supporters.

- *Key volunteers.* Involved people understand your organization. Volunteers often know the most moving stories about the people you serve and how your organization makes their lives better. Some volunteers view financial contributions as a natural extension of their commitment to your organization.

- *Staff.* Board members and other contributors are impressed when they become aware of generous staff contributions. Such donations bolster confidence in the philanthropic community. Donors know that if the staff is generous, the organization has inspired confidence in those most likely to know its weaknesses and strengths on an intimate basis. Hospital campaigns rely especially heavily on the staff effort. The staff, including physicians and top administrators, often donates up to 20 percent of the capital campaign total.

   Be cautious, however: Staff solicitations must be approached with sensitivity. As with volunteers, staff members must be comfortable with their decision to donate . . . or not to donate.

- *Current donors.* Your most likely future generous supporters are current donors. Contributors who believe in your cause expect to be asked for donations more often than once a year. Most organizations tend to ask too few times, not too often. Just be sure that you invite your current supporters to appreciation events and other happenings not connected with fundraising. It is rude to approach your supporters *only* when you are asking for contributions.

- *Lapsed donors.* A person who gave in the past but has not contributed in the most recent 12- or 18-month period is a lapsed donor. Some fundraising professionals estimate as many as 30 percent of these lapsed donors can be persuaded to donate again. A thoughtful and highly personalized approach helps. For capital campaign purposes, be aware that an affluent individual who gave in the past—even modestly—is a better prospect than one who never donated at all.

- *Vendors.* Businesses that sell goods and services to nonprofit organizations often donate when asked.

- *Those generous to similar organizations.* Start collecting donor lists. Board and staff fundraisers can find the names of philanthropists and community leaders in symphony program books, hospital annual reports, university publications, nonprofit newsletters, and on donor acknowledgment walls. A generous sponsor of one arts organization may be a prime prospect for another arts institution's capital campaign. Donor names are easy to come by. Addresses and phone numbers take more work. That said, many of your board members and key volunteers have the names, addresses, and phone numbers needed on their personal contact lists.

- *Affluent individuals with whom someone in your organization has a peer relationship.* Knowledge that someone is wealthy might be meaningless, especially if you have no link to that person. Conversely, the affluent individual's closeness to one of your board members or to a campaign leader can serve as a sufficient link to garner a pacesetting pledge to your capital campaign.

PROSPECT RESEARCH

Whether your nonprofit organization is a grassroots agency or a large institution, if you wish to raise money you will have to focus on four key areas of prospect research:

1. The prospective supporter's relationship to your organization
2. The prospect's interests and hobbies, especially as they relate to your organization
3. Networking (who in your organization is close to the prospect)
4. Capability (net worth, capacity to donate, and challenging contribution amounts to request)

At the early stages of prospect research, you should identify as large a prospect pool as possible. Concentrate on creating as complete and accurate a database as possible. Enter or clean up the gift history. As you put together your master list, remember to get the names of decision makers at the corporations and foundations you might approach. As you gather more information—spouse name, notes about giving to other causes, interests, network of associates (potential volunteer solicitors), and so on—enter this information into the database too.

Savvy fundraising professionals devote the majority of their limited research time on prospects capable of *major gifts* with whom the organization has a potential relationship.

Every organization has its own definition of a major gift. An institution with a $60 million capital campaign goal might define major gifts as pledges of $750,000 or more, whereas a nonprofit agency with a $100,000 fundraising goal might consider any gift of $1,000 or more to be a major gift. In general, fundraisers consider any gift of 1 percent to 1.5 percent of the goal to be a major gift. Pacesetting leadership gifts represent 10 percent, 15 percent, or more of the campaign goal.

PROSPECT RATINGS AND EVALUATIONS

In *The Complete Guide to Fundraising Management,* I outlined a powerful method for rating prospective donors' capacity to support your organization. The approach also provides staff and board members with valuable data concerning each prospect's network of associates and relationship to the nonprofit organization. Let me summarize the method here. It is imperative that capital campaign organizers gather this most important information.

First, create a cover sheet, key page, and Prospect Rating Form (see Exhibits 6.1, 6.2, and 6.3). The cover sheet summarizes your case for support and helps

---

EXHIBIT 6.1   PROSPECT RATING FORM COVER SHEET

PROSPECT RATING FORM

XYZ Nonprofit Organization is preparing for a capital campaign to build state-of-the-art facilities that will enable us to strengthen all of our programs for the people we serve, while at the same time maintaining our reputation for financial stability and sound management. The information gathered on this form will help us refine our plans. The campaign can only succeed with the generous support of a limited number of pacesetting contributors.

The information derived from this and other "ratings and evaluations" activities will be kept confidential and treated with the utmost discretion. The final decision concerning the correct amount of contribution to request will be based upon the prospective donor's capacity, philanthropic nature, and relationship to XYZ Organization. The correct choice of solicitor can only be determined with knowledge of the prospect's network of associates.

When rating capacity to give, keep in mind the prospect's total means, rather than past giving patterns. In other words, please indicate the *maximum* potential.

Thank you for your help. Your opinions are valuable to us.

EXHIBIT 6.2 PROSPECT RATING KEY

PLEASE USE THE FOLLOWING KEYS
WHEN FILLING IN THE FORM:

MAXIMUM CAPACITY (Base on Prospective Donor's Total Assets)

Enter number 1 through 8 based on your best guess. Leave blank only if you have no knowledge whatsoever.

1	$1,000,000	or more 3- to 5-year pledge capacity
2	500,000	or more 3- to 5-year pledge capacity
3	100,000	or more 3- to 5-year pledge capacity
4	50,000	or more 3- to 5-year pledge capacity
5	30,000	or more 3- to 5-year pledge capacity
6	15,000	or more 3- to 5-year pledge capacity
7	7,500	or more 3- to 5-year pledge capacity
8	Less than $7,500 3- to 5-year pledge capacity	

LEVEL OF INTEREST IN XYZ NONPROFIT ORGANIZATION
AND PHILANTHROPIC TENDENCY

Enter letter A through E based on your best guess. Leave blank if you have no knowledge of prospect.

A High level of interest in XYZ Nonprofit Organization
B Moderate level of interest (probably donates or attends organization activities)
C Low level of interest but with potential for cultivation (doesn't give or participate yet but is interested in the goals of the organization)
D Little known interest in the goals of the organization but has demonstrable civic pride
E No interest and no concern for community

YOUR RELATIONSHIP TO PROSPECT

Enter number 1 through 5 to indicate the phrase that best describes your relationship.

1 Best of friends, relative, or close business associate
2 Acquainted and friendly
3 Met once or twice
4 Never met
5 Hostile relationship

volunteers understand the process. The key explains how the volunteers are to fill in the columns on the Prospect Rating Form.

Having created these forms, the next step is to fill in the names of 300 to 400 individuals, foundations, and corporations thought to be likely prime prospects. Included on the list are current generous donors, the largest local or national

EXHIBIT 6.3   SAMPLE PROSPECT RATING FORM

VOLUNTEER'S NAME:_____

Donors and Prospects Name / Company	Maximum Capacity	Interest in Our Organization	Your Relationship	Willing to Visit?
Mr. Ronald P. Abelson				
Mr. Thomas N. Ackerly				
Dr. & Mrs. Arthur Q. Adelle				
Mr. & Mrs. Harry B. Allen, III				
Mr. Lawrence C. Amlen				
Mr. Stanley W. Ammson, Jr.				
Aphorism Industries Paul Epigram, President				
Mr. & Mrs. Robert O. Baxter				
Mrs. Evelyn T. Carter				
Harold Charles, Esq.				
Mr. & Mrs. Russell Clinett				
Mr. & Mrs. Steven Darnit, Jr.				
Mr. & Mrs. William Derby				
Mr. & Mrs. Frank Desstitute				
Staff fills in 300–400 names prior to the volunteer review				

corporations you are likely to approach, those who are generous to similar causes, wealthy individuals who have a relationship to one of your volunteers or board members, and other constituents discussed earlier.

Next, take the list to your board of directors or to a special rating committee. This special committee can be composed of bankers, real estate brokers, insurance agents, stock brokers, attorneys, people who have lived in your city a long time, and community or national leaders—in short, affluent and influential "movers and shakers."

Remind volunteers to put their names at the top of the Prospect Rating Form. A "Yes" in the Willing to Visit column is very frustrating when capital campaign organizers don't know who filled out the form.

The most sensitive information fundraisers want to capture deals with each prospect's "maximum capacity." After all, we were all brought up to consider conversations about other people's money to be rude. The Prospect Rating Form's number system softens this natural resistance. Even volunteers who would never discuss their opinion of another person's net worth are comfortable conveying such information using the less direct number key.

Just be sure that each committee member has the same understanding when using the form. The intention is not to determine the request amount. Rather, capital campaign organizers first need to determine who is *capable* of making commitments at the upper levels. With this in mind, the meeting facilitator might say, "If this were the prospects' favorite charity—perhaps their church or university—what might be the *most* they could contribute? Please do not fill in a number that represents what you expect the prospect to donate. Please focus on the maximum amount the person could afford to contribute."

Later in the campaign organizing process, a number of factors will help determine each actual amount to request. Every prospective donor is worthy of individual attention. In some cases, especially when the prospect has a very close relationship to your organization, the request amount will be equal to the maximum capacity. In other cases, the appropriate request amount is somewhat less than the maximum the prospect can afford.

The column that deals with interest in your organization and philanthropic tendencies is self-explanatory. Your staff should know most of the relevant information such as giving history and current involvement. However, there are times when board members or key volunteers have historical information about the prospect's relationship to the organization.

By using number codes and Prospect Rating Forms, a board of directors or special committee can review up to 400 names in 20 minutes. This 20-minute concentrated period is important to your capital campaign's success. By staying focused—and by not being swayed by extraneous comments—an organization can quickly discover who on its list of donors and potential supporters is most capable of generous gifts. As important, the organization will quickly know who on the list has the closest relationship to the organization and the most philanthropic tendencies. Perhaps the greatest knowledge obtained through this process is who in your organization has a relationship to specific donors and prospective supporters.

After the volunteers fill in the forms, the staff gathers the individual rating forms and summarizes the committee's work and creates the Compiled Prospect Rating Form (see Exhibit 6.4). Once the staff has summarized the committee's work in this form, it becomes relatively easy to determine preliminary request amounts and begin to think about volunteer assignments. Moreover, now that campaign leaders know "who knows who" they can speak confidentially to individual committee members and gather additional sensitive information concerning the organization's top prospects. There are some things that are best left unsaid at group meetings.

EXHIBIT 6.4   COMPILED PROSPECT RATING FORM

COMPILED PROSPECT RATING FORM

NAME/COMPANY	MAXIMUM CAPACITY	INTEREST IN ORGANIZATION	YOUR RELATIONSHIP	WILLING TO VISIT?
Mr. Ronald P. Abelson				
Mr. Thomas N. Ackerly	6 (Carr)	B (Carr)	2 (Carr)	
	5 (Harrison)	C (Harrison)	2 (Harrison)	
			3 (Hagard)	
			2 (Mitchem)	
			2 (Whitt)	
Dr. & Mrs. Arthur Q. Adelle	7 (Carr)		2 (Carr)	
			2 (Hagard)	
	3 (Herring)	D (Herring)	2 (Herring)	
Mr. & Mrs. Harry B. Allen, III	7 (Carr)		3 (Carr)	
			3 (Hagard)	
Mr. Lawrence C. Amlen	7 (Harrison)	C (Harrison)	2 (Harrison)	
			3 (Hagard)	
Mr. Stanley W. Ammson, Jr.	7 (Liddy)	C (Liddy)	1 (Liddy)	Y (Liddy)
	8 (Mitchell)	C (Mitchell)	2 (Mitchell)	Y (Mitchell)
	8 (Carr)		2 (Carr)	Y (Carr)
	8 (Harrison)	C (Harrison)	2 (Harrison)	
			3 (Hagard)	
			2 (Michel, II)	
Aphorism Industries	1 (Liddy)	B (Hagard)	2 (Hagard)	
Paul Epigram, President	2 (Carr)	A (Liddy)	2 (Liddy)	
	2 (Hagard)	A (Carr)	4 (Carr)	
Mr. & Mrs. Robert O. Baxter				
Mrs. Evelyn T. Carter				
Harold Charles, Esq.				
Mr. & Mrs. Russell Clinett	8 (Harrison)	C (Harrison)	2 (Harrison)	
			3 (Hagard)	
Mr. & Mrs. Steven Darnit, Jr.				
Mr. & Mrs. William Derby				
Mr. & Mrs. Frank Desstitute	8 (Liddy)	D (Liddy)	5 (Liddy)	

NETWORK OF ASSOCIATES

Often the ideal volunteer solicitor for a particular prospect was not part of the team that filled in the Prospect Rating Form. In such cases you can visit people on the ratings team or others who know the prospective supporter but have some reason not to volunteer for the visit. Ask questions such as, "Who are some of Mr. Prospect's good friends? Who, on our team, is close to Mr. Prospect? Who believes in our cause and has the right 'chemistry' to approach Mr. Prospect for a contribution to our capital campaign?"

DETERMINING THE CAPACITY TO GIVE

Determining the amount to request is one of the keys to capital campaign success. Your aim is to determine a challenging, yet appropriate, gift amount or gift range to request *prior* to any solicitation visit with a prospective supporter. This process begins with a determination of the prospect's capacity to support the campaign.

Begin your deliberations by estimating the prospect's maximum giving potential. Then consider all the other factors—closeness to the organization, philanthropic spirit, interest in the capital project, and relationship to the volunteer visitor.

When considering maximum capacity, remember that many people contribute 10 percent of their earnings to their church. Still, they manage to feed their families, take vacations, send their kids to school, and make their mortgage payments. Many tithers even save and accumulate wealth. And yet, on average, Americans donate less than 2 percent of their income each year.

From the preceding paragraph you might assume that most donors can contribute at least five times as much as they currently donate. For example, a supporter who contributes $1,000 annually might be able to afford $5,000 each year. Also remember that capital campaigns have a three- to five-year pledge payment period. So your $1,000 annual donor could be considered a prospect for $15,000 to $25,000 for the capital campaign.

In some cases, the estimates of maximum capacity are even more encouraging. *Annual support most often comes from the donor's earnings. Capital and endowment support comes from the donor's income* and *accumulated assets.* Affluent people who love your organization and are totally committed to the project might donate 500 to 3,000 times the amount they give annually. In other words, that same $1,000 annual donor might make a $500,000 or even a $3 million campaign commitment, especially if the organization encourages multiyear pledges for the capital campaign combined with planned gifts to the endowment fund.

Clearly, the prospective donor's net worth is a better indicator of giving capacity than the prospect's current giving level. I have seen a $50-a-year donor increase her giving to $100,000 the very next year. In one case, a supporter who had never donated to the organization made a $50,000,000 pledge that was quickly fulfilled. Also, if you discover that a prospect with a modest career has inherited wealth, do not underestimate that person's giving capacity. For example, a retired schoolteacher once donated $110,000 of inherited stock to a homeless shelter's capital campaign.

Here are some general guidelines that can help you determine *capacity* to give:

- A person with a net worth of $25,000,000 or more can afford to donate $1,000,000 without changing his or her lifestyle.

- People with a net worth greater than $30 million have the capacity to give 5 percent to 10 percent of their net worth—or even more—with no diminution in lifestyle.

- Most donors have the capacity to donate at least 15 to 25 times their annual support to a capital campaign with a three- to five-year pledge period. In other words, if the donor is giving your organization $300 a year, you can assume that they can commit $4,500 to $7,500 to the capital campaign. Because capital campaigns have a three- to five-year pledge period, it is often prudent to request $1,500 a year for three years rather than $4,500. Alternatively, the volunteer might request $1,500 a year for five years rather than asking for $7,500. People of modest means find it easier to make larger pledges when offered an opportunity to donate over a multiyear period.

  However, if you learn that the prospect contributes $1,000 annually to another organization, he or she might be able to pledge $15,000 to $25,000 for your organization's capital campaign. Again, the rule is estimate capital campaign capacity at 15 to 25 times annual giving.

- Committed supporters can frequently afford to pledge annually an amount equal to three weeks' salary. Therefore, campaign organizers might request the equivalent of nine weeks' earnings for a campaign with a three-year pledge period (three weeks' earnings each year for three years).

  You can get a good sense of what the donor's annual salary is by quietly gathering information about salary ranges in your area. And don't forget your reference materials; for example, corporate annual reports and SEC 8-K filings contain information about executive remuneration and stock control.

- Estimate capital campaign capacity to be 20 times the prospect's largest known political contribution. Someone who donated $5,000 to a political campaign usually can commit $100,000 to a nonprofit organization's capital campaign.

Key volunteers and staff rate each prospective supporter's giving capacity. However, only generous people succeed in this task; miserly people cannot imagine others donating generously. So be sure to fill your ratings committee with big-hearted and thoughtful community leaders.

DETERMINING THE REQUEST AMOUNT

Capacity to give is one matter; willingness to give is quite another. So how much should you request? One answer is, enough to make a difference. Aim high. Involve the prospect. Inspire the prospect. Offer the prospective supporter the opportunity to play a leading role in your campaign. Let this principle guide your decisions: *When determining how much to request, it is far better to err on the high side than to ask too little.* Experienced fundraisers know that people are not insulted if they are asked for a larger contribution than they can afford. Rather, these prospects often feel flattered.

Two mistakes cause even more harm than asking too little. The first is not being specific in the request. Donors frequently have no way of knowing if the organization needs $50 or $500,000. Many prospects simply don't know what it takes for a capital campaign to succeed, so don't leave such important issues unresolved. Offer the donor an opportunity to make a significant investment in your capital campaign.

The second—and most damaging—mistake is to not ask at all. Capital campaigns succeed when volunteers and staff make their solicitation visits and request specific amounts or gift ranges.

Here are some general guidelines for determining the request amount:

- If the prospective donor has a close relationship to your organization and its visionary capital campaign, request an amount equal to the donor's maximum capacity.

- If the donor is not already closely associated with your organization, intensify your relationship-nurturing activities and wait to request a higher-level gift. If your campaign has a pressing deadline and momentum is needed, consider requesting an amount one or two levels below the prospective donor's capacity.

- If the prospective supporter is a foundation, request an amount at the upper end of the foundation's gift range. When possible, confer with program officers concerning the project budget and your request amount.

- If your organization is relying on a volunteer who has a peer relationship with the prospective supporter, encourage the volunteer to "think big." Even prospective supporters who have not yet developed a close relationship to your organization can be encouraged to donate very generously, especially if they have a strong relationship with the community leader who asks for the capital campaign commitment.

- If your organization has 12,000 names on its in-house prospect list, it often makes economic sense to confer with a consulting firm that offers electronic screening services. This screening uncovers previously unknown sources of wealth on your list. The service's greatest value is its capacity to segment your prospects by giving capacity, thus helping the campaign leaders organize and prioritize their efforts.

PROSPECTIVE DONORS ARE PEOPLE

Perhaps the previous discussion sounded cold and analytical. Be cautious when using prospect research jargon. Readers will fall into a dangerous trap if they internalize all of this talk of suspects, prospects, ratings, and evaluations. The more important point is to know the organization's supporters as people. Philanthropic fundraisers understand their supporters' likes, dislikes, and motivations. See that your organization makes every effort to know what each supporter cares about.

Community leaders who are long-term residents of the region tend to know a great deal about prospective supporters. With this in mind, the prospect researcher's best tool is the telephone. Speak with these movers and shakers often. Take notes. Understand the nuances of human relationships. Begin to form judgments concerning the best volunteer to visit the prospect, the appropriate amount to request, the best timing of the request, and the gift opportunity that will most inspire the prospective supporter to make a generous commitment to your capital campaign.

NURTURING RELATIONSHIPS

Capital campaigns succeed when board and staff dedicate themselves to "friend raising." As prospective donors become more involved, they become more committed. Their donations increase as their sense of belonging grows.

Activities designed to nurture relationships are not driven by deadlines. When schedules get tight, organizations with small staffs push back or cancel luncheon meetings, gatherings of community leaders, and other cultivation activities. How unfortunate. Your organization's future is shaped by these relationship nurturing encounters. Opinion leaders, philanthropists, and thoughtful businesspeople welcome opportunities to speak with nonprofit leaders who are working to improve the level of programs and services available in the community, nation, and world. Your nonprofit will benefit from the advice and financial support these people can bring to your organization.

Friend-raising activities might include any or all of the following.

Newsletters and Mailings

Though printed materials and mailings are no substitute for personal contact, newsletters, annual reports, friendly letters, and other printed material do play an important role in the relationship-building process. Newsletters keep all stakeholders and prospective donors informed. As an additional benefit, these periodic mailings ensure that the organization maintains up-to-date mailing addresses and contact information. The other materials give the organization additional opportunities to stay in touch with constituents.

When planning your communications strategy, include prospects—not just donors—on your mailing list. And don't be attracted to false economies; mail to as many people as possible.

Include simple planned giving appeals in every newsletter. Also acknowledge donors and volunteers in your newsletters. This increases awareness of the importance of contributed income and stimulates even more donations.

Include interesting news concerning the organization's facility plans and capital campaign. Stress the institution's accomplishments. Testimonials and poignant stories are effective ways of telling your case for support.

Highly Personalized Mailings That Do Not Request Funds

These friend-raising mailings usually convey some brief positive organization accomplishment. For example, a letter might begin, "As an important member of San Francisco's business community, you may be interested to know that the XYZ Institution recently completed a study on ways of strengthening the Bay Area's economy . . ."

Development officers and other professionals who value relationships frequently write short personal notes. Sometimes the note is a brief thank-you; other times, they send a congratulatory note. Indeed, there are seemingly unlimited reasons for writing these friendly notes. Make this a habit and you will be amazed at the unexpected rewards that come your way.

Invitations to Tour the Nonprofit Organization's Facilities

Supporters enjoy a behind-the-scenes look at your institution. Consider inviting donors and potential donors to your organization's facilities. This is especially helpful if the visit helps the donor better understand the nonprofit organization's programs and services.

As supporters become more at home with the organization, they become more likely to make generous contributions to the capital campaign. They might even begin to understand why your current facilities need to be replaced or enhanced. Show people who are touring your facilities models and drawings of the proposed capital project.

Social and Informative Gatherings

Relationship-building events are not the same as fundraisers (although special-event fundraisers—events that actually require contributions—also aid in the relationship-building process). Many of the nonprofit organization's gatherings should eschew direct solicitation of funds. Rather, they should be social and informative. A gracious and fun buffet dinner with a guest speaker describing your organization's accomplishments and aspirations is ideal. A sample invitation to such a gathering is included as Exhibit 6.5. Board members and key volunteers should make personal calls to people on the invitation list. These warm and welcoming calls increase attendance. To assure that the key messages for the evening are clearly presented, organizers can prepare a simple run sheet and script for the presenters (see Exhibit 6.6).

Be sure that well-informed board and staff members also attend these cultivation gatherings. Great minglers help strengthen the organization's bonds with current donors and volunteers, and the organization's socially astute advocates attract new prospects and potential board members. After all, many community leaders become involved with nonprofit organizations as a means of building new and meaningful relationships.

Breakfasts and Luncheons

Nonprofit CEOs, board chairs, board members, development directors, and key staff frequently get together with community leaders and potential donors. Many business leaders enjoy breakfast meetings. These tend to be less disruptive of the workday. Lunch is still a favorite of many folks who find it enjoyable to meet and eat. (I once heard an old pro say, "What's the mystery about fundraising? Just take a rich person to lunch.")

Nonprofit organizations that need capital and endowment funds also need board and staff members who get out of their offices. Lunch and breakfast meetings need not be solicitations. More often, these get-togethers focus on personal updates, advice, and information sharing. The informal nature of the meeting allows the participants to exchange ideas in a pleasant setting.

Invitations to Annual Meetings and Appreciation Dinners

Take every step possible to be sure that your annual meetings and appreciation dinners are not boring, perfunctory affairs. Use these gatherings to stimulate enthusiasm. Invite donors, key volunteers, community leaders, and others important to your capital campaign's success. Send attractive written invitations. Follow up with warm and personal phone calls.

Plan a short meeting followed by a meal. Celebrate your victories. Thank your donors. Congratulate your volunteers. Share poignant stories. Keep the meeting and meal fast-paced.

EXHIBIT 6.5   INVITATION TO CULTIVATION GATHERING

August 23, 2004

Mr. and Mrs. Charles McDonald
1234 Prospect Lane
Las Vegas, NV 89107

Dear Chuck and Lucy:

Please join us for a very special evening—a gathering of our friends and key support-ers of the XYZ Nonprofit of Southern Nevada. Please mark your calendar.

What:	An uplifting social and informative gathering.
When:	Wednesday, September 8, 2004
	7:00 P.M.
Where:	Home of Jan and Stan Friendly
	5678 Lowell Drive
	(see map if needed)

The evening will include hors d'oeuvres, wine, refreshments, fun, fellowship, informa-tion, and inspiration. Come and hear the latest details about our plans for the XYZ Orga-nization, as well as our plans to garner the financial resources needed to make our vision a reality. There will be no solicitations and no offerings accepted at this time. We simply want to assure that our special friends have the most up-to-date information as soon as possible.

We are looking forward to seeing you.

With appreciation and warmest wishes,

Irving Gotinfluence
Board Chair, XYZ Nonprofit

RSVP by Friday, September 3, 2004
Please Call: xxx-xxxx

Individualized Strategies

If your donor or prospective donor enjoys being in front of groups, invite him or her to speak at one of your organization's events. Whenever possible, recruit your best prospects to serve on ad hoc task forces or special committees. The simplest cultivation strategy is to meet face to face and seek advice from the sup-porter. People are flattered when you ask their opinion.

EXHIBIT 6.6   SAMPLE CULTIVATION SCRIPT

XYZ NONPROFIT ORGANIZATION

RELATIONSHIP-BUILDING EVENT

Social Gathering
The Home of Jan and Stan Friendly
(I. Gotinfluence, Board Chair, Presiding)
Wednesday, September 8, 2004

Presentation Notes & Sample Language

7:00 P.M. People begin arriving.

7:45 P.M. Presentation begins. Board President's welcoming remarks [see example following].

Welcome. For those of you who haven't met me, I'm Irving Gotinfluence, president of the XYZ Nonprofit Organization Board of Directors. Thank you all for coming tonight. We will keep this part of the evening short so that you can enjoy the fine food and fellowship.

I'd like to begin by thanking my fellow board members and our Capital Campaign Steering Committee for their hard work in helping create state-of-the-art facilities that will help XYZ Nonprofit provide compassionate services and a loving environment for women and children experiencing homelessness. Let me also take this opportunity to thank our Campaign Chair, Ed Roberts. I especially want to thank Jan and Stan Friendly for their support and help in organizing this evening and especially for their graciousness in opening their lovely home for this gathering. Jan and Stan, would you like to say a word or two? [Make hand gesture calling Jan or Stan forward to speak.]

[Jan or Stan's remarks.] "We are proud to be associated with this project. We would like to personally welcome you and thank you for coming tonight." [At end of the remarks, turn attention back to I. Gotinfluence.]

[Irving's remarks continue.] Many of you know about the importance of the XYZ Organization. Some of you have even visited our shelter for women and children experiencing homelessness. And people who hear about our comprehensive counseling and job training services know how much we do to restore lives. I suppose you wouldn't be here if you weren't convinced of the vital role the XYZ Organization plays in responding with compassionate services for women and children. You also know how we have seen a dramatic increase in the requests for services during the last several years.

Our new facilities will help us strengthen our counseling and job training services. In addition to those services, we are beginning a new contract with the state to administer a job placement program for women who recently experienced homelessness. That's an important part of prevention also. But the sad truth is that, for years to come, we will still need improved facilities for the women and children who are entrusted in our care.

Our plans call for building new and expanded facilities and office space for our counselors. This will allow us to take care of the growing number of women and children being sent to the agency. As important, the enhanced facilities will be brighter, safer,

EXHIBIT 6.6 (CONTINUED)

and will allow us greater flexibility in how we use the space available to us. The children deserve the best our community can envision.

Thelma Smith, our Executive Director, will say a bit more about our vision for the future in a few minutes. But now I would like to introduce our guest, Donald Celebrity [Irving's own words to introduce Mr. Celebrity].

7:51 P.M. Sample Remarks for Donald Celebrity:

Thank you, Irving. I'd like to add my personal thanks to every one of you who came tonight. You are the leaders who mean so much to XYZ Organization's future.

Let me also express my appreciation to the board and staff for their outstanding contributions to the women and children who come to us for help. Very few people are aware of the sacrifice and tenacious commitment your leaders have made to this cause. Here are some facts you might not know:

- Volunteers at the XYZ Organization devote, on average, 300 hours each month to help run the agency and take care of the children.
- Of course, many of you know that nearly 1,750 women and children spend some time at the XYZ Organization shelter each year. Many of the women have been in abusive relationships. Others have just had bad luck and are experiencing the effects of unemployment.
- The XYZ Organization begins the healing process. Our aim is to begin the process of recovery and to show each woman and child that our society can work. People can be trusted. There are people in the world who understand the needs of women and love and care for children. And the XYZ Organization is staffed with compassionate people who make a difference in these women and childrens' lives.
- [Other personal observations Mr. Celebrity would like to share.]

When we started this presentation, Irving Gotinfluence told you we would be brief. Let me summarize why I feel that your presence is so important tonight: The board, staff, and volunteers at XYZ Organization have looked beyond our short-term needs. Their vision will provide for the needs of women and children. The plans you will be hearing more about in the months to come stress counseling and adequate resources to care for women and children, now and for generations to come.

In the months and years ahead, I hope many of you will support the XYZ Organization with your time, talents, and treasure. Your work and wisdom, combined with a healthy investment of financial resources, will help the XYZ Organization realize its vision—a new shelter and offices for XYZ. I came tonight to meet with you and to share my personal prayers and best wishes for the success of the capital campaign.

8:00 P.M. Thelma Smith, Executive Director.

Thank you Donald. I'm Thelma Smith, XYZ's executive director. Again, I want to thank each one of you for coming tonight and to express my heartfelt gratitude to Irving Gotinfluence for his leadership, and to Jan and Stan for being our gracious hosts this evening.

[Executive director's remarks: Briefly review plans and case for support.]

8:05 P.M. Thelma wraps up and encourages guests to get back to the food and conversation. NOTE: The entire presentation should take approximately 20 minutes. Not more!

Board and staff members might wish to think for a minute about all of the pleasant things they can do for people they really like. Treat your prospective supporters in this manner. That's all there is to it.

Publish Names and Photographs of Donors and Potential Donors

Don't underestimate the value of this relationship-building technique. Donor lists and more highly personalized acknowledgments in newsletters, annual reports, and other publications help the organization bond with community leaders.

Use photographs liberally in your newsletters. Take photos at special-event fundraisers. Take photos at committee meetings. Take photos of people receiving awards from your organization. Take photos of volunteers. Send people copies of their photos. Whenever possible, publish these photos.

Prompt and Generous Acknowledgment of Every Contribution

Organization leaders should acknowledge every contribution with a polite note or letter. The thank-you letter should be sent within 48 hours of the gift receipt, and it should never take more than seven days to acknowledge a contribution.

The gracious thank-you letter is a minimal standard. Organizations with more resources might also routinely thank mid- to upper-level donors with friendly phone calls. Some even attempt to call all donors. Major donors should receive a prompt letter and should also be thanked in person—preferably at a private lunch, breakfast, or dinner.

Some advice offered in *The Complete Guide to Fundraising Management* is worth repeating here. Many well-intentioned people make a special effort to thank their largest donors in a highly personalized manner. This is as it should be. However, a danger arises when the person responsible for sending thank-you letters interrupts the usual acknowledgment process. As a result, the person the organization wanted to thank first and foremost becomes the person whose gift acknowledgment is delayed—or even worse, lost. A colleague once told me of an embarrassing phone call he received from a $1 million donor. The generous benefactor asked the organization's CEO, "How much do you have to contribute to get a thank-you from your organization?"

Don't let this happen in your organization. Keep the large donors in the regular loop. *Then* send a second highly personalized letter. Also, be sure to follow up with a personal call and invitation to meet.

Participation in the Precampaign Planning Study

The precampaign study contains findings and recommendations designed to lay the groundwork for a successful campaign (Chapter 8 describes the study process). For the purposes of this chapter, suffice to say that planning study interviews are among the most important relationship-nurturing steps the organization can take. Recall that the top 10 donations will account for one-third to one-half of the campaign total. By interviewing 35 to 45 top prospects, the organization can assure that potential pacesetting donors have an opportunity to offer advice concerning the capital project. Their opinions about the organization, case for support, potential campaign leadership, and community attitudes help shape the campaign. Moreover, the confidential interviews provide a meaningful and flattering opportunity to create buy-in.

MONITORING RELATIONSHIP-BUILDING ACTIVITIES

Fundraising professionals track information concerning donor and prospect cultivation. They know who has been invited to which gatherings, who came, and the prospects' reactions to the organization's presentations. Thoughtful nonprofit leaders know that it is rude to communicate with people only when asking for money, so they schedule periodic social occasions for donors and prospects. They use these gatherings to keep the prospective supporters engaged and informed. Professionals assure that every major prospect is invited to a non-fundraising social gathering at least once every six months.

Building relationships with people capable of making major contributions is the highest payoff fundraising activity possible. And yet there is never a deadline for inviting someone to visit the organization. There is never a deadline to create a social informative gathering to which to invite them. For these cultivation activities to occur, those responsible for fundraising must proactively create and schedule them.

Development staff should create a computer code for everyone invited to each cultivation activity. Campaign staff and volunteer leaders also should track who actually came to each cultivation event or gathering. Organizations using fundraising software use the system's Comment field to record information about conversations or other encounters. Prospects who come to these informative gatherings are higher-priority prospects than those who have not yet heard about the nonprofit institution's capital project.

Many development professionals find it helpful to summarize their prospect research, develop a relationship-nurturing strategy, and track the cultivation steps. There are even numeric systems available to track each prospect's closeness to the organization.

EXHIBIT 6.7   PRIME PROSPECT TRACKING FORM

XYZ Nonprofit Organization Prime Prospect Tracking Form

Prospect: _____
(Last)   (First)   (Middle)

Address: _____
(Street)   (City)   (State/Zip)

Business Address: _____

Phone: (Work) _____ (Home) _____ (Fax) _____ (Email) _____

Giving History:

Grand Total	Number of Gifts	First Gift Date	Most Recent Gift Amount	Most Recent Gift Date	Largest Gift
$_____	_____	_____	$_____	_____	$_____

Family: _____
(Spouse)

_____
(Children)

_____
(Other significant relationships)

Interests: _____

Key Relationships with XYZ Nonprofit Organization: _____

Capability: _____   _____
(Estimate of net worth)   (Form of wealth)

_____
(Other factors and information)

Rating: _____   _____
(Preliminary)   (Final)

Network:

_____
(Closest friends)

_____
(Those close to XYZ Nonprofit who have common bond with prospect)

Solicitor(s) of Record: _____

Cultivation Strategy: _____

_____

_____

EXHIBIT 6.7 (CONTINUED)

Gift Opportunity or Project: _____

_____

Next Step: _____

_____

By: _____   _____   _____
       (Target date)   (Entered tickler)   (Done)

Summary Comments:_____

_____

_____

_____

Next Step: _____

_____

By: _____   _____   _____
       (Target date)   (Entered tickler)   (Done)

Summary Comments:_____

_____

_____

_____

Some years ago, two of our nation's most gifted capital fundraisers, David Dunlop and G. Taylor "Bunky" Smith, were discussing the need to refine the relationship-nurturing process. Out of this conversation, the two developed a positive and effective process and coined the phrase "moves management." Later, the term became popular but misunderstood. Some board members and volunteers thought the term sounded manipulative. David has since expressed regret that he ever used the term. He believes that nonprofit leaders need to be sensitive to how their words are interpreted.

David and Bunky developed their powerful management tool, moves management, to help large development staffs monitor relationships with numerous prospective donors. This is especially important in institutions such as universities that might have thousands of major gift prospects throughout the world. Unfortunately, some less mature development people still focus on the word "moves" and view the process as controlling or manipulative. Nothing could be further from the truth.

A "move" might be as simple as sending a birthday card or as significant as having a luncheon meeting with the president of the institution. Tracking involves recording the activity and making notes about the prospect's response and readiness to support the organization. There is no manipulation involved. Rather, thoughtful "moves management" is a system that helps the organization maintain gracious and meaningful relationships with its supporters.

A small organization can track its top 25 to 50 prime prospects using a simple Prime Prospect Tracking Form (see Exhibit 6.7). Larger institutions use their dedicated fundraising software to track donor information and cultivation steps. Never forget, however, that while we are managing the process, our real goal is to nurture warm and respectful relationships.

CHAPTER 7

The Case for Support and Campaign Materials

Keeping the facility planning and capital campaign preparation processes in synch isn't easy. In an ideal world, both processes would move forward inexorably toward the dual goals of having the perfect facilities to meet the organization's needs and having more than adequate funding to assure the project's success. But real life doesn't go that way. At times the nonprofit organization's facility planning committee will get far ahead of the fundraising preparation. In other organizations the capital campaign might get underway and the building planning committee might suffer a serious setback such as a land acquisition deal falling through or a denial of a zoning permit.

Still, it is helpful to keep the processes in synch as much as possible. By the time the organization has a fairly well-defined idea of its facility needs—including an understanding of the solution and total related costs—key board and staff members should also have begun the process of identifying and nurturing relationships with potential lead funders.

When the organization has a good idea of the scope of the proposed capital project and some knowledge of the prospective supporters, the organization can begin to create the most important precampaign document: the test case for support.

THE POWER OF THE DRAFT CASE FOR SUPPORT

A *case for support,* also called a *case statement,* is a body of language that describes the rationale for supporting a nonprofit organization. It is written from the donor's perspective, primarily the desire to support worthwhile projects and organizations that help enhance the lives of others.

The case statement answers these questions:

- How does the organization change lives and help people?
- Who benefits from the organization's programs?
- What vital services does the institution offer?
- What is the agency's track record?
- What are the organization's plans for the future?
- What facility challenges does the organization face?
- What is the proposed solution to the organization's facility and endowment needs?
- What is the rationale for capital and endowment support?
- Why does this organization merit support?

With such important questions, why do fundraising consultants stress the importance of the "draft" case for support?

Recall that a goal of every nonprofit is to engage and involve key stakeholders. Nurturing genuine relationships and creating a sense of buy-in are the underpinnings for successful organization development and capital campaigns. Prospective supporters who help strengthen the organization and who also offer advice concerning the capital project are more likely to make significant commitments to the campaign.

By sharing a draft case statement, the organization reinforces the idea that prospective supporters are valued for their advice and wisdom. The draft case for support is a test document that is used during the precampaign planning study described in the next chapter. For now, suffice to say that each potential pace-setting donor is invited to participate in a confidential interview and to comment on the draft case statement.

If the case statement looks too polished or finished, prospective donors think, "Why are they asking me for advice? They already decided what they want to do and have published a fancy piece to describe their project." So save the glitzy publications for later in the campaign, well after the planning study. Leadership donors want and expect to be involved from the earliest stages. An attractively word processed case statement marked "Draft for Review by Community Leaders" is appropriate.

But just because the case statement is labeled a draft doesn't mean that the organization should not take great efforts to create a strong and positive impression. It should be well written, attractively laid out, and easy to understand. Moreover, the case statement should have both a rational and emotional impact. A four-, five-, or six-page document, including a project budget, should suffice for most organizations. Any architectural sketches or floor plans can also be included. If the organization does not yet have floor plans or schematic drawings, try to punctuate the case for support with suggestive line drawings. For example, an arch suggesting an entryway or other sketchy generic features remind the reader that the case statement involves a building project. Organizations can choose from a number of simple binding solutions and may also wish to include several photos. Just remember not to go overboard. Keep it simple and attractive.

When writing your case for support, consider hiring a professional writer. Alternatively, the consultant you engage for your precampaign planning study might include developing the case statement as part of the services. Problems sometimes occur when less-experienced writers close to the organization prepare the case statement. When other committee members make suggestions, "pride of authorship" might raise its ugly head. The result might be a long, painful process that results in a case statement that sounds as if it were written by a committee.

A case statement might include the following sections:

- Mission and brief history, including any awards or outstanding accomplishments
- Services and programs
- Poignant stories or testimonials
- The challenge, including the need to overcome facility obstacles and to enhance lives
- The solution
- Call for action
- Budget
- Floor plans, elevations, schematic drawings

Because the draft case for support is used for the precampaign planning study, the "Call for Action" section should not directly request funds. Rather, it should request "time, wisdom, and advice" concerning how best to prepare for a successful project. Exhibit 7.1 is such a "Draft Case Statement for Review by Community Leaders." The words might vary, but the thoughts expressed should be gracious, open, and genuine.

Chapter 8 describes the Precampaign Planning Study and other steps needed to prepare your organization for a successful campaign. The draft case statement is used during the study. Following the study, the case statement is revised based on suggestions made by study participants.

NOTE
The remaining materials described in this chapter are used after the study.

EXHIBIT 7.1   SAMPLE CASE FOR SUPPORT

ALL FAITHS RECEIVING HOME

Safe Facilities and Compassionate Services
for
Children and Families

Draft for Review by Community Leaders

ALL FAITHS RECEIVING HOME

Safe Facilities and Compassionate Services for Children and Families

---

MISSION STATEMENT

All Faiths Receiving Home is New Mexico's preeminent nonprofit agency providing protection and rehabilitation services to abused and neglected children and their families. The home was established in 1956 by a group of private citizens to provide emergency residential care for children in crisis.

In New Mexico there is an epidemic of violence against children. New Mexico's homicide rate for children under four years of age is more than 50 percent higher than the national average. And, according to the New Mexico Pediatrics Society, abuse and neglect in the home is the leading cause of death for children aged four and younger. For children five to fourteen years old, New Mexico's homicide rate is nearly 40 percent higher than the national average.

At All Faiths, we work to prevent child abuse and neglect. We are dedicated to developing healthy children and families. Throughout our 41-year history, All Faiths has expanded programs to address the challenges of nurturing and treating troubled children who are victims of physical, emotional, and sexual abuse, as well as neglect.

Today, All Faiths is a comprehensive child abuse intervention, prevention, and treatment agency serving more than 1,000 children and 400 parents each year through an integrated continuum of sensitive and caring programs.

> *When I came to All Faiths I immediately felt a sense of warmth, safety, and belonging. . . . While I was there, I learned to love and trust other people, and I learned I had value as a person. I will be grateful the rest of my life to All Faiths for these lessons.*
>
> Melody, a former Crisis Shelter resident

EXHIBIT 7.1   (CONTINUED)

Countless lives have been touched by the compassion of All Faiths workers. . . . Albuquerque is fortunate to have this haven for children—a haven that has provided warmth and love to children who desperately needed help.

Albuquerque *Journal*

All Faiths Receiving Home—with an annual budget of $2,700,000—relies on various sources of funding including local, state, and federal contracts, the United Way, our own Endowment Foundation, as well as private and corporate donations. Two special events, the All Faiths Auxiliary Apples & Arts Festival and the Active 20/30 Club's Equestrian Cup, raise significant financial support for All Faiths and have become popular fall traditions for Albuquerque citizens.

PROTECTIVE SERVICES

THE CRISIS SHELTER provides short-term emergency care for children from infancy to age twelve. In our safe and comfortable residential setting, we shelter, feed, clothe, and help heal 15 to 20 children daily—more than 400 children each year for an average stay of three weeks each. All Faiths believes that a child who has suffered the trauma of abuse deserves the best care in the most positive environment the community can offer.

For the past 41 years, the All Faiths Receiving Home's Crisis Shelter has been a safe, dependable place where law-enforcement and social service agents can take children in urgent need of emergency shelter, love, and care.

THE CHILDREN'S SAFEHOUSE offers a safe refuge for interviewing children who are alleged victims of sexual abuse or who have witnessed a violent crime. Each year, trained specialists conduct more than 500 confidential forensic interviews. These interviews are witnessed by law enforcement, social services, counseling, prosecutorial, and medical personnel and are audio- and video-recorded for possible future legal proceedings. This capability assures that the children need relive their traumatic experience only once rather than over and over as was often required in the past.

TREATMENT AND PREVENTION PROGRAMS

FAMILY SERVICES provides outpatient treatment, counseling, and support for children, adults, and families affected by abuse and neglect. The home's comprehensive offerings include individual, family, and group therapy, and numerous issue-specific peer support groups. These programs, which serve nearly 150 children and 400 adults annually, are designed to break the cycle of abuse, prevent future crises, preserve the family unit, and promote healthy families through rehabilitation.

RESIDENTIAL SERVICES offers intensive home-based counseling and therapy to families coping with multiple behavioral issues that significantly complicate a child's recovery from abuse and neglect. Specially trained and licensed practitioners spend many hours per week working with children and families to resolve adverse situations and restore appropriate family functioning.

EXHIBIT 7.I   (CONTINUED)

TREATMENT FOSTER CARE offers family-based treatment for children who are behaviorally disturbed as a result of long histories of abuse and neglect. These special needs children are placed in a loving home with carefully trained foster parents. All Faiths provides ongoing intensive professional support and supervision for the child and parents. This program promotes reunification with the natural family whenever possible and permanent family placement in all cases.

ONE CHILD'S STORY

One winter evening, a police cruiser delivered five-year-old Amy and her younger sister to All Faiths' Crisis Shelter. Alarmed neighbors had alerted authorities that the parents hadn't been seen for several days . . . and the girls were left all alone. The children were malnourished and dirty. While in All Faiths protective care, the girls were given food, clothing, and medical treatment in a safe and nurturing environment.

While at All Faiths' Crisis Shelter, Amy told a counselor a troubling event. At the Children's Safehouse, she told the clinical interviewer about her sexual abuse by her stepfather. As a result of this intervention by All Faiths, her assaulter was apprehended, convicted, and put in jail . . . thus preventing his sexual abuse of the younger daughter. During this process, Amy and her sister were placed with one of the home's Treatment Foster Care families.

It was determined that the girls should be reunited with their mother if she could be rehabilitated and taught proper parenting skills. So Amy and her family received intensive home-based therapy from All Faiths. With this support the children began their recovery from the downward spiral of abuse and neglect. Later, the family continued to receive treatment and support from All Faiths' Family Services program.

The family has remained intact and abuse-free for three years. All remain involved with support groups sponsored by the home. And the children's social skills have caught up with norms for their ages. Amy's family seems to have successfully broken the cycle of abuse—because All Faiths was there when they needed us.

PROGRAM INITIATIVES

To respond to growing needs and to better serve families and children, All Faiths Receiving Home is restructuring some services and implementing several major program initiatives. After extensive internal study, we have concluded that the following actions must be taken as soon as possible.

- **Integrate the work of the Children's Safehouse and Family Services and locate the services at a single upgraded facility.**

With the recent purchase of our Moon Street Complex, the Children's Safehouse and Family Service offices can now be housed in the same facility. When the services were miles apart, family members often did not seek needed and prescribed therapy. By combining the Safehouse and Family Services into one program at one facility we are healing families and *helping end the cycle of abuse.*

EXHIBIT 7.1   (CONTINUED)

This initiative is also designed to:
- ✓ Improve Safehouse interview recording capabilities, security, and privacy.
- ✓ Permit simultaneous forensic interviews in settings appropriate to children of different ages.
- ✓ Improve communications and coordination with the District Attorney's Office; Albuquerque Police Department; Children, Youth, and Family Department; and other agencies.
- ✓ Provide a seamless, supervised system of support for those families struggling with sexual abuse issues.
- ✓ Share staff and administrative support.

- **Preserve the natural family if possible or transition children into permanent homes.**

This initiative will:
- ✓ Help reduce expensive and unnecessary institutional placements.
- ✓ Provide intensive home-based therapy to families who are at risk of having their children removed from the home and to families adjusting to their children's return.
- ✓ Teach parenting and coping skills.
- ✓ Encourage networking with other community resources for those families that need additional services.
- ✓ Require families to participate in support and education groups designed to prevent child abuse.

THE CHALLENGE

In addition to the Residential and Safehouse facilities at our Trellis site, All Faiths Receiving Home also, until recently, rented administrative offices at 1330 San Pedro. Family Services and Treatment Foster Care offices are six blocks south at 601 San Pedro.

Unfortunately, improvement and expansion of the home's facilities have not kept pace with community needs. And, the Moon Street Complex must be renovated to accommodate the new Safehouse and Family Services.

As All Faiths Receiving Home prepares for the next millennium, our most pressing need is to provide safe and pleasant facilities for our children. At the same time, we must assure that our facilities support our mission and programs. Given the rapidly changing healthcare and social services environment, All Faiths' overall facilities plan must offer maximum flexibility and make better operational and economical sense. Simply put, we must address the following challenges.

The Crisis Shelter buildings are old and in need of enlargement and renovation. Current space layouts and usages do not adequately, much less comfortably, meet the needs of our children, staff, and volunteers. We must make numerous substantial improvements related to facility safety and security. The West Building must be remodeled as a flexible, multipurpose space that can be adapted to respond to the changing needs of our constituencies. The entire Trellis Street campus must be upgraded to relieve crowding and enhance amenities. Our children and the people who serve them deserve a more secure, accommodating, and cheerful environment.

The Children's Safehouse is a crowded, small building, completely inadequate for our needs. It has many serious functional problems, including severe privacy and climate

EXHIBIT 7.1   (CONTINUED)

control deficiencies. The Safehouse is located at the Trellis site, which is distant from Children's Hospital and not convenient for many families or other agency officials. Most importantly, the Safehouse is isolated from the Family Services location now in a rented space on south San Pedro Street that is inhospitable and uncomfortable for clients. These two programs must be united in one comprehensive treatment facility so that abused children and their families may be transitioned readily into rehabilitative and preventive therapy. The effectiveness and efficiency of these related services will be greatly enhanced in a single facility that is designed to address the specialized needs of each program.

Treatment Foster Care currently functions out of the same undesirable site on south San Pedro. It needs to be relocated to the Trellis Street campus so that all residential care programs are consolidated in one location.

Administration, Public Relations, and Development offices are housed in yet another isolated location, a situation that inhibits efficient communication and coordination with programmatic services and personnel. Furthermore, facilities and equipment use economies—such as shared office equipment—are not feasible with management and program services in separate sites.

CORE ISSUES

Through an intensive planning process involving a broad spectrum of child care professionals and community leaders, All Faiths Receiving Home has identified the following core issues:

- **The Crisis Shelter must be expanded and renovated. Our vision is to create a safer, more flexible and attractive environment for the children we serve. We must also be prepared to accept the increasing number of children who will come to All Faiths Receiving Home.**
- **The Children's Safehouse and Family Service Offices must be housed together. This will help us ensure that child abuse victims and their families receive counseling and other related services.**
- **The overall facilities plan must offer the greatest flexibility to enable All Faiths to adapt and respond to increasing demands and changing needs.**

OUR SOLUTION

After examining numerous options, All Faiths Receiving Home has focused its facilities planning on the following main elements:

Priority 1:   **Purchase—and eliminate the mortgage as soon as possible—a 15,000-square-foot building to house the Children's Safehouse, Family Services, and Administration.** Remodel approximately 3,600 square feet of the Moon Street Complex specifically for Safehouse activities.

Priority 2:   **Enlarge and renovate the Crisis Shelter on Trellis Street.**

Priority 3:   **Remodel and upgrade other facilities at the Trellis Street campus.**

EXHIBIT 7.1   (CONTINUED)

Priority 4:   **Demolish the current Safehouse. Construct a new building at the Trellis Street site for Treatment Foster Care and Home-based Services.**

The total investment required for our facilities plan is approximately $3,200,000.

CALL TO ACTION

The improvement of our facilities is absolutely vital to All Faiths Receiving Home's ability to provide compassionate services for children who are victims of abuse and neglect and for families seeking to end the cycle of abuse.

We have an opportunity to make a difference. All of us with All Faiths Receiving Home know that you share our concern for children and families. As we refine our plans and prepare for our capital campaign, we need your advice and wisdom.

Please join us as we prepare for *Safe Facilities and Compassionate Services for Children and Families.*

Printed with permission from All Faiths Receiving Home.

REVISING THE CASE FOR SUPPORT

Soon after the precampaign planning study is completed, the organization should review suggestions made by study participants and revise the case for support. Often the changes are small. At times study participants will suggest more specific information about the number of people the organization serves and how many more can be served with the new facilities. Or study participants might read a phrase embedded in the text and suggest that the phrase be printed in bold or used as a heading for a section.

In other situations, the suggestions might be more extensive. If prominent supporters do not believe the organization has the capacity to raise the full amount, the study participant might suggest completing the work in phases or stages. If such a plan is adopted by the organization, the case statement would need to be revised to reflect the new plans. Similarly, if the architect has revised the floor plans or schematic drawings, the revised case statement should include the most recent drawings.

After the study, the organization also begins the board campaign and the "quiet phase" of the capital campaign. Even during these early key meetings and solicitations, the attractively word-processed case for support will suffice. If the organization wants to make a somewhat more polished presentation, one cost-effective solution is to produce presentation folders. These can be used for capital campaign purposes or for other presentations to groups or individuals. Attractive two-pocket presentation folders with slits for business cards can be produced for approximately $1.10 a piece. Exhibit 7.2 is one example of a presentation folder used during a capital campaign for a homeless shelter for women and children.

MARKET-SPECIFIC CASE STATEMENTS

Many nonprofit organizations find that one version of the case statement is not sufficient for the campaign. A community of Catholic priests in New Mexico prepared two case statements. One version was responsive to local needs; the theme was "A Critical Shortage of Priests." The second version was geared to long-time supporters from Wisconsin, the main home of the priests' order; the theme for that case statement was "From Wisconsin to New Mexico—A Rich History and Mission." The two case statements spoke well to their respective constituencies. The community was successful in securing leadership level commitments from people residing in both states.

Sometimes the changes you make in the case statement are simple. For example, it is often helpful to prepare a case statement for corporate leaders that stresses the economic benefits of the proposed project. The case statement prepared for others can contain the same information but might stress other points more prominently.

One advantage of spending a bit more on the presentation folder is that market-specific case statements and support material can be easily revised during the campaign and customized for individual donors. The organization need not spend a great deal of money on one master case statement but can still make a strong impact with a well-designed presentation folder. Some small to medium-sized nonprofit organizations find it possible to raise millions of dollars using these presentation folders and customized campaign materials. Exhibit 7.3 shows a case for support cover customized with the name of the individual prospect.

THE "ULTIMATE" CASE FOR SUPPORT

Prestigious institutions and organizations that have an international reputation for excellence need campaign materials that reflect their values. Several years ago, Susan Duncan Thomas, CFRE, a former partner of mine, was working with The Santa Fe Opera. During its $21 million capital campaign, the organization produced a four-color brochure that included a spectacular 37-inch fold-out color drawing of the state-of-the-art new home for The Santa Fe Opera.

EXHIBIT 7.2 SAMPLE PRESENTATION FOLDER

Printed with permission from the Barrett Foundation, Ken Wilson Design, and Timeless Images Photography.

EXHIBIT 7.3   PERSONALIZED CASE STATEMENT COVER

ALBUQUERQUE

HISPAN@

CHAMBER OF COMMERCE

BARELAS JOB OPPORTUNITY CENTER

NEIGHBORHOOD REVITALIZATION
&
ECONOMIC DEVELOPMENT

Information Prepared for
MR. ALEX ROMERO

Printed with permission from the Albuquerque Hispano Chamber of Commerce.

Time magazine referred to The Santa Fe Opera as "the handsomest operatic setting in the western world." Anyone who sees the magnificent capital campaign booklet—with its large color foldout, dramatic photos of New Mexican skies, colorful photos of opera scenes, pithy quotes from prominent artists, and awesome detailed diagrams of the rich facilities—instantly knows that this is no ordinary project. This is a campaign that reflects "the combination of adventure and tradition that have become the signature of The Santa Fe Opera."

One other feature of note in The Santa Fe Opera brochure is its inside back cover, which has a flap that enables the organization to use the booklet as a presentation folder. Highly personalized requests and gift opportunity information can be placed in the booklet. This makes sense. As dramatic as the materials might be, each visit to a prospective supporter must be personal. Relationships, not materials, lead to pacesetting gifts.

COMMITMENT FORMS

One of the earliest orders of business after the planning study is to secure multiyear commitments from 100 percent of the members of the board of directors. The best approach is to have the board chair, one or two generous board members, and the CEO divide the board list based on personal chemistry and strength of relationship. To assure that the capital campaign gets off on the right foot, two-person teams of visitors should personally call on each board member. Team members discuss the revised case for support, listen to the board member's concerns, explain the importance of 100 percent participation, and ask the board member to consider a generous multiyear commitment to the campaign. A sample board commitment card is shown as Exhibit 7.4. Be sure *not* to refer to your forms and cards as "pledge cards." Many people find the word "pledge" intimidating. They are fearful to enter into a legal obligation. Anecdotal evidence and the personal experience of many leading capital campaign consultants indicate that "commitments that may be revised" or "statements of intent that may be adjusted should circumstances require" are fulfilled to the same or greater extent as old fashioned "pledges." And many people reluctant to sign a pledge card will sign a commitment card with the appropriate language.

An alternative to the board commitment card is a one-page commitment form that could be used by board members or others who have made their commitment. This type of commitment form is illustrated in Exhibit 7.5.

FACT SHEETS

In our high-tech age with its frenetic tempo, most people will not read your longer campaign pieces. Have you ever noticed how many people never get

EXHIBIT 7.4   SAMPLE BOARD CAMPAIGN COMMITMENT CARD

COMMITMENT CARD

YES! To help in **Building Futures for Women and Children**—and in recognition of my special role as a Board member—I will commit $_____ to the Barrett Foundation Capital Campaign. Enclosed is my first contribution of $_____.
I/we will contribute the balance as follows:

Monthly_____ Quarterly_____ Annually_____ Other_____

This commitment is for: 1 year_____ 2 years_____ or 3 years_____

Name: _____

Address: _____

City, State, Zip: _____

Phone: _____

Signature: _____ Date: _____

Please mail contributions to:
Barrett Foundation, Inc.
P.O. Box 25823
Albuquerque, NM 87125
(505) 246-9244

Printed with permission from the Barrett Foundation.

EXHIBIT 7.5   ONE-PAGE COMMITMENT FORM

Barrett Foundation
Building Futures for Women and Children
P.O. Box 25823 · Albuquerque, NM 87125-5823
(505) 246-9244 · fax (505) 246-9272

Barrett Foundation, Inc. (Barrett House) is grateful for
your support and financial commitment to

Building Futures for Women and Children

Yes! I am pleased to participate in the Barrett Foundation, Inc. Campaign to help ensure
its financial future. My gift, along with others, will further the mission and goals of the
Barrett House.

In consideration of the gifts of others, joining together to build a new Barrett House,

I/We make a gift of $_____ to the Barrett Foundation, Inc./Barrett
House Capital Campaign   (cash or securities; if other, please specify).

I/We pledge to the Barrett Foundation, Inc. a gift of $_____ over a
___ one-year period, ___ two-year period, ___ three-year period, ___ five-year period.
We will honor our pledge as follows:

$_____ paid with this pledge, with subsequent payments as follows:

$_____ to be paid _____ (month, year)
$_____ to be paid _____ (month, year)
$_____ to be paid _____ (month, year)
$_____ to be paid _____ (month, year)

I wish my gift to be anonymous _____
                                                    Signature
I wish my gift to name _____ in honor/memory of _____
                                          (circle one)

Please make all gifts payable to the Barrett Foundation, Inc.

_____
Name (as you wish to see it in print)

_____
Address   City, State, Zip

_____
Telephone   Email   Fax

_____
Signature   Date

All gifts will be acknowledged, by gift level, in Barrett Foundation, Inc. publications and in other appropriate places
unless otherwise specified by the donor. I understand that my gift may be used to inspire gifts from additional
individuals, corporations, and foundations.

| Barrett House Emergency Shelter | Bridges Supportive Housing | Casa Milagro Transitional Living | Casa Verde Permanent Housing | Barrett House Attic Shop of New and Used |

Printed with permission from the Barrett Foundation.

beyond the first two sentences of any email message? "I don't scroll" seems to be their mantra. With this in mind, it behooves campaign organizers to reduce key messages and the case for support to a one-page fact sheet.

In addition to being useful on visits to prospective donors, the one-page fact sheet helps simplify volunteer orientation. Many volunteers are uncomfortable with longer campaign pieces. The one-page version of the case statement helps them grasp the main "talking points." On cultivation or solicitation visits, volunteers can say something like, "This brochure tells the whole story about our campaign. I'll leave this with you. By way of introduction, this one-page fact sheet will give you the broad overview." Exhibit 7.6 shows a simple version of a one-page case statement or fact sheet. Fancier versions are possible, but the single page with bullets is the easiest for the reader to absorb.

COMMEMORATIVE GIFT OPPORTUNITIES

Acknowledgment planning is crucial to campaign success. Donors often respond more generously when they are offered an opportunity to name a significant architectural feature or to make a gift in honor or memory of a loved one.

Thinking strategically, campaign organizers assure that there are an equal or *greater* number of named gift opportunities corresponding to their gift pyramid. In other words, if the campaign requires one $1 million lead gift to succeed, the gift opportunities will include one or perhaps two $1 million gift opportunities. This principle carries forth through the remainder of the gift pyramid. Exhibit 7.7 illustrates a gift pyramid for a campaign for a bit more than $5 million; Exhibit 7.8 illustrates a description of gift opportunities for the same campaign.

Exhibit 7.9, "Gift Opportunity and Prospect Management Tracking Form," is an illustration from another campaign. This prospect management tool links the organization's top prospects to possible gift opportunities. It is clearly *not* a campaign piece that is shared with the public. However, it is a powerful communication and management tool that keeps campaign leaders focused on the most important prospects and gift opportunities. Also note that some of the prospects listed may not choose to participate at the targeted gift levels. When offered the opportunity, some may choose a named gift that requires a larger investment. Some might choose to participate at a more modest level.

As the campaign proceeds, the staff will need to revise the gift opportunities page to keep track of which rooms or other commemorative gift opportunities have been committed and which remain. It is important that key volunteers receive this up-to-date information. It is embarrassing to offer the same room

EXHIBIT 7.6   ONE-PAGE CASE STATEMENT/
FACT SHEET

International Institute of Asian Arts

Capital and Endowment Campaign
Preservation, Education and Inspiration

Campaign Summary: Did you know . . . ?

- The International Institute of Asian Arts (IIAA) has more than 700,000 visitors each year. Our main facility in Santa Barbara, California, is recognized as one of the world's leading repositories for Asian art objects and artifacts.
- With the addition of the Lambert Collection, IIAA now has the largest collection of works related to Japanese Buddhism in North America.
- The IIAA is open 7 days a week, 365 days a year. Our holiday celebrations have become an integral part of Northern California's social and cultural life.
- IIAA's current facilities allow us to display only a small fraction of our total collection.
- Moreover, our aging building does not have the climate control features expected of a world-class institution such as IIAA.
- Our new home at Montgomery Pkwy. and Lowell Dr. will have double the exhibit space of our current facility. Additionally, the new IIAA will house expanded space and research facilities for the hundreds of scholars who visit us each year.
- Our capital campaign encompasses $12,000,000 new construction, $3 million acquisitions to complete core collections, and $5 million in endowment funds. **Therefore, our campaign goal is $20 million.**
- Generous supporters from throughout the nation and world have already contributed $14,000,000. And an anonymous donor has issued a $3 million Challenge Grant. The donor will donate the final $3 million when we have raised the next $3 million in new contributions and pledges.
- Your pledge will be matched dollar for dollar—and will be an investment in preserving and interpreting some of our world's most transcendent art. Please join us with your time, talent, and financial support.

EXHIBIT 7.7 SAMPLE GIFT PYRAMID

HILLSIDE FREE WILL BAPTIST COLLEGE

STANDARD OF INVESTMENTS
NECESSARY TO ACHIEVE $5,250,000 GOAL

Number of Gifts Required	Investment Level Three-Year Pledge Period	Annual Amount	Value
1	$1,000,000	$333,333	$1,000,000
2	500,000	166,667	1,000,000
2	300,000	100,000	600,000
2	150,000	50,000	300,000
2	100,000	33,333	200,000
2	75,000	25,000	150,000
10	50,000	16,667	500,000
10	30,000	10,000	300,000
15	15,000	5,000	225,000
21	10,000	3,333	210,000
22	7,500	2,500	165,000
44	6,000	2,000	264,000
55	3,000	1,000	165,000
114	1,500	500	171,000
302			**$5,250,000**

The honored tradition of significant public causes supported by special funds dates back to biblical times. Using an approach common among hospitals and academic institutions, the Hillsdale Free Will Baptist College will establish Named Gift Opportunities. Major investments will be named in perpetuity in honor or memory of the donor family or loved one.

Pacesetting gifts at the top investment levels will assure that Hillsdale Free Will Baptist College will reach or exceed its goal.

Donors wishing to make pledges of $500,000, $1,000,000, *or more* may also be acknowledged with special named gift opportunities tailor-made for their unique circumstances.

Printed with permission from Hillsdale Free Will Baptist College.

for naming to more than one major donor. It is even more embarrassing when two major donors independently name the same room. Exhibit 7.10 shows an updated gift opportunities page. An alternative is to mark rooms that are taken on a floor plan that is used to indicate the remaining gift opportunities. Exhibits 7.11 and 7.12 shows this approach.

EXHIBIT 7.8   GIFT OPPORTUNITIES RELATED TO EXHIBIT 7.7

NAMED GIFT OPPORTUNITIES
HILLSDALE FREE WILL BAPTIST COLLEGE

Honorary or Memorial Naming Opportunities	*Minimum Gift (Paid over 3–5 Yrs.)*
The Complex	$1,000,000
The Chapel/Auditorium	1,000,000
Overall Name for Endowment Fund	1,000,000
Educational Center	500,000
Amphitheater and Bell Tower	500,000
Dining Hall	300,000
Community Room	300,000
Activities Center	300,000
Faculty Center	150,000
Administrative Suite	150,000
Recital Hall	125,000
Lobby I	100,000
Lobby II	75,000
President's Office	75,000
Conference Room	50,000
Each Classroom	50,000
Each Administrative Office	30,000
Each Faculty Office	30,000

Additional Wall of Honor Categories

Guardian	$15,000
Steward	7,500
Fellow	6,000
Good Samaritan	3,000
Friend	1,500

Hillsdale Free Will Baptist College
For more information, contact the Development Office of the Hillsdale Free Will Baptist College
P.O. Box 7208 • Moore, OK 73153-1208 • (405) 912-9000

Printed with permission from Hillsdale Free Will Baptist College.

EXHIBIT 7.9   GIFT OPPORTUNITY AND PROSPECT
MANAGEMENT TRACKING FORM

GIFT AMOUNT	NUMBER OF GIFTS NEEDED	NUMBER OF PROSPECTS NEEDED	GIFT OPPORTUNITIES	PROSPECTS
$1,000,000	1	4	East Wing, or Endow Music Director	M/M Steven Charles M/M Robert Bryant George Crane, Sr. M/M Roger Kroth
$500,000	1	4	Auditorium, or Endow Concertmaster	The Kresge Foundation Mrs. Roberta Blitz M/M Ed Williams Charles M. Wyatt
$300,000	2	8	Recital Hall or Lobby, or Endow Principal Chairs	Mabee Foundation M/M Dennis Thelander Charles Higbee Ed Cox M/M Ken Burns ABC Corporation Sam Maxwell M/M Juan Dinero
$150,000	3	12	Upper Lobby or "Green Room" or the Board Room	Albert Smith 1st National Bank M/M Charles Baxter Linda Hughes Scott Herron M/M Hulk Hogan Melvyn Barber M/M Michael Wexler Fabian Del Jiorno Helen Webb M/M Mark Carter M/M Bruce Zink

(CONTINUE FOR ALL TOP GIFT LEVELS)

PRICING NAMED GIFTS

Consultants are often asked how the named gift opportunities are priced. While there are no rigid rules that always apply, some general principles serve well as guideposts. The first of these is to avoid the mistake of equating gift opportunities with the actual construction costs. In a large project, it is very difficult, if not impossible, to determine the cost of a specific room. Besides, campaign organizers need not obtain the full costs of an architectural feature to offer the naming opportunity. Many recommend that a contribution equaling one-half the

EXHIBIT 7.10　UPDATED GIFT OPPORTUNITIES PAGE

NAMED GIFT OPPORTUNITIES

HILLSDALE FREE WILL BAPTIST COLLEGE

Honorary or Memorial Naming Opportunities		*Minimum Gift (Paid over 3–5 Yrs.)*
The Complex		$1,000,000
The Chapel/Auditorium	**Subscribed**	1,000,000
Overall Name for Endowment Fund		1,000,000
Educational Center	**Subscribed**	500,000
Amphitheater and Bell Tower		500,000
Dining Hall		300,000
Community Room	**Subscribed**	300,000
Activities Center	**Subscribed**	300,000
Faculty Center	**Subscribed**	150,000
Administrative Suite		150,000
Recital Hall		125,000
Lobby I	**Subscribed**	100,000
Lobby II	**Subscribed**	75,000
President's Office		75,000
Conference Room		50,000
Each Classroom		50,000
Each Administrative Office		30,000
Each Faculty Office		30,000

Additional Wall of Honor Categories

Guardian	$15,000
Steward	7,500
Fellow	6,000
Good Samaritan	3,000
Friend	1,500

Hillsdale Free Will Baptist College
For more information, contact the Development Office of the Hillsdale Free Will Baptist College
P.O. Box 7208 • Moore, OK 73153-1208 • (405) 912-9000

Printed with permission from Hillsdale Free Will Baptist College.

EXHIBIT 7.11   UPDATED FLOOR PLAN

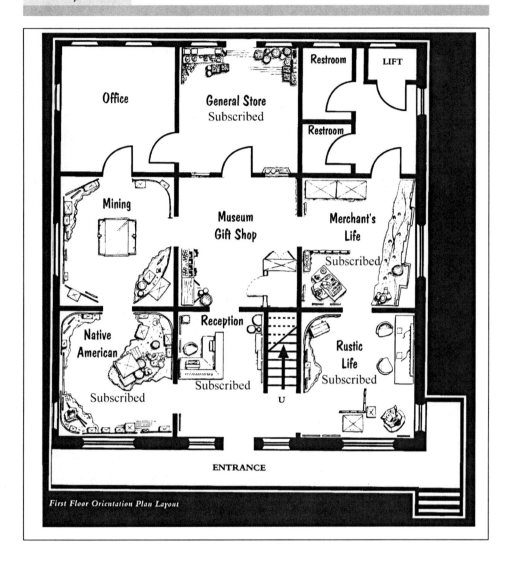

Office

General Store
Subscribed

Restroom

LIFT

Restroom

Mining

Museum
Gift Shop

Merchant's
Life

Subscribed

Native
American

Reception

Rustic
Life
Subscribed

Subscribed

Subscribed

U

ENTRANCE

First Floor Orientation Plan Layout

estimated construction costs should be required in order to name a building, room, or wing.

Required contributions for naming opportunities can be further refined. Organizers may wish to put a somewhat higher investment level on a less costly feature. For example, a small memorial garden might be more attractive to potential donors than an administrative office that might have higher actual construction costs. In such cases, the campaign organizers might request a higher gift level for the memorial garden than the administrative office. So the helpful rule is to price gift opportunities from high to low based on their attractiveness to the philanthropic community.

EXHIBIT 7.12   UPDATED FLOOR PLAN

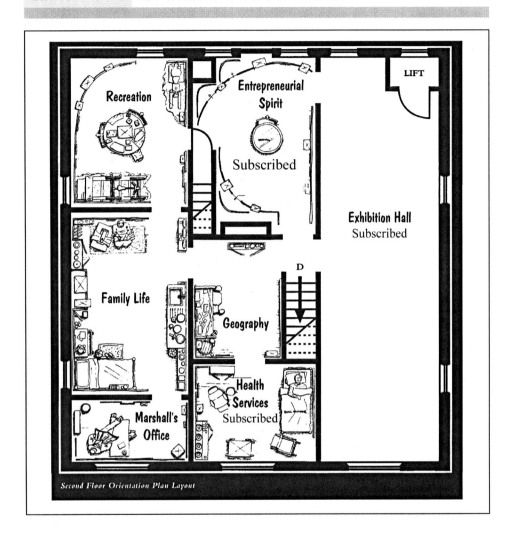

Second Floor Orientation Plan Layout

Campaign organizers might wish to adopt a pragmatic approach relative to overall levels. If the organization's top prospects cannot donate one-half the cost of each actual architectural feature, perhaps they are capable of gifts that match the most generous gift pyramid levels. In such cases, consider pricing the gift opportunities in line with the gift pyramid—even though these levels do not match the "one-half the actual costs" recommendation. Some organizers are reluctant to name a $10 million building for less than $5 million. Others reason that a $2.5 to $3 million lead gift that assures the campaign's success would be adequate to name the facility. Each nonprofit organization must make these decisions based on its circumstances and prospect pool.

CAMPAIGN STATIONERY

Many nonprofits use their regular stationery for communications during the capital campaign, while others print special stationery that lists the members of the capital campaign steering committee and board of directors down the left-hand margin of the letterhead. Of course, any new campaign logo and campaign theme is displayed prominently.

Campaign organizers will want to use the logo and theme on any number of campaign communication pieces. For example, invitations to cultivation events, as described in Chapter 6, might appear on campaign letterhead. The important point is to maintain a consistent message and image throughout the campaign. The campaign materials should constitute a family of communication pieces.

DVD AND VIDEO

Many capital campaign experts believe that videos and DVD case statements are powerful campaign tools. Videos or DVDs can be mailed to prospects too distant to visit in person. For that matter, videos or DVDs left with prospective supporters after a cultivation visit reinforce the visitor's message. A well-produced video or DVD can be expected to bring the prospect closer to your cause.

Consider the following: A development officer called six times to set up an appointment with a prospect and the board chair. Six times the prospective supporter did not return her calls. The campaign consultant suggested she call again—using a different approach. The consultant advised the development officer to "schmooze" with the prospect's secretary and promise that the meeting would not take more than 15 minutes. On the seventh call, the prospect did call back and set up the appointment.

During the visit, the development officer and board president arrived with a video case for support. The development officer and board president used the brief meeting to introduce themselves and to summarize the need for the capital project. They also left the video case statement. The next morning the supporter called and made a $75,000 commitment.

Considering the original resistance, one can conclude that the video case statement played a major role in the prospect's conversion process. In all probability, the dramatic turnaround was at least in part due to the power of the visual message.

The steps for producing a video or DVD case statement are as follows:

1. Determine your communication goals.
2. Identify the primary audiences.
3. Determine the length—usually six to nine minutes.
4. Define a few key messages.

EXHIBIT 7.13   NOTES FOR VIDEO OR DVD
CASE STATEMENT

INTERNATIONAL INSTITUTE OF ASIAN ARTS

Preliminary Notes for Video Case Statement

Objectives
- Indicate to the donor public why the International Institute of Asian Arts (IIAA) deserves their financial support.
- Create an emotional bond with major donors.
- Let prospective donors understand the need for IIAA's Capital Campaign.
- Tell prospective donors how the capital project will help IIAA display more of its collection, preserve some of Asia's most significant art objects/artifacts, and better serve visiting scholars.

Audience
- Current and potential donors—especially affluent individuals
- Corporate and foundation leaders

Maximum Length 7 to 9 minutes

Key Messages

IIAA is a "world-class" museum

Potential Images and Interviews:
* Objects from Japanese Collection (accompanied by Shakuhachi music)
* Interview international guest dignitary and/or visiting scholar
* Brief walk-through with CEO's remarks

Current facilities too small—climate control issues

Potential Images and Interviews:
* Continue CEO's walk—point out challenges and obligation to preserve
* Shot indicating delicate nature of some of IIAA's artifacts

New facilities at Montgomery and Lowell—visionary solution

Potential Images and Interviews:
* Board chair on vacant site
* Model of new facilities—computer-generated tour
* Conversation with lead architect, board chair, and CEO

EXHIBIT 7.13   (CONTINUED)

Sample Script Outline

TIME	SCENES
20 seconds	Titles—Music Opening: Montage of art objects.
40 seconds	Art montage continues as narrator begins. "The International Institute of Asian Arts is recognized as a world-class institution and North America's preeminent repository for some of our world's most priceless treasures . . ."
3 minutes	Guest remarks and CEO's walk-through. Point out strong points, then problem statement.
	Current facilities too small. Climate control problem. Delicate works entrusted to IIAA. Scholars need more appropriate facilities.
2.5 minutes	Capital project explained: Board chair on vacant site. Computer-generated walk-through of new facility while architect, board chair, and CEO continue conversation.
1 minute	Reiterate strong points. Indicate expansions to collection.
1 minute	Appeal for support: "Your financial commitment is an investment . . ."

5. Describe possible images or interviews that correspond to key messages.

6. Outline a sample script or video case statement concept notes (see Exhibit 7.13).

7. Develop a budget. (Count on spending $1,200 to $2,000 per finished minute. Alternatively, find a video producer—such as a TV station, a university's communications department, or other provider of pro bono services—to donate all or part of the work.)

8. Allow the producer and copywriter great flexibility in shaping the video or DVD project.

OTHER CAMPAIGN COMMUNICATIONS

Many churches use monthly or even weekly campaign update newsletters. These can be simple single-page, two-sided updates, as illustrated in Exhibit 7.14. Side one can contain a brief description of the project and a campaign update indicating how much has been committed from the number and percentage of households participating. Inspirational messages are also appropriate. Side two is largely devoted to acknowledging families that have already pledged.

EXHIBIT 7.14   SAMPLE CHURCH CAMPAIGN BULLETIN

Risen Savior Church
A Spiritual Journey . . . *By Faith We Build*

Building Campaign News and Notes

CAMPAIGN GOAL: $2.7 MILLION

AMOUNT RAISED AND PLEDGED TO DATE: $1,323,000

(That's 49% of Our Goal from only 98 Families or 7% of our Parish's 1,400 Families)

Thank you Risen Savior!

BUILDING BANQUET SET FOR SATURDAY, SEPTEMBER 4, 2004

All members of our parish are invited to a very special afternoon—the Sacred Heart Church Building Banquet. Please mark your calendar and plan to attend the Building Banquet on Saturday, September 4, 2004, from 6:30 P.M. to 8:30 P.M. The Building Banquet will be held at the Marriott Courtyard.

The evening will include food, fellowship, information, and inspiration. And there will be no solicitations, no charge for the meal, and no offering taken at this uplifting gathering. **Please join us for this most important gathering in the history of our church.** Our goal is to have as many church members as possible join together on this most special day. To make it easier for parishioners to attend, we are also having a Pizza Party for youngsters under 13 years of age.

You will be called by a Building Banquet volunteer who will help count the number of Building Banquet attendees and the number of children in each age group. All family members 13 and over are encouraged to attend the Building Banquet. We are looking forward to seeing you. If you do not hear from a volunteer in the next two weeks, please call Jan Murphy at 278-1234 or Maria at the Church office 278-4321.

CAMPAIGN CABINET LEADS THE WAY

Any campaign such as this one requires a significant commitment from our volunteer leaders. Let's all express special thanks to our Campaign Cabinet:
Mr. & Mrs. Vincent O'Leary, Co-Chairs
H. B. Mumford, Advanced Gifts Chair
Debra Moore, Communications Chair
Becky Smith & George Berry, Co-Chairs, Visiting Stewards
Jan Murphy, Arrangements Chair

WHAT IS MY PART?

Many of you may be wondering how you can help your parish in achieving the goal of raising $2.7 million to enlarge our Church, upgrade the old Parish Center, and build a new Parish Center.

EXHIBIT 7.14 (CONTINUED)

Actually, this is a question that only you can decide.

There is only one way for each of us to determine our commitment. It should be large enough to represent a real sacrifice. It must be a part of our very life. Our commitment should show our willingness to do without something—to give up some small or large pleasure and make a significant three-year contribution to the Church we love.

CAMPAIGN COMMITMENTS

All of us at Risen Savior Parish wish to express our gratitude to the following people who have made early three-year commitments to the Building Campaign:

Greg Abler	Richard Fernandez	Mr. and Mrs. Franklin Riddel
Mr. and Mrs. Kevin Adams	Mr. and Mrs. Ralph G. Finley	Andre Segovia
Mr. and Mrs. Dan Adelo	Mr. and Mrs. Dale Gurule	Charles Sena
Mr. and Mrs. Royce Albin	Mr. and Mrs. Jack Gutierrez	Mr. and Mrs. William Sharpe
Anonymous (2)	Mr. and Mrs. Paul Hand	Mr. and Mrs. Jeffrey Schriver
Mr. and Mrs. David Azari	Mr. and Mrs. Michael Hanson	Mr. and Mrs. Ron Sigler
Anastasia Baca	Mr. and Mrs. George Hsu	Mr. and Mrs. Eduardo Sosa
Mr. and Mrs. George Barton	Mr. and Mrs. Albert Knight	Mr. and Mrs. John P. Sousa
Barbara Beason	Mr. and Mrs. Robert Krawiecki	Mr. and Mrs. Franz Springer
Rev. Brad Bodner	Mr. and Mrs. Jason Leong	Mr. and Mrs. Robert Spurlock
Mr. and Mrs. Herbert Brennan	Mr. and Mrs. Edward Lesher	Mr. and Mrs. Russell Stanley
Mr. and Mrs. Rex M. Brennan	Carolyn Linn	Mr. and Mrs. Kevin Stanton
Mr. and Mrs. Arthur Camden	Mr. and Mrs. Arthur Little	Mr. and Mrs. Frederick Steel
Mr. and Mrs. Gordon Campos	Mr. and Mrs. David Lopez	Mr. and Mrs. Archie Stevens
Mr. and Mrs. Howard Campos	Mr. and Mrs. Frank Lopez	Zelda Strong
Mr. and Mrs. George Costello	Mr. and Mrs. Richard Lopez	Mr. and Mrs. David Subia
Dr. and Mrs. Edward Dees	Mr. and Mrs. George Mason	Mr. and Mrs. Howard Thompson
Mr. and Mrs. John Degani	Mr. and Mrs. Stanley Masters	Mr. and Mrs. Leland Thompson
Mr. and Mrs. Andrew DeSantis	Mr. and Mrs. Scott Mathias	Mr. and Mrs. Henry Trujillo
Father Raymond Donoghue	Mr. and Mrs. Robert Mullin	Mr. and Mrs. Roberto Trujillo
Margaret Douglas	Mr. and Mrs. Stephen Mumford	Mr. and Mrs. Irving Tucker
Mary Ellen Duplentis	Mr. and Mrs. Derrick Myerson	Mr. and Mrs. Anthony Vigil
Mr. and Mrs. Greg Escobar	Dr. and Mrs. Milton Nail	Mr. and Mrs. George Washington
Mr. and Mrs. Frank Ezell	Mable Newbill	Mr. and Mrs. Douglas Weaver
Mr. and Mrs. H. B. Farmer	Mr. and Mrs. Michael Newsom	Mr. and Mrs. Franz V. Weber
Mr. and Mrs. John Farrar	Mr. and Mrs. Patrick O'Keefe	Richard Wexler, Jr.
Dr. Elizabeth Farrell	Mr. and Mrs. Ed O'Leary	Barbara Yager
Mr. and Mrs. Ed Fast	Maxwell Phillippi, Sr.	Dr. and Mrs. Philip Yarbrough
Henrietta Fauci	Mr. and Mrs. Artemus Phillips	Mr. and Mrs. Andrew Young
Joann Ferando	Mr. and Mrs. Robert Puckett	Mr. and Mrs. Darrell Zachary
Mr. and Mrs. Dave Fernandez	Jerrold Reynolds	
Mr. and Mrs. Ray Fernandez	Mr. and Mrs. Ted Richers	

THOUGHTS FOR THE MONTH

Give, and it will be given to you . . . For the measure you give will be the measure you get back.

Luke 6:38

Glory be to him whose power working in us can do infinitely more than we can ask or imagine . . .

Ephesians 3:20

EXHIBIT 7.15   SAMPLE CAMPAIGN THERMOMETER

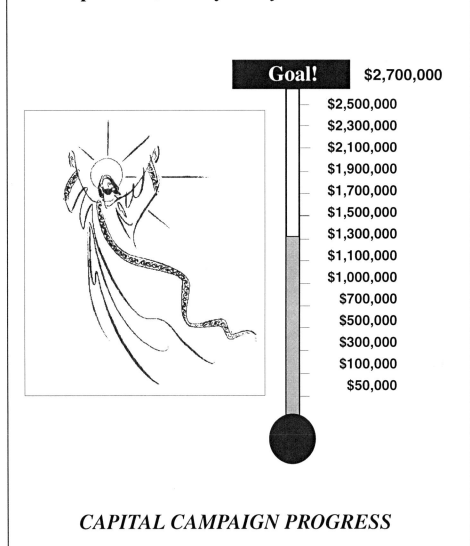

Risen Savior Church

A Spiritual Journey . . . *By Faith We Build*

Goal! $2,700,000

$2,500,000
$2,300,000
$2,100,000
$1,900,000
$1,700,000
$1,500,000
$1,300,000
$1,100,000
$1,000,000
$700,000
$500,000
$300,000
$100,000
$50,000

CAPITAL CAMPAIGN PROGRESS

These capital campaign pieces are distributed along with the regular church bulletins to all members of the parish or congregation.

Secular organizations can use a similar approach to update campaign volunteers and key constituents. Alternatively, organizations that produce regular newsletters can write preliminary articles during the planning and quiet phase of the campaign. Early on, articles might describe facility needs and planning processes. During the quiet phase, campaign leaders might describe the capital project and state that the organization is beginning to organize for the capital campaign and is "quietly recruiting volunteers and approaching a small number of financial supporters who will help in the early phase of the effort." After the organization has secured more than 50 percent of the total, and the campaign has "gone public," regular campaign updates can honor major donors and key volunteers. As important, these regular newsletter capital campaign articles help build a strong sense of momentum.

Another common tool in capital campaigns is the "campaign thermometer." Exhibit 7.15 illustrates such a communication tool. One note of caution, however. Do not introduce the campaign thermometer too early. It should only be used late in the public phase of the campaign, when momentum is well established.

Precampaign Planning Study and Campaign Readiness

Experienced fundraising professionals estimate that 90 percent or more of all successful capital campaigns are preceded by a planning study—often called a *feasibility study*. This figure holds up well for secular campaigns. Many church campaigns are undertaken without the planning study. This is possible because the members of the congregation already have close ties to the church and experienced fundraisers can calculate the giving potential based on the congregation's record of support.

Some nonprofit leaders believe that the term "feasibility study" sends a negative message. Potential donors get the impression that the organization might *not* go forward with a campaign, or could even have doubts as to the validity of the project. To avoid these negative connotations, many consultants and campaign organizers refer to the interview process and report as a "precampaign planning study," "philanthropic planning study," "market survey," "philanthropic assessment," or some variation of these.

If organization leaders wish to know whether to proceed, conduct a feasibility study. If the organization must proceed with its capital projects, conduct a *precampaign planning study*. In this latter situation, call it what you will, but avoid the term "feasibility study."

At the heart of the planning study is a number of confidential interviews—usually 30 to 50—with selected individuals representing key prospective donors, board members, and community leaders. Because so much of the campaign's success depends upon the top 10 or so gifts, the vast majority of the interviews should be with potential lead gift donors. Prior to the interview, the organization mails each potential interviewee a summary of the case statement. Exhibit 8.1 is a sample cover letter requesting the interview.

To assure objectivity and confidentiality, the interviews are conducted by an external consultant. The confidential nature of the interviews allows the interviewees to speak candidly and have maximum input into the planning process.

EXHIBIT 8.1   LETTER REQUESTING INTERVIEW

International Institute of Asian Arts

2100 Mitchell Ave., Santa Barbara, CA 93105, 805-256-1776

January 9, 2004

Mr. Samuel Adams
1234 Prospect Lane
Santa Barbara, CA 93105

Dear Sam:

I am writing to ask your advice.

The International Institute of Asian Arts (IIAA) is working to build a new home at Montgomery Parkway and Lowell Drive. This visionary project will help us create a world-class facility for our internationally renowned collection of Asian artifacts and art objects. As important, the new facilities will allow us to solve the challenges related to preserving some of our world's most delicate treasures.

Our planned campaign also encompasses increasing our endowment funds and acquiring some important works of art needed to complete our core collections.

In response to these pressing needs, the leadership of IIAA is embarking on a process designed to help refine our plans and integrate the best advice from friends and leaders throughout the international community. To help us with this process, Mary Langlois of Stanley Weinstein & Co. will conduct a number of confidential leadership interviews.

Your advice and perspective mean a great deal to us. I would be most appreciative if you would meet with Ms. Langlois for a confidential interview to hear your frank opinions. The interview will take no more than 30 to 45 minutes. We will contact you in the next few days to arrange a time that is convenient for you.

Enclosed is a summary of IIAA's current situation and our vision for the future. I hope you have an opportunity to look this over prior to your interview. Thanks for your time and help.

With appreciation,

Aaron Fieldhouse

Aaron Fieldhouse
Board Chair

BENEFITS OF THE
PLANNING STUDY

There are three essential purposes of the planning study:

1. *The study helps the organization understand what steps are needed to assure success.* Study participants offer advice concerning the case for support, volunteer leadership, campaign timing, potential donors, organization development, community perceptions, communications, the organization's image, administrative acumen, governance, and a host of issues related to campaign readiness.

   Beyond offering advice, some study participants respond favorably to questions concerning volunteer involvement. Their responses are tantamount to volunteering to be a campaign leader or participant. Some also identify potential major gift donors, new prospects with whom the organization might not be familiar.

2. *The study helps the organization determine its fundraising potential.* After a number of open-ended questions, and after establishing trust, the interviewer shows the study participant the gift pyramid and says something like, "We are not soliciting contributions at this time, but what would be an appropriate range—low to high—that you might consider as a three-year pledge to the campaign?"

   The responses to this question and others give a strong indication as to how many prospects there are for each of the upper gift levels required for success. This is crucial information in establishing a realistic campaign goal.

3. *The study is important to the relationship-nurturing process.* It is easy to see why the precampaign study process is a key to establishing stronger relationships with potential lead donors and opinion leaders. Potential study participants receive a letter that informs them that their advice is needed. They then get a well-planned phone call to set up the interview. The call is followed up with a short note confirming the interview time and place. The interview is structured to elicit meaningful advice on a broad range of issues. Each study participant receives a thank-you note for the interview. And when the study is complete, organization representatives call on interviewees to inform them of the study results. In short, prospective lead donors are engaged in six gracious contacts that create an opportunity for buy-in. Throughout the study process, potential lead donors and volunteers become familiar with the organization's case for support and rationale for the capital campaign.

STUDY PROCESS

To understand how these three main purposes are achieved, let's examine the planning study process. To begin with, the organization forms a planning study committee, task force, or other appropriate body to guide the precampaign planning study. A job description is included in Exhibit 8.2. The committee works to prepare and refine a preliminary case for support. Chapter 7 contains practical advice concerning this test draft case for support. The planning study committee also helps refine the list of people to be interviewed.

To get approximately 40 interviews, most organizations must contact 55 to 80 potential study participants. Marilyn Bancel, in *Preparing Your Capital Campaign,* states that the organization should have at least 100 good names prior to finalizing the interview list. If not, the organization "will be wasting time, money, and momentum to continue along a campaign path."

This may lead you naturally to ask the questions, "How can the organization be sure that it has 100 good names? Who are they? Who should be invited to participate in the interview process?"

To answer these questions, list the organization's most generous current and past donors, current and past board members, prospects identified by board and staff, potential new donors, key staff, and community philanthropists. If the organization relies on government funding, also list political figures and government agency administrators.

After the committee approves the case for support, the cover letter, and the list of prospective interviewees, the organization sends the personalized letters and case statements to the selected people.

During the scheduling phone call, a representative of the organization—a person with good people skills—responds to any questions the potential interviewee has concerning the study. Frequently, study participants need to be assured that the study is *not* a solicitation. As mentioned previously, the interviewees receive a letter confirming the appointment. During the interview, the consultant asks a number of open-ended questions (see Exhibit 8.3), introduces a gift pyramid, and seeks advice concerning potential campaign donors and potential campaign leaders. Interviewees are not solicited during the interview; however, most give an indication as to their potential range of support.

Following the interviews, the consultant summarizes the findings, conclusions, and recommendations. To indicate the breadth of information included in a precampaign planning study, a sample study table of contents is included as Exhibit 8.4. Upon completion of the writing, the consultant delivers a written and verbal report to the nonprofit organization's board of directors or other appropriate decision-making body.

EXHIBIT 8.2   PRECAMPAIGN STUDY—WORK GROUP
JOB DESCRIPTION

INTERNATIONAL INSTITUTE OF ASIAN ARTS

Philanthropic Planning Study

Study Team Job Description

Overview: The Philanthropic Planning Study is designed to garner advice from community and national leaders concerning potential pacesetting supporters for the IIAA Capital and Endowment Campaign. Approximately 35–45 people participate in confidential interviews. The findings and recommendations are crucial to the success of the campaign. As importantly, the interview process will help create buy-in and commitment for IIAA and the campaign.

Time Commitment: The committee will meet three times. We will find three convenient meeting times and dates during a period from late November 2003 through early January 2004.

Committee Composition: Approximately seven members total, composed of members of the board of directors together with other community leaders. This study team is composed of people who know the pool of prospective supporters well. Some of the committee members should be long-term residents of Santa Barbara. Committee members should be philanthropic individuals who are "plugged in" and able to offer advice about potential sources of generous support.

Study Team/Working Group Responsibilities:

✓ Decide on the list of people to be interviewed.

✓ Review and refine the case for support. (Staff and fundraising counsel will produce a preliminary written document that tells of the important work of IIAA and creates a sense of urgency for the capital campaign. This study team suggests broad themes and refinements in the case for support. The committee-approved version is distributed to study participants prior to the interviews.)

✓ Review and refine the questionnaire and other materials used during the interviews. Fundraising counsel will work with you to develop an interview format that elicits the information needed, while building positive relationships with the study participants.

✓ Help secure appointments for interviews if necessary.

EXHIBIT 8.3   PRECAMPAIGN INTERVIEW QUESTIONS

INTERNATIONAL INSTITUTE OF ASIAN ARTS PRECAMPAIGN CONFIDENTIAL INTERVIEWS

Name of Interviewee: _____

INTERVIEW QUESTIONS

1. How have you been associated with the International Institute of Asian Arts (IIAA)?
2. How would you characterize your relationship with the IIAA?
3. What, in your opinion, is the IIAA's image with people in Santa Barbara? If you have any knowledge of IIAA's international reputation or reputation among scholars, please comment on that also.
   Excellent_____ Good_____ Fair_____ Poor_____
4. What is your judgment of how well the IIAA has carried out its mission?
5. With which IIAA's collections, exhibits, or programs are you most familiar? Which are strong? Which are weak?
6. Are there any IIAA programs underway of which you disapprove? If so, why?
7. Are there specific projects you would like to see the IIAA undertake?
8. What is your opinion, if any, of the administration?
9. What do you think of the case for support? (Is it clearly written? And do you find the projects compelling?)
10. Does any part of this project and case for support have greater appeal for you (personally, your company, or foundation) than any other?
11. Which conditions or factors would you point to that would *help* assure a successful capital campaign at this time? (Follow-up question: How would you rate the local and national economy?)
12. Which environmental factors would you point to, such as competing campaigns, that could *harm* a capital campaign at this time?
13. Do you think a $20 million IIAA capital and endowment campaign, payable over a three-year period, will be successful?

(PRESENT GIFT CHART)

14. Gifts by individuals account for most of our nation's philanthropic support. Could you, confidentially, identify the best prospects for the IIAA to approach who might give in these ranges?

(List Gift Range)   Names   Best Contacts

            Which organizations, corporations, or businesses might be approached?

            Names   Best Contacts

       Foundations?

            Names   Best Contacts

EXHIBIT 8.3 (CONTINUED)

15. We are not soliciting contributions at this time, but what would be an appropriate range—low to high—for you to consider as a gift to the IIAA's campaign by virtue of a pledge payable over a three-year period?

(PERSONAL GIFT) Lows   Highs   Pledge Period

16. Would you consider a gift based on noncash assets such as stocks, bonds, Israel bonds, land, or as a result of estate planning? (Also ask if there is possible interest in a planned gift for the endowment fund.) Yes_____ No_____

17. Can you recommend a few names of people who would help assure the success of the campaign if they assumed a volunteer leadership position?

18. Would you act as an intermediary to reach them? Yes_____ No_____ Maybe_____
    Which ones?

19. Would you be willing to participate in such a campaign by making three to five introductions for fundraising purposes? (If yes, discuss willingness to assume a leadership position.)

20. Finally, and again in confidence, is there any advice you care to give the board on policies, priorities, programs, methods, staff, or anything else?

Name of Interviewer: _____ Date: _____

EXHIBIT 8.4   PLANNING STUDY TABLE OF CONTENTS

INTERNATIONAL INSTITUTE OF ASIAN ARTS
PRECAMPAIGN PLANNING STUDY

TABLE OF CONTENTS

EXHIBIT 8.4 (CONTINUED)

The Findings section is made up largely of study participants' responses to interview questions. Many consultants also summarize the findings with tables or charts indicating the percentage of respondents who express concerns vis-à-vis those who were unabashedly enthusiastic supporters. Exhibit 8.5, *in abbreviated form,* illustrates the consultant's summary and respondent quotations concerning a nonprofit organization's case for support.

EXHIBIT 8.5   SAMPLE PAGES FROM STUDY

B. APPRAISAL OF THE CASE FOR SUPPORT

A case for support is designed to inform and involve the potential donor. The appeal must be clear; it also must be compelling. An effective case for support will reflect the uniqueness of the International Institute of Asian Art. To assess IIAA's case for support, *Preservation, Education, and Inspiration,* study participants were asked the following questions:

"What do you think of the case for support?

Is it clearly written?

And do you find the project compelling?"

The following table shows the results in summary form.

PERCEPTIONS OF THE PROPOSED PROJECT

RATING	NUMBER	PERCENTAGE
Favorable or Enthusiastic	33	79%
Favorable, but Expressed Concerns	6	14%
No Opinion of Case Statement	2	5%
Unfavorable Opinion	1	2%
Total	**42**	**100%**

Favorable and enthusiastic comments included:

"This is long overdue. IIAA has such great treasures. We have a special obligation to preserve them. And the new museum will be spectacular."

"The case was very clear and professional. It created such a great impression. I am particularly pleased that IIAA will be able to display so much more of its collection."

"Very well done. Although I was familiar with a lot of the information, I didn't realize how delicate some of the artifacts are. My wife and I look forward to the new facilities. Montgomery and Lowell is where IIAA belongs."

"This is very important."

EXHIBIT 8.5   (CONTINUED)

"A fine document. We need to raise the endowment funds because the new IIAA deserves to be on a solid financial footing."

"Loved it."

"It is a clear statement of the need."

"Well done. Clear and compelling."

"Wow. Lots of programs and exhibits I didn't know about."

"I like our challenges and solutions."

Positive statements that also expressed concerns included:

"The greatest challenge is to convince people that we are not competing with other pressing community needs. Santa Barbara has some social service agencies that need help. But I am committed to this project."

"Overall positive. But, I'm afraid that some people might be attached to our existing facilities. IIAA will really have to stress the need for preservation and expanded exhibit space."

"It's okay, but IIAA doesn't appear to be clear about the need for endowment funds. That part of the campaign might not appeal to everybody."

No opinion or neutral: (Two of the study participants either didn't read the document or expressed neutral comments on the case for support.)

The one unfavorable opinion expressed was:

"Every time I turn around, another nonprofit organization gets bitten by the 'edifice complex.' I'd have to know a great deal more about the organization before I felt comfortable that the need is real."

Another key question in the Findings section is the one concerning potential ranges of support. Exhibit 8.6 illustrates how the responses to this question might be described in the Findings section of a precampaign planning study.

The Recommendations section of a precampaign planning study contains the consultant's recommendations concerning campaign goal, timing, volunteer structure and recruitment, refinements to the case for support, organization development, the board of directors, key issues, and campaign policies.

During the presentation to the board, the consultant outlines the highlights of the report, focusing on key findings and recommendations. The consultant then answers questions concerning the conclusions and report. Savvy boards then meet to discuss next steps and approve the recommendations contained in the study.

One early step that almost every organization should take is to meet again with study participants to brief them. These briefings sometimes evolve into the

EXHIBIT 8.6   SAMPLE POTENTIAL GIFTS
SECTION OF STUDY

Willingness to Give

During each interview, study participants were shown the Standard of Investments (Appendix D). Fundraising counsel stressed the importance of attaining pledges in the ranges needed.

Each study participant was told that he or she was not being solicited during the interview. However, those who indicated support for the project were asked, "What would be an appropriate range—low to high—that you might consider as a gift to IIAA's campaign by virtue of a pledge payable over a three-year period?" The following table summarizes the results:

RANGE OF POTENTIAL GIFTS AS INDICATED BY STUDY PARTICIPANTS

GIFT LEVEL	NUMBER	PERCENTAGE
$3,000,000 or more	1	2%
$1,000,000–$1,500,000	1	2%
$500,000	0	0%
$300,000	3	7%
$100,000	1	2%
$50,000	4	10%
$30,000	7	17%
$5,000–$15,000	13	31%
Less than $5,000	5	12%
Did not say	4	10%
Will probably not give	3	7%
Total	**42**	**100%**

During the study period, one person committed $3,000,000 for a challenge grant. It should be noted that all the other figures do not represent firm financial commitments from those interviewed, nor do they suggest that these are the only potential gifts that could be realized. Based on our research, IIAA also has the potential to secure commitments from foundations not interviewed. During the campaign, many of the above might commit at levels somewhat higher or lower than the potential gift range indicated during the interview.

first explicit solicitations. The conversation might include a suggestion like this: "Community leaders responded enthusiastically to this study and the XYZ Nonprofit's capital project. With this in mind, our board chair and I hope that you might be in a position to play an important role in the campaign and consider one of these leadership gift opportunities."

In summary, the planning study process engages prospective supporters through six steps taking place in a brief period of time. These six steps bring people closer to your organization. They provide valuable advice concerning campaign readiness. Moreover, the information gathered during the interviews helps establish the campaign fundraising goal.

PREPARATION FOR THE PLANNING STUDY

Even before the planning study, organization leaders must accomplish a number of important tasks. The following early steps will enhance the response to the precampaign planning study and assure the institution's readiness to undertake a successful campaign:

1. Review all issues related to board development. Strengthen nominating criteria and processes. Seek people with affluence and influence. Seek diversity. Strengthen, expand, and activate the board's committees.

2. Intensify the project planning. At every step involve as many board members, volunteers, and potential large supporters as possible.

3. Prepare preliminary written materials describing the project, its history, rationale, and case for support. Stress the project's benefits to the community.

4. Prepare a number of project budgets. Examine the total contributed income necessary to operate the organization and accommodate your capital and endowment requirements. Use a spreadsheet program to examine a number of what-if scenarios.

5. Refine your preliminary materials based on your discoveries during the preliminary budget formulation process.

6. Prepare the following draft materials:
   • A test case for support
   • A project plan and timeline (Consider obtaining architects' sketches or preliminary elevations and floor plans and schematics, if applicable.)
   • Spreadsheets or draft budgets illustrating various options
   • Tentative income requirements, including the first estimate of the campaign goal
   • An understanding of your needs on a prioritized basis
   • An understanding of how the project fits into the institution's overall long-range plan
   • A preliminary gift pyramid

Often, the capital campaign counsel helps develop the early draft materials. The consultant might also offer services to assure that the organization is well positioned in the philanthropic community. The organization's objective is to keep volunteers, advisory committees, governing bodies, and potential supporters actively involved in the planning process.

If organization leaders have not yet identified the institution's top prospects, now is the time to get to work. (Chapter 6 covers prospect identification and research.) Capital project planning and capital campaign preparation are parallel processes. By the time the organization has a good sense of its facility needs and related costs, the organization should also have a reasonable idea as to who will fund the project.

CHOOSING A CAPITAL CAMPAIGN CONSULTANT

Choosing the right consultant is critical to the success of the organization's precampaign study and capital campaign. In fact, this is perhaps the most important precampaign task. Even organizations with a large experienced fundraising staff find it helpful to work with a consultant experienced in capital campaigns. Outside objective counsel helps the nonprofit organization's staff and volunteers lay the groundwork for a successful capital and endowment campaign, one that maximizes the institution's fundraising potential.

The services provided during the planning phase—including the feasibility or precampaign planning study—are integral to the success of the campaign. The confidential interviews provide potential pacesetting donors an opportunity to help shape the project and campaign. To make a wise and thoughtful decision concerning the choice of consultant, consider the following nine-step process.

1. *Form selection committee.* Recruit three to five visionary, wise, generous, and decisive people to serve on the capital campaign consultant selection committee.

2. *Develop a request for proposal (RFP).* A simple one- or two-page letter can serve as a model request for a precampaign planning study. The RFP should state your expectations. Describe your situation. Include your initial estimate of the goal. State any concerns that are unique to your organization. Also state when you wish to begin and end the study. Remember, the process takes three to five months. Moreover, the nonprofit organization should have a well-defined facilities need and *at least* 100 top prospects.

   Request information concerning the consultant's experience and approach to precampaign studies. RFPs should have a due date. The RFP should also request the name and background of the consultant who will be assigned to the project. The RFP should request references.

3. *Identify well-qualified consultants.* It is best to avoid sending 25 to 50 RFPs to consulting firms across the nation. A more productive strategy is to identify not more than seven respected consultants or firms to approach. Sources of suggestions you may look to include:

   - *Consultants the nonprofit organization has dealt with in the past.* You may not need to conduct a full formal search if you have a strong relationship with a successful consulting firm or independent capital campaign consultant. Such experts who know your organization's situation and prospects very well can give your project a jump-start.
   - *Referrals from colleagues.* Ask colleagues who have conducted capital campaigns for referrals.
   - *AFP referrals.* The Association of Fundraising Professionals can furnish a list of member consultants in your region.
   - *AAFRC members.* The American Association of Fund-Raising Counsel can furnish background information concerning member firms.

4. *Screen RFPs.* Eliminate any obviously unqualified or nonresponsive RFPs. Also note if any of the proposals appear to be pure boilerplate. Firms that prepare cookie-cutter proposals tend to adopt a "one size fits all" approach to project implementation. After the initial screening, the committee can reach consensus on approximately three finalists.

5. *Check references.* Checking references prior to final selection can help you eliminate a wasted interview. Ask:

   - What services did the consultant provide in preparing the organization for the precampaign study?
   - If the consultant helped prepare the case statement, was it well written and well accepted?
   - Were most of the interviews in person? Or, did the consultant overly rely on phone interviews?
   - Did the study result in a thoughtful report that included insights into donor attitudes?
   - Did the study contain useful information about potential volunteers?
   - Did the study contain specific information about the study participants' capacity and willingness to donate?
   - Did you engage the consultant for support services after the study?
   - Did the campaign meet or exceed the goal recommended in the study?
   - Was the consultant always objective?
   - How would you rate the consultant's flexibility?
   - Was the consultant a good listener?
   - How well did the consultant relate to the board, staff, and volunteers?
   - How well did the consultant develop solutions to the problems you faced?
   - Would you hire the consultant again?

6. *Conduct the interview.* Have the entire committee present for all interviews. A simple format for each 40-minute interview might be as follows: Committee chair opens with introductions and a five-minute summary of the organization background and project status; the consultant is then asked to provide a 7- to 10-minute overview of the firm's background and proposal; allow an additional 5 minutes for the consultant to ask questions of the committee; the remaining 20 or so minutes are devoted to the committee's questions to the consultant. Ask each consultant the following questions:

- *Who will conduct the interviews and write the report?* Be cautious in hiring firms that cannot answer this question. Some have very polished salespeople who make a strong favorable impression. Unfortunately, some of these firms employ less experienced people to conduct the study.

- *How much time will you devote to the interviews?* Expect a firm to devote at least nine days to the interview process. Two weeks is even better. Firms that devote only five days to interviews tend to schedule too little time for each interview and rely heavily on telephone interviews. With more time, some of the interviewees will give expansive responses to each question. Often, older supporters enjoy the opportunity to speak with the interviewer. The interview should be gracious and guided by the study participant's tempo—not pushed along just to meet a consultant's tight schedule.

- *When you are conducting a feasibility study and the interviewee appears reluctant to answer your question about a giving range that the interviewee might consider, how do you respond?* Experienced consultants find it easy to explain how they handle this situation. They will have developed persuasive language that will, in most cases, overcome the interviewee's reluctance to discuss a potential giving range.

- *Tell us about two studies you conducted where you concluded that a campaign was not advisable or should be delayed. What were the circumstances? What advice did you give? And how did the client respond?* Firms that can't describe such circumstances are not being intellectually honest. There is a possibility that such firms view the feasibility study as a marketing tool—a means of gaining a profitable long-term capital campaign support contract. These firms recommend that even weak organizations proceed with a campaign. Consultant selection committee members should ask themselves if the firm seems more interested in securing work or in providing objective advice.

- *Have you worked in a fundraising campaign where the volunteers were simply not making their calls? What steps did you take to assure that the campaign reached its goal despite this obstacle?* The answer to this question will tell committee members a great deal concerning the consultant's organization skills and approach to training, timing, and motivation.

- *When you recommend a capital campaign goal, what factors do you consider? Please be as complete as possible in your explanation of how you establish your recommended goal.* The consultant should be able to describe a thoughtful process. The criteria should comprise a combination of quantitative analysis and qualitative judgment. Committee members should be cautious if they hear a reply such as, "I don't really have a method. I rely on my intuition and years of experience."

When possible, look at previous studies written by the consultant. Ask, "Did the study indicate potential gift levels? Were the positive and negative interview responses separated so the organization could more readily gain a sense of the range of responses? Did the recommended fundraising goal flow naturally from the findings?"

Again, structure the interview so that the prospective consultant has an opportunity to ask questions. The questions asked will reveal a lot about the nature of the consultant's thought processes. Additionally, the consultant's questions will reveal what homework the consultant did prior to the interview.

7. *Make a decision.* Focus on the four Cs: competence, confidence, chemistry, and cost. The consultant must have the *competence,* experience, and knowledge needed to accomplish the work. The consultant must inspire *confidence.* The *chemistry* must be right; the consultant must be a person who relates well with your board, staff, and volunteers. And, finally, the consultant's proposal must be *cost-effective.*

To make a decision, committee members ask the following:
- Will the candidate inspire our board and staff to make any changes needed?
- Does the candidate have the knowledge and experience needed?
- Did the candidate receive good references?
- Will the candidate work well with our board, staff, and volunteers?
- Will the candidate "tell it like it is?"
- Does the candidate have a demonstrable record of helping similar organizations dramatically increase their contributed income and successfully complete their capital and endowment campaigns?
- Does the candidate thoroughly understand capital campaigns?

8. *Draw up the contract.* The consultant's response to your organization's RFP forms the basis of the contract. The final contract should be clear as to start and stop dates. The final contract should define the scope of work to be accomplished. Build in some flexibility, but assure that the final

contract is as specific as possible as to deliverables and due dates. The contract should be specific as to the services the consulting firm will perform. The contract should include a description of the nonprofit organization's responsibilities. The study schedule should be included. The fees and payment timing should be as specific as possible. The contract should clarify which party pays for which expenses. The contract might specify the geographic bounds of the interviews. Precampaign study contracts should also specify the number of bound written reports to be delivered.

9. *Notify consulting firms.* As a courtesy to the consulting firms that responded to your RFP but were not chosen to perform the work, send a gracious letter acknowledging the proposal and informing the firm or consultant of the outcome of your search.

RESPONSE TO FINDINGS AND RECOMMENDATIONS

This chapter began with a description of the planning study and its benefits, then we went back in time to be sure that the organization laid a strong foundation for a productive study and successful campaign. Now, let's turn our attention to some additional points contained in the Findings and Recommendations sections of the precampaign planning study. Careful attention to these issues will further help the organization prepare for the campaign.

Confidence

Chapter 2, which contains a full discussion of the ways in which nonprofit organizations can inspire confidence, stressed two main points: that the organization should first strive to be worthy of support; second, that the organization should improve its internal and external communications. In every case, special attention should be given to highly personalized contacts and communications with potential pacesetting contributors.

The precampaign planning study includes questions concerning the study participants' confidence in the institution. Many will be positive. Others will have recollections of past unfavorable incidents. Organization leaders can experience some comfort in the knowledge that the healing process began when the study participant was given the opportunity to retell the offending story. Simply listening with empathy goes a long way toward reestablishing a positive relationship. Capital campaign consultants and organization leaders should also find other ways to let prospective donors know that the organization is serious about seeking continual improvement.

Don't go into campaigns with unnecessary old baggage. Be realistic and thoughtful about solutions to past challenges. Get together with the organization's top prospects and bring them up to date about institutional progress. Be positive about the future.

Case

Study participants don't hesitate to let you know how they feel about the organization's case for support. Some are enthusiastic. They often marvel that the organization has not yet begun the important work described. They want to be part of the project.

Others will be somewhat favorable but might express concerns. They will ask if other nonprofits are working on the same problem. They might ask if the organization examined a wide range of planning options when it arrived at the proposed campaign. Some might request more information about the organization's priorities or the number of people served.

A few key people may even express negative reactions to the project. This shouldn't occur too often if the organization did its homework, involved community leaders, and consulted with people known for their wisdom and integrity.

The important point is to take all suggestions seriously. Two issues are at stake: Does the project make sense—representing the best solution for the people being served? And do the written materials clearly state what the organization proposes? The first issue is one of substance. The second issue deals with communication skills and the quality of the message. Both have to be on target.

Capacity and Willingness

The precampaign planning study should include detailed information concerning the organization's potential top donors. The report should explicitly describe the study participants' response to the question concerning the range of possible gifts each might consider. If the nonprofit organization receives a report without such information, it probably engaged the services of the wrong consultant. It is imperative that organization leaders know whether they have a pool of qualified prospects willing to support the campaign at the levels necessary for success.

If the organization has such a qualified and willing top prospect pool, the test campaign goal can be confirmed. In some cases, the consultant might even recommend a higher goal than the one originally contemplated. If the organization is weak in regard to top prospects, it can consider a number of alternatives, including: scale back the project; proceed in phases; proceed with a longer campaign process that includes a prospect identification and cultivation period; postpone the campaign; seek public funding; seek several special donors who might donate a large percentage of the total needed; or devise some solution unique to the organization.

The organization can increase its fundraising potential by implementing the specific suggestions in the Recommendations section of the precampaign planning study and the general advice offered in Chapter 6, "Prospect Identification and Cultivation."

Philanthropic Environment

When speaking of the environment for philanthropic fundraising, two issues are most frequently mentioned: the economy and competing campaigns. Both of these factors can have an impact on a proposed capital campaign. However, the impact is often based more on perceptions than reality. But public relations professionals remind us that "perceptions are reality." So let's address both of these factors.

The Economy.   When study participants speak about the economy, they often distinguish between global issues and local or regional concerns. Many leading philanthropists and community leaders have a truly global perspective. They know how world trends affect their businesses and the overall economic climate.

Other interviewees focus more on local or regional issues. They might point to factors that keep the local economy strong, or they might point out that a particular local industry is weak or flat.

In any case, readers of the precampaign planning study should relate the study participants' responses to the probable outcome of the campaign. When the global or local economy is perceived to be weak, study participants are less optimistic—or are even pessimistic—concerning the campaign goal. When the economy is booming, study participants tend to be effusive and optimistic. When the economy is somewhat flat or growing at very modest rates, study participants are split in their opinions, or they focus on issues other than the economy.

The good news is that campaigns can succeed in good times, ordinary times, and even under poor economic circumstances. That said, during poor times, the organization may wish to accommodate a longer pledge period—perhaps five rather than three years. Surprisingly, many of the longer pledges will be contributed sooner than originally planned. As the economy turns upward (business cycles are part of the natural order of things), many donors find their economic circumstances improved to the point where they prepay the pledge.

If a campaign is getting organized during a downturn, the organization will need to strengthen all of the key success factors to the extent possible. Special attention should be given to prospect identification, cultivation, and strengthening the case for support. Thoughtful planners assure that affluent and influential people have a favorable relationship with the organization and develop a passion for the capital project.

Competing Campaigns. Study participants are asked, "Do you know of any competing capital campaigns that might have an impact on this proposed campaign?" In response they sometimes say to the consultant, "You know this region pretty well. I bet you know more about that than I do." Perhaps. Still, the organization needs to know which other campaigns are important enough to interviewees that these campaigns have registered on their radar screens. We want to know which campaigns are attracting our prospects' interest.

Some interviewees seem plugged in and know about many local campaigns—even ones in their precampaign phases. Conversely, there are studies during which interviewees don't have a clue concerning competing campaigns. (This latter case may indicate that the people selected to be study participants are not community leaders and prominent philanthropists.) During most precampaign studies, typical interviewees will have knowledge concerning selected campaigns for organizations with which they have a relationship.

Many board members, volunteers, and study participants express concern about the number of competing campaigns. Most consultants will tell you that it is a rare time that they don't observe numerous simultaneous capital campaigns even in limited geographic regions. And yet, well-organized campaigns succeed or even exceed their goals.

How is this so?

A number of factors make it possible for so-called competing campaigns to succeed. Some projects appeal to vastly diverse constituencies. For example, a Jewish Community Center, Catholic church, ballet company, and homeless shelter might have prospect lists with very few overlapping names. Even when the same people are prospects for multiple capital campaigns, the prospects may support two or more campaigns generously. Philanthropic people rarely give to only one nonprofit organization. They have multiple interests and the capacity to prioritize their giving. Besides that, donors can pledge different amounts to different organizations and still help both meet their goals. One donor might pledge $5 million to his or her university's $100 million campaign, and $50,000 to a local social service agency with a much more modest capital campaign goal. In both cases, the commitments were major gifts. The donor was a significant factor in helping each organization reach its goal.

Capital campaigns become much more competitive when two major efforts appeal to very overlapping constituents in a local community. For example, if two museums with many of the same volunteers and donors wish to have a capital campaign, both might suffer if the organizations don't resolve the timing issue. Alternatively, the institution that organizes first and best might attract the campaign leaders needed for success.

Timing

Precampaign planning studies contain recommendations concerning campaign timing. The study should let the organization know when the campaign should start and finish. A strong Recommendations section will also inform the organization as to how much time to devote to each phase of the campaign.

A number of factors go into decisions concerning timing. We have already mentioned that it might be prudent to organize quickly to avoid competing with similar campaigns in your community. Recall, too, that most concern for "competing" campaigns is more of a perception than a reality.

Additionally, the organization might consider timing relative to its most recent previous capital campaign. For example, an institution that completed a capital campaign may decide *not* to begin another effort until after at least three years have elapsed since the last pledge payment. In other words, if an organization accepts capital campaign pledges that are to be fulfilled during calendar years 2004, 2005, and 2006, the next campaign should not begin until after calendar year 2009. Of course, there are exceptions to every rule. A university might have a capital campaign for its School of Engineering. A similar campaign for the History Department might take place at the same time. Again, if the prospect lists are different enough, timing is not an issue.

Another reason to consider postponing a campaign is scandal or recent adverse public opinion. Many professionals will recommend a period of time devoted to rehabilitating the organization and its image. Institution leaders should also work to assure that their relationships with major donors have been restored to the extent possible. If the organization has undergone recent negative press scrutiny, it is probably preferable to focus on strengthening the institution rather than undertaking a capital project at that time.

Most organizations do not face extraordinary reasons to delay. They should begin to develop strong relationships with potential lead donors and proceed in a stepwise manner. Others may have compelling reasons to delay but need to begin immediately because of circumstances beyond their control. Such situations include: loss of current facilities, expiring leases, and pressing economic or facility needs that seriously threaten the institution. In such circumstances, the organization has no choice but to proceed, remain focused on its mission, keep the troops as optimistic as possible, and persevere.

Staff

During the precampaign planning study, the consultant and organization leaders begin to address the question of staffing the capital campaign. To begin with, it is axiomatic that executive directors of small agencies can be expected to devote

30 percent or more of their time to the capital campaign. Development staff needs to be strong. The organization will benefit from an experienced director of development, a person who gets out of the office and participates with key volunteers during cultivation and solicitation visits. At the same time, the staff will be expected to continue and enhance the organization's ongoing annual campaign programs.

In response to these demands on staff time, many organizations engage the services of consultants who provide "hands-on" support. This support can be in the form of resident campaign counsel, that is, a nearly full-time consultant who provides staff support for the campaign. Alternatively, the firm can provide consulting and support services on the basis of one to five days per month. This cost-effective solution works well when the organization has sufficient staff to follow up between the consultant's site visit days.

As early as possible, the organization must make every effort to improve its record-keeping ability. Staff should assure that the organization has a fundraising information system that can support the capital campaign. Dedicated fundraising software, such as DonorPerfect and Blackbaud's The Raiser's Edge work well. Nonprofit organizations preparing for capital campaigns need a system that can accommodate detailed information about each current and potential supporter. An information system capable of segmenting prospective donors by giving potential and other criteria is a necessity. An effective system helps fundraising staff track all volunteer solicitor assignments, generate reports, record pledges, and track pledge balances and payments.

Board

Chapter 3 discusses important issues related to developing a strong and committed board of directors. The precampaign planning study might also contain specific recommendations that respond to your nonprofit board.

Board giving is of utmost importance as the organization moves from the planning study phase to the quiet phase of the capital campaign. Some of the organization's earliest and most generous gifts should come from members of the board of directors. Their multiyear commitments should help inspire confidence. Of equal importance is the organization's ability to secure pledges from 100 percent of the board. Foundation directors and experienced philanthropists in the community will expect no less.

Board members should also become familiar with fundraising principles and practices—especially the prerequisites for capital campaign success. The board might form a resource development committee to help shape the organization's comprehensive fundraising strategy. This committee should seek advice and work with counsel to formulate the organization's approach to ongoing support, as well as the capital campaign strategy. Strong boards develop a core of knowledgeable people who help avoid the common mistakes in preparing for a capital campaign. This is the group of people that will remind other board members and volunteers to focus on leadership gifts. This committee will also remind others to seek support from individuals, as well as from foundations and corporations, and remind volunteers that the appropriate strategy for capital campaigns is personal contact—not mail, phone, or special events. They will also stress the importance of a multiyear pledge period.

In short, board members play a key role in assuring the capital campaign's success. Their leadership and giving inspires others. Their wisdom helps assure a well-planned project. And their knowledge of fundraising keeps the capital campaign focused on strategies that lead to success.

When organizations follow the recommendations from their precampaign planning studies, the results are often spectacular. Universities raise hundreds of millions of dollars—even a billion dollars or more. Large healthcare institutions garner tens or hundreds of millions of dollars for buildings, endowment, and equipment. Arts institutions, independent schools, YWCAs, YMCAs, churches, synagogues, and nonprofit institutions of every ilk have the potential to raise millions of dollars. Even organizations with little fundraising experience have successfully completed multimillion dollar capital and endowment campaigns. In almost every case, a most important factor leading to success was the precampaign planning study.

CHAPTER 9

Staff and Volunteer Solicitation Training

Every staff member and campaign volunteer with solicitation responsibilities should attend at least one campaign orientation and training session. This is such an important point that many organizations adopt a policy establishing this requirement.

That said, a note of caution is in order. Avoid inviting people to a "fundraising training meeting." With any hint that a meeting is solely devoted to such training, the attendance will drop to a point approaching zero. Consider this alternative: invite people to an "uplifting and inspiring capital campaign orientation session." Or, include orientation time in regularly scheduled board and capital campaign meetings. Let the agenda show the usual business, but keep these items short so as to devote sufficient time to volunteer training.

One of the aims of the volunteer orientation is to eliminate fear and increase comfort. Fearful and uncomfortable people don't show up for the "fundraising training sessions." But they often discover ways in which they can participate when they attend the sessions that are integrated into regular meetings.

Language is important. Many people have an aversion to "training," whereas few react negatively to "orientation." Experienced community leaders often don't feel the need to be trained, but they do appreciate an orientation opportunity that gives them the tools they need to succeed.

There are four main parts to the capital campaign orientation session: (1) institution and project overview; (2) instruction concerning securing appointments; (3) how to ask for a capital campaign commitment; and (4) follow-up and campaign procedures. Exhibit 9.1 shows an agenda for a capital campaign orientation meeting. Let's look at each of the main components of the orientation session.

EXHIBIT 9.1   ORIENTATION SESSION SAMPLE AGENDA

International Institute of Asian Arts

Capital and Endowment Campaign

Preservation, Education, and Inspiration

Orientation Session
Agenda

I. Institution and Project Overview
   A. IIAA's rich history (Joel Schuster, CEO)
   B. Our challenges (Aaron Fieldhouse, Board Chair)
   C. The solution—our new home (Yoshi Yamamoto, Architect)
   D. Capital campaign, strategy, timeline, and structure—brief review (Joel Schuster)
   E. Prospect selection and assignment review (Barbara Young, Campaign Chair)

II. Securing Appointments
   A. Importance of in-person visits (Stanley Weinstein, Campaign Consultant)
   B. "What and how-to" advice: "Don't slip into a solicitation . . ."
   C. Staff support for the appointment and solicitation process

III. The Solicitation Process (Barbara Young and Stanley Weinstein)
   A. Build rapport
   B. State the case
   C. Encourage involvement: ask questions
   D. Handling objections
   E. Seeking advice
   F. Closing

IV. Follow-up and Campaign Procedures (Susan Walton, Director of Development)

V. Identifying Potential Causes of Inaction and Their Solutions (volunteer attendees, Young and Weinstein facilitating)

VI. Thank You and Adjourn (Aaron Fieldhouse)

INSTITUTION AND PROJECT OVERVIEW

Always review the case for support—even when working with people who know the organization reasonably well. Reviewing organization achievements and the rationale for the project provides a context for the campaign. If the schedule allows, discuss the case statement fully. If the orientation session is less than an hour, briefly review the organization's one-page capital campaign fact sheet and refer participants to the larger document, which is also distributed. In any case, be sure that the participants have a solid background of information concerning the capital project.

If the architect is available for the orientation session, great! Alternatively, invite an articulate and impassioned member of the facilities planning commit-tee to briefly review the capital project. Stress how the new facilities will help the organization achieve its objectives to provide enhanced services. Paint verbal pictures that allow participants to envision the organization serving real people who benefit from the nonprofit's programs.

If your campaign encompasses an endowment goal, review the importance of endowment funds and briefly review the organization's policies concerning planned gifts. If time permits, explain the benefits of charitable gift planning. Also let volunteers know of any special materials available and introduce them to team members who can go on selected visits to planned gift prospects.

Introduce campaign leaders. Briefly describe the campaign structure and strategy. The orientation overview should also remind participants of key capi-tal campaign principles—the importance of multiyear pledges, the importance of face-to-face meetings, the importance of volunteer commitments prior to solicitation visits, and the importance of maintaining the campaign timeline.

SECURING IN-PERSON APPOINTMENTS

An old, somewhat crude, maxim states, "To get milk, you have to get next to the cow." This certainly holds true for capital and endowment campaigns. To secure generous multiyear commitments, campaign volunteers and staff must be able to get face-to-face appointments. To assure these in-person visits, consider the following advice:

- Whenever possible, recruit a volunteer to whom the prospective supporter cannot easily say no.

- Offer the prospective donor a choice of dates. Example: "We can get together late this week or late afternoon on Monday or Tuesday. What works best for you?"

- Do not slip into a telephone solicitation when calling for an appointment. Know what to say if the prospect begins to discuss contributions. For example, if the prospect asks, "Are you going to solicit me for a campaign contribution?" reply, "The most important thing now is that key people such as yourself have a good idea of XYZ Nonprofit's vision and plans. Should you decide to invest in the campaign later, that would be your decision. And I won't take more than 20 minutes of your time. Which works best for you, Monday or Tuesday?"

- Define success as getting the appointment. In all volunteer and staff training, stress that your organization's most important indicator of capital campaign success is the ability to get face-to-face appointments with potential major donors.

Staff Support for the Appointment Process

Staff support is critical for the success of the capital campaign and its personal contact strategy. At a minimum, campaign staff and the institution's CEO can call volunteers and urge them to make the appointments. These calls are made "on behalf of the capital campaign chair."

At times, the director of development or CEO might also offer to set up the appointment. In such cases, the staff person gets a number of dates that are available for the volunteer and then calls the prospect. During the call to make the appointment, the staff member might include words such as, "Bob Gotinfluence, a member of our board, asked me to give you a call and find a convenient time for the three of us to get together." By using the volunteer or board member's name, the staff person lets the prospect know that the campaign is organized with strong community leaders. Moreover, prospects know that effective people often delegate tasks such as coordinating schedules.

A third alternative is to urge the volunteer to make the appointment calls when the volunteer and the staff team member are together. This can be arranged in a seemingly casual way when the staff member says, "Why don't you call Mr. Prospect now? I have my calendar with me and we can set up a time that's good for all three of us." Or, "Let's get together with your prospect list on Tuesday morning and see how many appointments we can get."

Realistic campaign organizers know that many volunteers are uncomfortable calling for appointments and going on solicitation visits. Gracious urging and occasional prodding keep the process moving. With this approach, maintaining momentum is possible. With momentum, the campaign moves inexorably toward its goal.

HOW TO ASK FOR A CAPITAL CAMPAIGN COMMITMENT

Prior to any solicitation, campaign leaders and the volunteer visitor determine the appropriate request amount and gift opportunity. The choice of solicitation team is based on chemistry and peer relationships. Volunteers and key staff make their personal commitments prior to participating in solicitation visits. Finally, campaign organizers determine when the timing is right to approach the prospective supporter for a capital campaign commitment.

Volunteers and staff members participating in the solicitation process easily understand that no two visits will proceed in exactly the same way. At times, the solicitation visit is with people who know the organization and the case for support very well. At other times, the visit might be with a prospect who knows very little about the organization or the capital project. In most cases, the representatives of the nonprofit organization will know the prospect fairly well. In a few situations, the visitation team might need to introduce themselves to the prospect. And every prospective supporter will respond differently to the appeal. Many will be supportive. Some will have objections. Many will have questions. Some will offer advice. Some will be decisive. Many will need some time to make a decision.

Later we will discuss listening skills and ways in which the solicitor might respond to the prospect's concerns. For now, let's examine the steps of a "model" solicitation.

Building Rapport

The first step of the solicitation visit is taking the time to reestablish your relationship and to break the ice. This is a very natural process. When meeting at the prospect's home or business, it is easy to find an opening question. Just look around. What looks interesting? Perhaps a photo of the prospect shaking hands with the president of the United States. Perhaps a basketball signed by all the members of the prospect's favorite team. Nearly every prospect has photos of family and loved ones nearby. Every prospect's environment offers clues as to what is important to that person. Simply ask, "Where was that photo taken?" Or say, "That's an interesting basketball. There must be a story there." Then be quiet and be prepared to hear an interesting story.

Spend more time listening than talking. Don't try to top the prospect's story. When through with their stories, prospects often say something like, "Oh, but enough about that. You must have something to say about the capital campaign." The words won't always be the same but prospects usually indicate when it is time to move the conversation forward.

Stating the Case for Support

After building rapport, experienced fundraisers move the conversation forward by describing the nonprofit organization's achievements and capital campaign aspirations. The nonprofit's spokesperson can refer to the organization's written materials. The one-page fact sheet might work well. If time permits, briefly review the longer case for support. Volunteers and staff people should always find their own words to explain the elements of the case that they find most moving and persuasive.

Many solicitation visitors find it helpful to hold on to the campaign materials. They point out highlights while continuing to speak. In this way, they avoid the awkwardness of speaking while the prospect is thumbing through the case for support.

Effective solicitors speak from the heart. They know how the capital project will help the organization better serve people—often one person at a time. Motivated fundraisers focus on the stories and facts that moved them. Prospective campaign supporters sense the volunteer or staff person's sincerity and enthusiasm. Many prospects respond with their own stories of meaningful philanthropy and a restatement of the rationale for supporting the campaign.

Encouraging Involvement

During the visit, ask lots of questions. Pause and listen. A volunteer or staff solicitor raising funds for a youth facility might ask, "Do you think it makes sense to invest more in positive programs for young people?" Or, "What kind of programs do you think work best for youth-at-risk?" If you are raising funds for an educational institution, you might ask, "Where does education fit in to your philanthropic priorities?" Or, "What did this institution mean to you when you went to school here?" Experienced fundraisers might also ask open-ended questions such as, "Does any part of our organization's case for support especially appeal to you?" Or, "What part of the capital and endowment campaign most interests you?" Questions such as these frequently encourage the prospective supporter to state the case for support in his or her own words.

When the prospect is speaking, listen intently. Don't jump to conclusions or make assumptions about the prospect's meaning and concerns. Hear the actual words. Watch the body language. If you are not sure of what the prospect is saying, ask questions. As Stephen R. Covey says, "Seek first to understand then be understood." As he explains in his writing about empathic communication, "Most people do not listen with the intent to understand; they listen with the intent to reply. They're either speaking or preparing to speak. They're filtering everything through their own paradigms, reading their autobiography into other people's lives" (*The 7 Habits of Highly Effective People,* Simon and Schuster, 1989).

A few more words about listening might be helpful here. In all training and orientation sessions, devote some time to listening skills. Encourage staff and volunteer visitors to listen to the prospect's stories. These are fascinating and instructive. One of the great joys of fundraising is the opportunity to meet colorful people, successful people, and compassionate people, many of whom are great storytellers.

Also encourage campaign workers to hear the prospect's concerns. If the prospect speaks about the university's history department, don't keep trying to shift attention back to some other gift opportunity. If the prospect asks questions about the institution's fiscal health, make sure you supply accurate and up-to-date information that helps assuage these concerns.

If the prospect has a positive impression of the organization, move forward with the request for funds. To the extent possible and natural, use the prospect's own words and thoughts to state the case for support.

Handling Objections

Prospective supporters' concerns or objections should be handled with tact and courtesy. Arguments and attempts at persuasion rarely, if ever, work. Communications experts also remind us to avoid "yes . . . but . . ." phrases. Most people never hear a word after the "but." It's a complete turnoff. Instead, consider "yes . . . and . . ." phrasing. Example: "Yes, I have heard your concern before. And the organization has made considerable progress addressing that issue."

Many people find it helpful to use the "feel, felt, found" model for responding to objections. The "feel" phrase indicates that the listener understands the prospect's concerns. The "felt" phrase assures the prospect that he or she is not alone—and places the concern in the past tense. The "found" phrase offers the nonprofit representative an opportunity to supply new information.

To illustrate, imagine a capital campaign volunteer visiting a potential lead gift donor for a performing arts organization who says, "I am troubled about the organization's seemingly continual fiscal crises." Using the "feel, felt, found" approach, a representative of the performing arts institution might say, "You *feel* distressed that the organization had so many problems with its financial affairs. I can tell you that you're not alone. Others have *felt* that way. What they *found* out was that the organization has adopted a new set of policies based on solid management principles. In fact, the organization has eliminated its accumulated deficit and has enjoyed several years with operating surpluses. Our next step is to secure the facilities and endowment we need to better serve the community while maintaining our new reputation for fiscal responsibility."

Because it is impossible to anticipate every objection, it is helpful to learn what has become known as "Weinstein's bottom-line" reply. Here's how it works:

- Upon hearing a new and upsetting objection, admit that you have not heard it before and that the situation sounds serious—even horrific.
- State that you are going to look into the matter and report the concern to the organization's board and management team.
- Assure the prospect that the administration is working to make the organization as strong as possible.
- Let the prospect know that you speak to many people who believe in the organization's "bottom line," that is, the institution's strongest and shortest rationale for support.
- Conclude by citing the bottom line as the reason that everyone will work to overcome the problem and do everything possible to strengthen the organization—including support for the capital project.

To illustrate: Imagine a volunteer solicitor raising funds for a youth and family recreation and health facility who hears a prospect say, "A friend's kid went there and said that they offered very little for middle school students. In fact, they decided to look elsewhere. I would have thought that the organization would offer a wider range of programs for kids of all ages."

In situations such as these, the volunteer can begin by acknowledging the seriousness of the issue and the depth of emotion. You might say something like, "I have not heard that before. It surely sounds like a serious issue. I'll try to find out more about that for you."

You might now transition to the bottom-line reply. You can continue, "Everyone I know on the management team is dedicated to continuous improvement and to developing strong programs. So I know they'll want to hear about your concerns. I speak to a lot of people about this organization. And their bottom line is that this facility is the only organization working to provide lifelong recreation and fitness programs for the entire family. It is crucial to all the people in our region—kids, adults, and seniors. We've got to work together to make it as strong as possible."

By returning the conversation to the organization's strongest points, fundraisers can often overcome objections. Moreover, prospects who feel they were heard and understood frequently become the organization's strongest supporters.

Asking Advice

Some time during every cultivation and solicitation visit should be devoted to asking advice. Helpful questions include: "Is there something our organization should be doing that we're not doing?" "When speaking with other community leaders, what points concerning our capital campaign would you stress?" "Do you have any advice on how we can recruit more volunteers?" "Do you know of other people who might be interested in our organization?" "Would you be willing to introduce our organization to some of your friends or business associates?"

Perhaps the most important advice capital campaign staff and volunteer solicitors might ask concerns the solicitation itself. Consider the following questions:

- "I know you have a family foundation; would it be best to approach you individually or would you prefer a written application?"

- "Might you consider a personal commitment in addition to the corporate pledge?"

- "What is the best way to approach your company?"

- "We were thinking about requesting $25,000 a year for three years from your company; is this a realistic amount to request?"

Capital campaign fundraisers who ask questions such as these find that most prospects respond favorably. Their answers provide crucial information concerning how much to request and how best to complete the solicitation.

Closing

Savvy staff members and volunteers recognize the words and body language that indicate that the prospective supporter is responding positively. The clearest sign of acceptance occurs when prospects state the case for support in their own words. Other signals may be more subtle. Prospects who shift body position and lean closer to the solicitor are unconsciously informing the visitor that the response is favorable. If previously the prospect's arms had been folded across the chest, then he or she adopts a more open posture, that too is a positive sign. Also note if the prospective supporter is beginning to ask positive questions about your organization. Just listen and watch. You will soon develop a sixth sense about the prospect's attitude.

Less experienced fundraisers continue speaking well after the prospect has indicated a willingness to support the cause. A better approach is to graciously request the multiyear commitment soon after the prospect has indicated a positive attitude toward the capital campaign.

When speaking with prospects who have affirmed their support for your case, you may say something such as, "You have a good grasp of how much our organization does for the people of our region. And to continue our programs we are going to need gifts at these leadership levels." (Bring forward the gift opportunities page indicating investments at the rated range and higher.) "Where do you see yourself participating?"

Alternative language might sound something like this, "You know how important this capital and endowment campaign are to XYZ's ability to serve our community, nation, and world by providing excellence in education. So I hope you are in a position to endow the Faculty Research Fund with a three- to five-year pledge totaling $300,000." Or, "You know how important the YMCA is to families and kids living in our community. And we'd like to offer you an opportunity to name the new multipurpose training room with a commitment of $50,000 a year for three years."

When speaking with a long-term, loyal supporter of your organization, you might wish to close with words such as, "You have been so supportive of our organization, and you know how much this capital campaign means to the people we serve, so our campaign leaders want to offer you the opportunity to make a significant investment in this cause. Your $3 million contribution will allow us to have the strongest possible start to the capital campaign and will also allow us to name the new center in memory of your wife, Emily."

Successful fundraisers rehearse their closing statements prior to going on calls. They know the amount they are going to request. They also know the words they will use.

Being good listeners, successful fundraisers are also flexible. If the prospect indicates an aversion to naming opportunities, the staff member or volunteer will respect the wish for anonymity and will shift focus to the level of investment needed for campaign success. Rather than emphasizing the naming opportunity, the solicitor will stress the benefits the campaign will bring to the people who are served by the nonprofit. Listening and responding appropriately are the keys to success.

Note the benefits of the three recommended capital campaign closings:

1. *"To better serve those who come to us for help, we will need gifts at these levels. Where do you see yourself participating?"* This closing allows the volunteer or staff member to rely on a gift opportunity page that has been customized for the individual prospect. For example, solicitors planning to request $15,000 or more may show a gift opportunities page with all of the investment levels from $10,000 to your top ranges. Many of your prospects will choose an amount greater than your rating.

   The other benefit of this approach is that many people can never bring themselves to actually ask for a specific gift amount or range. The "where do you see yourself participating?" question avoids any direct mention of the dollar amount. Therefore, many volunteers find this a very comfortable and gracious way of indicating the gift request range.

2. *"I hope you are in a position to consider a pledge of $30,000 or more to help us."* Notice that this phrase has every conceivable word to soften the impact of the direct request. The phrases "I hope," "you are in a posi-

tion," and "to consider," when strung together, create the impression that the volunteer solicitor has not judged the prospect's capability to give. Moreover, these words even imply that the solicitor hopes that the prospect is doing so well financially that he or she can make a significant contribution.

"I hope you are in a position to consider a pledge of $XX,XXX . . ." is a priceless addition to anyone's fundraising vocabulary. This golden phrase is well worth memorizing and practicing until it sounds entirely natural.

3. *"We would like to offer you an opportunity to make a significant investment in. . . . Your pledge of $XXX,XXX will allow us to . . ."* Douglas M. Lawson, Ph.D., author of *Give to Live* (ALTI Publishing, 1991), likes to stress the importance of the two "Os"—Offer Opportunities. Successful capital campaigns grow out of a sense of involvement. Donors who want to make a wholehearted investment in your cause appreciate being offered an opportunity to play a significant role in shaping your institution and enhancing its services and programs.

After the Close, Silence!

Successful fundraisers know how important it is to be silent after the closing question or statement. They don't say a word until the prospect speaks. They wait quietly and patiently for the prospect's response.

What might happen if the fundraiser speaks too soon? What is an inexperienced volunteer or staff member likely to say? It is human nature to project one's greatest fear and even put forward a response to a concern that the prospect never even mentioned. In role-playing situations, you might hear something like this, "I hope you are in a position to consider a pledge of $25,000 or more. (Pause very slightly.) But I know you are very generous to so many other charities, and anything you can do would be appreciated." In this example, the fundraiser talked him- or herself out of the gift before the prospect even had a chance to think about the request.

Some people find it very difficult to wait for a response in utter silence. They become very uncomfortable. Seconds seem like hours. Still, don't speak. If, in the very rare event, the prospective supporter appears to have also decided not to speak first, and the long silence becomes too tense, you might ask, "Well, Sherman, what are you thinking?" Or you might say, "I once heard that silence means consent. Can I safely assume that your silence means that you have decided to contribute the amount we have requested?" Words such as these can break the ice in this rare situation. You might even get a laugh *and* the multiyear commitment you requested.

Respond Appropriately

Fundraisers who wait for the prospect to respond learn what the prospect is thinking. In general terms, prospects have three choices upon hearing the request for a capital campaign commitment. They can reply "yes," "no," or "maybe." The staff or volunteer fundraiser's task is to listen carefully and respond appropriately.

If the prospect's response to the request for a capital campaign multiyear commitment is yes, repeat your understanding and tie down all of the details. You might say, "Thank you so much. That's very generous. Let me make sure I have all of the correct information. You are pledging $10,000 a year for five years. Would you expect to be making your contributions monthly, quarterly, semiannually or annually? (Wait and record reply.) By the way, do you prefer your acknowledgments as Mr. and Mrs. I. M. Giving, or would you prefer that we list you as Irving and Matilda Giving?"

The most important first step in cementing the supporter's bond with the nonprofit institution begins when sensitive solicitors repeat their understanding of the commitment terms. Pledge totals, payment schedules, and acknowledgment details are important. Long-term relationships and pledge fulfillment depend on getting the information right in the first place.

If upon hearing the request for capital campaign support, the prospect responds "no," the solicitor's first task is to determine the meaning of that no. Recall that the solicitor used words such as, "I hope you are in a position to consider an investment of $25,000 a year for three years to support our capital campaign." If the prospect says "I don't think I could do that," you can ask yourself what it is he or she is saying no to. A moment's reflection will tell you that the prospect has declined to donate at the level requested. Nimble campaign workers might respond, "What level of support would you be comfortable with?" Or, "Of course we need gifts at all levels; might you be more comfortable with a pledge of $10,000 a year—or perhaps staying at the $75,000 level but paying it over five years instead of three?"

If the prospect appears to be saying no to a contribution, you might suggest that the prospect not make a final decision at this time. The solicitor might say, "Please don't decide not to support the campaign today. Let me get you more information and we can speak again in six months or so. Perhaps then your circumstances might have changed." Of course, when you hear a final no, graciously thank the prospect for his or her time and say something like, "I hope you will be in a position to help sometime in the future."

Many prospects' "maybe" responses are requests for time to consider the contribution. Some of these maybes can be avoided by setting appointments with both spouses or with all known decision makers. However, experienced fundraisers know that if they are getting predominantly yes responses, they are probably asking too little. So effective capital campaigners want and expect to hear lots of responses such as, "I'll need to think about that," "Let me talk that over with Jan," or "That's a bit more than I thought you were going to request; let me think that over." Upon hearing these prospect responses, effective fundraisers know to say, "I thought you might want some time to think about this commitment. That's why I put together these materials for you to look over. I'll leave these with you. And I can call you in two or three weeks to discuss your participation. Would that work for you?"

The Commitment Card

Whether the prospect responded to the capital campaign with a "yes," "no," or "maybe," it is prudent to recall that most important fundraising maxim: *Do not leave a pledge card!*

Prospects who say, "Give me a pledge card and I'll send something in," rarely do. So don't lose control of the solicitation process by leaving the pledge card or commitment form with the prospective supporter. Learn how and when to use the pledge card or commitment form.

First, do not put the pledge card or commitment form in the presentation package you will leave with the prospect. Staff members and volunteers should keep these in their possession.

When the prospect responds "yes" to the capital campaign request, the staff member or volunteer can clarify all the details, as described in this section. As the prospect responds, the representative of the nonprofit organization can fill in the details and then hand the commitment form to the prospect for his or her signature. In such cases, the capital campaigner leaves with the signed commitment form. If the commitment is made during a follow-up phone conversation, the nonprofit representative can verbally affirm the details, see that a prompt thank-you letter is sent, and have the commitment form signed soon after.

If the prospect responds "no," "maybe," or "I'll need to think about that," there is no reason to leave a pledge card. Campaign workers need not even mention pledge cards or commitment forms until the prospect has made a decision. By not leaving pledge cards, capital campaigners do not lull themselves into a false belief that they have completed their tasks. They know that they need to follow up.

Finally, know that many contributions are lost because of a lack of follow-up. Successful capital campaign workers keep the solicitation process moving forward by pinning down the date or time frame when they will call back for follow-up appointments or decisions. Campaign support staff keep track of pending decisions and follow-up dates. Campaign leaders stay focused on these contacts, outstanding requests, and follow-up steps. Campaigns succeed when solicitors stay in contact with their prospects and help lead them to a decision to be as generous as possible.

FOLLOW-UP AND CAMPAIGN PROCEDURES

Send a brief note of thanks after every capital campaign visit. Of course, if the prospect said "yes" to the request, the thank-you should also acknowledge the contribution or pledge.

If the prospect said "no," the thank-you note can serve to establish or strengthen the prospect's ties to the nonprofit. For example, the note can say, "Thanks for your time and advice yesterday. I understand why this is not the best time for you to consider a commitment to XYZ Nonprofit's capital campaign. However, let me send you some information from time to time. XYZ's services and programs are so inspiring. I believe you might enjoy hearing about the organization as it moves forward with its plans to enhance its facilities and better serve the people in our community."

If the prospect said "maybe" or requested time to make a decision, the thank-you note can say, "Thanks for meeting yesterday. Your advice and good humor are always welcome and refreshing. Thanks, too, for considering our request for capital campaign support. I know that you and Jan will be as generous as possible. You do so much for our community. I'll give you a call in about two or three weeks to set up a time when we can get together again and to hear your thoughts about XYZ Nonprofit's capital campaign, 'Pride and Excellence for the Future!' "

The more personal the thank-you note, the better. Even late in the public phase, when the volume of pledges might necessitate automated acknowledgments, computer-generated thank-you letters can be written to sound warm and personal. And volunteer and staff solicitors can be reminded of the importance of handwritten notes to those they personally visited.

Call Reports and Campaign Record-Keeping

In addition to writing thank-you notes, campaign solicitors make sure that the campaign staff knows about the outcome of the visit. In particular, solicitors and support staff make sure that they record the necessary follow-up steps and dates. Notes can be as simple as "Call Mike and Lana for a decision during the third week of March."

At the orientation sessions, be sure to explain your nonprofit organization's record-keeping policies and processes. Confirm that every volunteer and staff member knows how commitment forms and acknowledgments are to be handled.

Many also find it helpful to use call reports, which can be simple or complex. But as Exhibit 9.2 indicates, the purpose of the call report is to assure that the

EXHIBIT 9.2   CALL REPORT FORM

International Institute of Asian Arts Call Report Form

Volunteer or Staff Name: _____

Person Visited: _____

Date of Visit: _____

Notes:

Follow-up Action Needed:

By When:

> Please return to IIAA office or call Susan Walton (805) 256-1776.
> Use other side for additional notes.

---

campaign support team knows what happened on each visit and what follow-up steps might be indicated.

Follow-up might also involve invitations to the nonprofit organization's special cultivation gatherings or to regularly scheduled events. Whenever appropriate, representatives of the nonprofit can recruit the prospective supporter for an active role. In all cases, effective campaign workers keep prospects well informed about the organization and the capital campaign's progress.

TRAINING, ORIENTATION, AND ROLE-PLAYING ACTIVITIES

In all probability, the people serving on the board of directors and capital campaign team are intelligent people with above-average social skills. Many should be community leaders; all should be dedicated to your cause.

For these reasons, capital campaign leaders must be careful not to "overtrain" team members or undermine their confidence. Do we really have to teach community leaders how to build rapport? The actual solicitation is a natural process that can be handled any number of ways. The most important aspect of training is to stress the importance of getting the appointment. Next, devote as much time to role-playing as possible to increase everyone's comfort level. Keep your training materials concise. The sample "Advice to the Volunteer or Staff Solicitor" memo (see Exhibit 9.3) might become the basis for the orientation session. Again, keep it simple. Inspire confidence. And reap the rewards.

Another point: To the extent possible, don't lecture. Most volunteers and staff members know the answers to their most common concerns. They just don't know they know until a skilled facilitator elicits their concerns and responses.

EXHIBIT 9.3   ADVICE TO THE VOLUNTEER OR STAFF SOLICITOR

Please begin to make your appointments with your prospects. Alternatively, you may wish to encourage your prospects to attend one of IIAA's cultivation gatherings and follow up with a solicitation visit. Please remember that we are requesting three-year commitments.

Please consider going on your calls with a team member. If you decide to go "solo," the following suggestions might prove helpful.

BEFORE THE SOLICITATION
- Please make your three-year financial commitment prior to calling on your prospects.
- When calling for the appointment, offer the prospective donor a choice of dates. Example: "We can get together late this week or late afternoon on Monday or Tuesday. What works best for you?"
- Please do not slip into a solicitation when you are calling for the appointment. The most important objective now is to get the appointment. If the prospect asks, "Are you going to solicit me for the campaign?" reply, **"The most important thing now is that key people such as yourself have a good idea of what's happening at the International Institute of Asian Art. Should you decide to invest in the campaign later, that would be your decision."**
- KNOW YOUR FACTS. Be familiar with the case for support. Be sure to read the literature in your solicitor's kit. More importantly, decide on a few key points that move you personally.
- KNOW WHAT YOU ARE GOING TO ASK YOUR PROSPECT. Decide on a challenging yet feasible amount to request.

  Some examples of the most gracious ways to ask for the gift are: "I hope you are in a position to consider a pledge of $10,000 a year for three years to help us build our new facilities, support the scholars who come to us, and preserve some of the world's greatest treasures." Or, "For this campaign to succeed, we will need gifts at these levels (present Gift Opportunities page). Where do you see yourself participating?"

  Please memorize the closing sentence that works best for you. Remind yourself about the *silence* after the ask.

AT THE SOLICITATION
- First, relax. Build rapport. Chat about the prospective donor's interests and any common interests you may share.
- Speak about the campaign and how the new facilities will help IIAA fulfill its mission. Ask some involvement questions. Listen to the prospective donor's thoughts about IIAA.
- Discuss the prospect's concerns. Don't argue. Remember, "feel, felt, found."
- As soon as you have heard the prospect state a positive opinion, *close.*

  Present the Gift Opportunity page and ask for a contribution by suggesting a specific amount. Or say, "I hope you're in a position to consider a pledge of $10,000 a year for three years to help us build our new museum and preserve

EXHIBIT 9.3 (CONTINUED)

some of the great treasures entrusted to us." *Silence.* Wait for prospect to reply.

- TIE DOWN any loose ends. *(Never leave a pledge card!)* Repeat your understanding of the total commitment and the approximate anticipated pledge payment schedule (annually in December, quarterly, or any special arrangements).

  If the prospective donor needs more time to think about his or her decision, set up a date for a follow-up meeting, or reconfirm when the decision will be made.

  Again, thank the prospect for his or her time.

AFTER THE SOLICITATION

- Record the total gift or pledge and expected payment dates. Have the prospect sign the commitment card. If the prospect has not yet made a firm commitment, make note of the follow-up date. Inform the office of your results.
- If time permits, please send a short personalized thank-you note to the person you visited. Of course, we will promptly thank all pledges and contributions.

If there is something you don't understand or are unsure about, don't hesitate to call IIAA or Stanley Weinstein 505-256-3231 or 1-800-325-2117. If you want any other team member to make the solicitation visit with you, please let us know. Team visits work best.

Thanks and Good Luck!

Consider this process: First, ask orientation participants to list their concerns. Ask them why they might be reluctant to make a solicitation visit. Ask them to also list any questions or objections they might anticipate. Record these, leaving lots of space on flip charts. At the end of this first step, record only issues and concerns. After the second step—recording participants' solutions—the flip chart would appear as follows:

- Discomfort with rejection: afraid of "no."

Responses and solutions:

- Remember, "no" might be no to the request amount. You can always ask, "What amount might you be comfortable with?"
- The "no" is not personal.
- Every salesperson and anyone advancing a project knows that not everyone says yes. Some donors give less than requested. Some prospective donors have circumstances that make them unable or unlikely to give at all.
- Intensify prospect research.

- "I might be too close to the prospect to feel comfortable asking for a pledge. I don't want to jeopardize my close relationships."

Responses and solutions:
- Don't go to your closest friends or relatives.
- Solicit affluent people with whom you have respectful peer relationships.
- Remember that you are not asking for yourself. You are offering an opportunity for the prospective supporter to make a significant investment in the region's well-being.

- "I might not be able to answer every question about the organization and capital project."

Responses and solutions:
- Go with a staff member.
- Read your solicitation materials. Learn as much as possible beforehand.
- Be prepared to say, "I don't know but I can find out for you."

- "I'm not experienced in asking for charitable contributions."

Responses and solutions:
- Staff and board members can engage in role-playing activities.
- Go in a team setting.
- Go with someone who has been on solicitation visits in the past.

- "The prospect might treat the solicitation as a quid pro quo and ask me for a contribution to his or her favorite charity."

Responses and solutions:
- Remember that both you and the prospect have the right to say yes or no.
- This doesn't occur as frequently as some believe. Besides, experienced community leaders know that each prospect decides how much he or she wishes to donate to specific causes.
- If you are quite sure that the uncomfortable reciprocal solicitation will take place, don't take that volunteer assignment. Choose prospects you are comfortable with.

- "I'm not comfortable speaking about large amounts of money or requesting specific pledge requests. I was taught not to talk about other people's money. And I don't want to show knowledge of the prospect's worth."

Responses and solutions:
- Speak in terms of community benefits.
- Never discuss the prospect rating process.
- Use solicitation materials that make requesting higher dollar amounts easier and more automatic.
- Use printed gift opportunities with larger donation levels. Use language

such as, "We need gifts at these levels in order to have a successful capital campaign and enhance our services for the people who have come to rely on us."

- Alternatively, use language such as, "I hope you are in a position to consider a pledge of $25,000 a year for three years to help us get the strongest possible start to this campaign."

- "So many nonprofits are asking. Won't we annoy people with too many requests?"

Responses and solutions:
- Don't worry. Most nonprofits aren't so well organized that prospects are asked to participate in many face-to-face solicitations.
- If the prospect is really overextended, he or she will probably not want to meet—or might simply make a smaller gift when asked.
- Don't overplay your chips. If you have personally solicited someone three or four times recently, you might not wish to go back.
- Clear visits with staff.
- Remember, you can offend someone by *not* asking.

- "Our organization is not well connected with the multiple power structures in our large region."

Responses and solutions:
- Interview known community leaders throughout the region.
- Identify power base—that is, movers and shakers.
- Uncover personal linkages; find people who are close to XYZ Nonprofit and who can make introductions.
- Ask local movers and shakers to host "cultivation" events, that is, social and informative gatherings at their home (friend-raising not fundraising).
- Invest in prospect identification, research, and cultivation prior to soliciting gifts.

Remember, the facilitator first listed the concerns, then got the answers and solutions from the capital campaign orientation participants. In most cases, someone in the room will suggest a perfectly acceptable solution. Experienced facilitators know not to get too hung up over their role. If they know a workable solution that was not suggested, they might suggest it, saying, "Those are great solutions you came up with. At another meeting such as this, a volunteer made a suggestion you might also wish to consider." Again, the objective is to avoid lecturing. The goal is to tap into the participants' experience and good sense.

Finally, consider alternatives to traditional role-playing. Recognize that most volunteers do not want to rehearse their presentations with a group watching. One alternative is to prearrange a model solicitation. Have two board or staff members demonstrate a typical capital campaign solicitation visit. The demonstration can include a few prearranged "rough spots" to indicate how objections might be handled. A way to make the demonstration even more meaningful to participants is to have a facilitator monitor the solicitation and be given the power to stop action and conversation at any point. Frozen poses during these breaks provide levity to the orientation session. (I first saw this training technique at an AFP International Conference, demonstrated by Edith Falk of Campbell & Company.) During the pauses, the facilitator can lead group discussions concerning what just happened, what was good, what might be improved, next steps, and questions the orientation participants might have.

TEAM SOLICITATIONS

Throughout the capital campaign—and certainly at all training sessions—campaign leaders emphasize the importance of team solicitations. Also recognize that while teams work well, campaign organizers never want to overwhelm their prospects. Two representatives of the nonprofit visiting one prospect is fine; three is overkill—and likely to make the prospective supporter uncomfortable.

Perhaps the most effective solicitation team is the board chair accompanied by the nonprofit CEO, but, other teams are frequently equally effective. These might include: two volunteers who have a peer relationship with the prospect; a very experienced capital campaign worker with a newer member of the team; a member of the board accompanied by a key staff member, especially one who knows the programs well; a well-connected volunteer teamed with a campaign worker who is knowledgeable concerning charitable gift planning, planned giving, and endowment building; or an experienced staff fundraiser teamed with a retired volunteer who can participate in many solicitations.

The advantages of such teams are clear. The board chair accompanied by the nonprofit CEO is the most knowledgeable and prestigious team possible to visit potential pacesetting prospective supporters. Two well-informed volunteers with the right chemistry and a peer relationship can always get appointments and inspire generous multiyear commitments. New campaign workers teamed with experienced fundraisers increase their comfort level, gain experience, and become more effective when approaching their network of contacts. Staff members who accompany board members and volunteers often can answer questions that the prospects might have. As important, staff members often share poignant stories of the nonprofit organization's impact on the people served.

Staff and volunteer fundraisers who are knowledgeable of charitable gift planning, planned giving, and estate planning make great team members for selected visits to prospects who might consider commitments to the endowment portion of the campaign. The simplest approach is a request that the prospect consider remembering the organization's endowment fund in his or her will or estate plan. In addition, experienced charitable gift planners can suggest ways in which prospects can better provide for their family and loved ones while being generous to the nonprofit organization.

Every campaign can benefit from teaming a staff fundraiser with a retired volunteer. Committed retired volunteers can attend numerous solicitations, add credibility to the staff request, and articulate the case for support from the community and public's perspective.

Consider these additional benefits. With team solicitations, the nonprofit organization has two sets of ears to listen to the prospect. Team members are more likely to hear the prospect's concerns and respond appropriately. With team solicitations, the nonprofit organization increases the probability that the predetermined gift amount is requested. Often, unaccompanied volunteer workers get cold feet. When it comes time to request a generous commitment range or gift opportunity, they might take the more comfortable route of requesting less or simply being vague.

In sum, campaigns succeed when campaign visitors listen to the prospect's concerns and when they urge each prospective supporter to be as generous as possible. These principles and the resulting outcomes—generous campaign commitments—are best observed with team solicitations.

CHAPTER 10

Managing the Campaign

In a very real sense, nonprofit leaders begin to manage the campaign process when they agree to conduct a feasibility study or precampaign planning study. Several major issues critical to campaign success are integral to the planning study process: refining the case for support, identifying potential pacesetting donors, giving these prospects an opportunity to offer advice on the project, and identifying steps needed to strengthen the organization.

Be sure to take the study seriously and work intensely to implement the recommendations. Devote time and energy to board development, refining the case for support, public relations, prospect identification, and nurturing positive relationships with key stakeholders—especially top prospects. Also work to strengthen the organization's fundraising record-keeping and reporting systems.

When the study is complete and the nonprofit agency has made progress implementing the study recommendations, campaign organizers can move more directly into the solicitation phases of the capital campaign: the *quiet phase, intermediate phase,* and the *public phase.* These campaign phases are also called, respectively, the *advancement phase, special gifts phase,* and the *general phase.*

THE ADVANCEMENT, OR QUIET, PHASE

The first order of business of the quiet phase is volunteer recruitment. The organization's objective is to enlist the volunteer commitment of 7 to 11 dedicated people to serve on the *capital campaign steering committee* or *capital campaign cabinet.* There are no official definitions of these terms but a subtle distinction might be made. A steering committee guides the campaign's earliest steps, including the board campaign and recruitment of a campaign chair, if that person has not already been enlisted. Of course, when the campaign chairperson has been recruited, that most important volunteer becomes the chair of the steering committee. A campaign cabinet is formed when all co-chairs, vice chairs, and division chairs, if any, have been recruited.

If the steering committee has fewer than seven volunteers, it lacks the resources needed to contact the 50 or so top prospects. Beginning with more than 11 is also problematic. The organization that recruits too many volunteers too soon risks diminishing enthusiasm. Large steering committees are somewhat unwieldy and are ill-suited to the task of rating prospective donors' capacity to support the campaign. That task requires a great deal of confidentiality. (If a larger campaign committee has been recruited, the rating process can be delegated to a smaller committee.)

If the organization recruits the entire campaign volunteer structure all at once, many volunteers would not be able to begin until earlier phases of the campaign are completed. The largest number of volunteers are not needed until the intermediate and public phases of the campaign.

During the quiet, or advancement, phase, early generous and pacesetting supporters are identified, cultivated, and graciously solicited. The steering committee is formed. This core group, in turn, intensifies the organization's other cultivation and leadership awareness activities.

As noted, at this stage, the nonprofit organization has not yet recruited the entire capital campaign leadership and volunteer team. Capital campaigns are sequential in nature. During the advancement phase, the organization can adopt policies and timelines, complete the board campaign, recruit key campaign leaders, and approach potential pacesetting contributors.

So who should be recruited to serve on the steering committee? The most obvious choices include the organization's board chair, several of the most generous and influential members of the board of directors, the chair of the capital campaign (if recruited shortly after the planning study), and one or more key volunteers who are very respected in the community. The organization's CEO, director of development, and the campaign consultant also participate as team members working with key volunteers.

The Campaign Chair

Perhaps the most important decision made early in the campaign is the choice of campaign chair or co-chairs. A brief look at Exhibit 10.1, "Capital Campaign Chair Job Description" reminds the reader of the chairperson's substantial responsibilities. But beyond these, the chair sets the tone for the campaign in a number of less tangible ways. The choice of campaign chair sends a signal to the philanthropic community. A well-respected chair informs community leaders that this campaign is a worthy cause—worthy of the chair's attention and worthy of the community's support. The credibility of the campaign chair makes it easier to recruit additional effective volunteers. The right choice of campaign chair facilitates access to decision makers capable of large donations or of influencing pacesetting leadership commitments.

EXHIBIT 10.1 CAPITAL CAMPAIGN CHAIR JOB DESCRIPTION

- Work with the institution's CEO, capital campaign consultant, and fellow campaign cabinet members to refine the capital campaign plan, timeline, volunteer structure, and strategy.
- Help recruit additional volunteer leaders.
- Review the capital campaign case for support and other campaign materials. Help assure that all materials accurately convey the information presented. Also remind those responsible for campaign materials of the importance of clear and compelling images and language.
- Serve as an advocate for the campaign. Be available to speak at key campaign relationship-nurturing gatherings.
- Participate in meetings designed to evaluate prospective donors' capacity to support the campaign. Recommend generous "request amounts." Help others set their sights high.
- Make a self-satisfying financial commitment to the campaign.
- Chair campaign cabinet meetings.
- Participate in selected cultivation and solicitation visits with the campaign's most important prospective donors.
- Urge key volunteers to complete their tasks.

Prior to discussing how to recruit the capital campaign chair, let's think about *when* this most important task should take place. Many organizations prematurely recruit a capital campaign chair early in the planning process. At times, a board member or interested community volunteer steps forward or is recruited prior to the precampaign planning study. This choice may work out well. However, there are some risks involved. If the campaign chair is chosen prior to the engagement of a capital campaign consultant, the organization may set its sights too low. Most consultants advise organizations to "go for the gold" and recruit the most respected and admired community leader to serve as campaign chair. Moreover, the precampaign planning study helps identify people willing to serve and people willing to help recruit potential leaders. And at times, the early choice may have some subtle negative baggage that was not known to the organization. Potential pacesetting donors use the confidential interview to state whom they admire and who may have disappointed them in the past. Interviewees will also let the consultant know who may be extremely overcommitted. In short, we ask community leaders for advice during the confidential interviews. It is best to consider that advice—and to ignore it at the organization's peril.

Perhaps this is overly dramatic. Organizations usually choose reasonably wisely. Still, many fundraising professionals agree that it is best to recruit the campaign chair *after* the precampaign planning study, if possible. Why make such a crucial decision before it's necessary?

Exhibit 10.2 lists capital campaign chair attributes. Note that keys to success place importance on clout, control of time, moral suasion, reputation in the community, and commitment to the project. As you can imagine, people with these attributes are rare and in great demand. But don't hesitate to recruit a busy person. Just be cautious that the potential campaign chair is not overcommitted to other nonprofits. A community leader serving on five or more boards of directors and helping with other capital campaigns can't be effective for your organization. Also, be cautious in approaching elected officials. Politicians can be helpful in many ways, but they often use their network of associates to raise political contributions. Moreover, even very well-respected political leaders will agree that nearly half or more of the general population will oppose them at one time or another.

So focus on nonpolitical, well-respected community leaders who may be busy but are not wildly overextended. And be sure to recruit your best candidate in a gracious and thoughtful manner. Have two people with peer relationships

EXHIBIT 10.2 CHAIRPERSON ATTRIBUTES

SEVEN ATTRIBUTES OF THE IDEAL CAPITAL CAMPAIGN CHAIR

1. **The ideal chairperson is a respected community, national, or world leader.**
   We're not talking about political leaders. They usually don't work out well for capital campaigns. Rather, look for people recognized for the positive role they play. These can be business leaders, philanthropists, or volunteer organizers. The best are all three.

2. **The ideal chairperson controls his or her time.**
   Recruit a person who does not have to punch a time clock. The ideal leader answers to him- or herself. The person must also be a gifted time manager.

3. **The ideal chairperson is known for his or her generosity.**
   Enough said.

4. **The ideal chairperson is one to whom people say, "Yes."**
   This person has the moral suasion to ask others and have them respond positively.

5. **The ideal chairperson lends credibility to the institution's cause.**
   Go for the Gold! Recruit a known winner.

6. **The ideal chairperson has strong organization skills.**
   This person knows how to build teams, run meetings, and get things done.

7. **The ideal chairperson is a strong communicator.**
   Recruit a passionate and articulate leader, someone who appreciates good staff support but also brings a lot to the table. People should enjoy hearing this person speak and should appreciate his or her written messages.

to the potential campaign chair call on the candidate. The two-person recruitment team members are often chosen from among the following: already committed and respected community leaders, the board chair, generous board members, and nonprofit CEOs. Decide which two people will have the best chemistry and the best chances of securing an in-person visit.

During the recruitment visit, explain the importance of the campaign and responsibilities thoroughly. Listen. Listen. Listen. Assure the potential chairperson that staff and consultant support will be extensive and professional. Share the results of the precampaign planning study. Describe what the organization will do to help maximize the campaign chair's effectiveness and control the time commitment.

Many recruiters find it helpful to say something like, "Please understand that you are not our 'first choice.' You are the *only* candidate for campaign chair. So many people will benefit from this project that we hope you will find a way to join us in this meaningful campaign. You'll feel good about your commitment. We can have fun together. You will be well supported. And together we will raise the significant funds needed for this most important project."

After making your impassioned appeal, be quiet. Listen some more. Respond appropriately. Find ways to help the candidate come to a "yes." Again, be sure that the organization sends recruiters with peer relationships. Potential campaign chairs are flattered when their peers ask them to serve.

Recruiting the Remainder of the Campaign Leadership

At times, the newly recruited campaign chair will suggest one or two people to be recruited for the capital campaign steering committee or campaign cabinet. When possible, have the chair go in person with someone already close to the organization and recruit these additional community leaders.

Knowing who might be willing to serve is not difficult. During the precampaign planning study, the consultant interviewed key board members, potential pacesetting donors, and community leaders. Study participants were asked if they were willing to serve as campaign volunteers. Experienced consultants inform interviewees that this question is not as confidential as the others. Study participants who are willing or eager to serve have no problem letting the organization know their intentions. When conducting precampaign planning studies, I include a listing of all names suggested by study participants as potential campaign volunteers. The list also includes all interviewees who indicated that they might be interested in volunteering. These names are integrated into the larger potential volunteer list and are marked with an asterisk. Typically, a study involving 35 or more interviews will produce a list of 70 or more respected community leaders. With a well-developed case for support, more than half of the interviewees will indicate possible volunteer involvement. Thus, the study will frequently include 17 to 23 names of people willing to serve marked with an asterisk. Even consultants who don't follow this protocol should be able to help the organization identify potential campaign leaders and volunteers.

Thus, when forming your steering committee or campaign cabinet, look to your board chair, current and past board members, precampaign planning study interviewees who indicated a willingness to serve, people who served on the facility planning committee, and people who served on the precampaign planning study working group. Have a small number of people, including the campaign consultant, review all the possibilities. Graciously recruit the 7 to 11 people who are best connected to your community's philanthropic leaders.

Quiet Phase Tasks

Some of the critical tasks that take place during the advancement phase include:

- Identify the organization's top prospects. Intensify prospect research and determine each prospect's capacity to support the campaign. Determine request amounts and gift opportunities for specific donors. (This is an extension of work begun prior to the interviews. Chapter 7, Exhibit 7.9, illustrates gift opportunities tied to specific prospects. This is a most important management tool to use throughout the campaign.)

- Recruit campaign leaders. First, get the steering committee in place. Later, in the quiet phase, the organization can recruit additional volunteers and create the entire structure for the intermediate and public phases.

- Reconcile project plans to financial projections as determined by the feasibility study. Reach agreement on the project budget, project phases, and fundraising goals.

- Revise the case statement based on suggestions from interviewees.

- Develop and refine campaign strategies, organization, plans, and timelines. Stress the importance of "sequential campaigns." Those closest to the project and those capable of lead gifts are solicited first.

- Adopt campaign policies and procedures. Policies should include: commitment period; gift acceptance policy, encompassing types of deferred gifts accepted for the endowment fund; campaign total reporting policies, including how deferred gifts are reported; naming opportunity policies; and other policies unique to the organization. Your consultant can help your organization develop these. Also, consider ordering the Counsel for Advancement and Support of Education (CASE) campaign standards. These can be purchased by visiting the CASE Web site, www.case.org.

- Refine your gift pyramid and assure that you have a sufficient number of gift opportunities that correspond to the various gift levels.
- Plan public relations activities and acknowledgment events.
- Produce brochures and other visual materials. (Don't go overboard too soon. Early on, professionally produced presentation folders and attractive word-processed materials are sufficient—although, a well-produced video or DVD can serve your organization well at this stage.)
- Conduct the board campaign. Secure multiyear commitments from 100 percent of the board members.
- Secure pacesetting leadership commitments.

The Board Campaign

The board of directors typically donates 15 percent or more of the capital campaign total. Some members of the board may be people of modest means; others may be affluent community leaders. All should donate generously relative to their own situation. If the organization has a particularly affluent and committed board, several of the lead gifts will come from board members.

The board campaign is important for a number of additional reasons. First, experienced community leaders expect the board to make early generous commitments. In part, they judge the seriousness of the appeal based on the organization's board members' commitments. Every capital campaign consultant has been asked, "How much has the board pledged? Do you have commitments from 100 percent of your board members?" Anticipate those questions. Let board members know that their gifts will inspire others.

A second, less frequently discussed, reason for placing importance on early board commitments is a practical matter relating to cash flow. Some significant expenses occur early in the campaign process. The precampaign planning study, support services, and materials development require early outlays, yet solicitations don't always begin right away. Rather, early months are devoted to volunteer recruitment, prospect identification, and leadership awareness activities. Even when the first pledges are secured, the funds might not flow to the organization immediately. A supporter who makes a three-year $150,000 commitment in April may not intend to make the first $50,000 contribution until December of that same year.

Perhaps the organization can handle the early capital campaign expenses from its operating surplus or operating funds. Perhaps the organization can borrow against early pledges. In other situations, the organization may receive a grant to cover some of the organizing expenses. And there are times when several board members get together to commit the funds needed to cover the precampaign planning study and the early months of the campaign.

An old saying has it that, "When the going gets tough, the tough get going." In board terms, this could translate, "When the cash gets tight, board members prepay their pledges."

So who conducts the board campaign? And what is the best way to approach board members?

Usually, the board chair, campaign chair, nonprofit CEO, and one or two generous board members conduct the board campaign. As always, the choice of the ideal solicitor is one based on chemistry and peer relationships. At a special meeting of the steering committee, board members should be rated as to capacity and request amount. Identify gift opportunities that correspond to each board member's interests and request amount. Decide which committee member or two-member team can follow up with a personal solicitation. To the extent possible, arrange in-person visits with each board member. Also, provide the staff and volunteer visitors with solicitation training.

Group solicitations at board meetings with letter and phone follow-ups are *not* the ideal way to approach board members. Group techniques tend to elicit somewhat smaller commitments than might have been secured with personal solicitations. A greater harm comes when board members' introduction to the capital campaign begins with letters, phone calls, and group appeals. During the campaign, when stress is placed on personal contact, board members recall how they were approached, and push for letters and phone calls, even when reminded that those approaches yield substandard results.

If organization leaders want board members to personally visit their prospects, they should model that behavior. Make every effort to personally visit *each* board member. Breakfasts and lunches work well. Meetings with individual board members and their spouses are also effective.

To reinforce the importance of 100 percent giving, a board campaign thermometer, like the one shown in Chapter 7, Exhibit 7.14, can be displayed at board meetings indicating what percentage of the board has made their commitments.

Lead Gift Cultivation and Solicitations

Members of the steering committee are responsible for nurturing relationships and soliciting approximately five prospective leadership donors each. Thus, the 7-to-11-person group of volunteers and key staff can manage a solicitation process for board members and approximately 35 to 55 top campaign prospects. Many of these will be well prepared for a visit because they were interviewed during the precampaign planning study. From these board members and prospects, the organization might expect to secure the 10 lead gifts that will account for 33 percent to 50 percent of the goal.

Relationship-building activities closely accompany or precede the actual solicitations. Breakfast briefings for businesspeople, focus groups, social/informative gatherings, and personal visits bring potential pacesetting donors closer to the nonprofit organization and its capital/endowment campaign.

During the advancement phase, the core group makes their initial approaches—most commonly, several in-person visits—to potential pacesetting donors. The early visits are informative. Frequently, volunteers might suggest gift levels to consider. They might say, "Later, when you have learned more about our organization and we have had an opportunity to answer all of your questions, we hope you might be in a position to consider one of our leadership-level gift opportunities." During preliminary cultivation meetings, volunteers do not push to close; rather, they inform and begin to set high expectations. Later visits are devoted to more detailed discussions of gift opportunities, pledge requests, pledge payment schedules, and other circumstances unique to the donor.

During the quiet phase, it is best to set high goals and expectations. Offer the organization's best prospects opportunities to make pacesetting leadership gifts. Encourage them to consider the top naming opportunities. Let them tell you what they wish to do. Don't listen to naysayers. Politely ignore committee or staff members who say, "Let's not ask that much." Or find gracious ways of raising their sights.

Throughout the quiet phase—and indeed throughout the entire campaign—provide solicitation training and role-playing opportunities, as described in Chapter 8. Complete the board campaign. Secure multiyear commitments from members of the steering committee. Revisit many of the people interviewed during the feasibility study. Also, seek pledges from key administrative staff. Secure pacesetting leadership gifts. Continue to host cultivation gatherings and expand the number of volunteers as you transition into the intermediate phase.

MEETINGS AND RECORD-KEEPING

As the organization transitions from the quiet phase to the intermediate phase, meetings and reports begin to take on a familiar flavor that carries on through the entire campaign. Common questions asked are:

- Who is on our prime prospect list?
- What is the appropriate gift amount to request from each top prospect?
- Which corresponding gift opportunity will appeal to the prospective supporter?
- Who will make up the ideal solicitation team? Who has the best chemistry?

- In addition to a financial commitment, might we ask this person to also serve as a campaign volunteer? Can the prospect help us by making three or more introductions for fundraising purposes?
- When might be the best time to solicit this contribution?
- Are there any cultivation gatherings to which we can invite the prospect? Or should we arrange a very personal briefing or luncheon with a top representative of the organization?
- If a team member has already visited the prospect, what happened and what should happen next?
- Summarizing our next steps, who is going to do what, by when?

These detailed conversations dominate nearly every capital campaign meeting. As a result, a great deal of data is generated concerning prospect identification, the prospect's relationship to the organization, request amounts, gift opportunities, cultivation strategies, and volunteer assignments. All of this information must be presented in a manner that facilitates the cultivation and solicitation process. Accurate note-taking is important. Careful data entry is essential. And the ability to generate understandable reports is crucial to the success of the campaign.

Some campaigners find ways to work with spreadsheets to maintain and report the information. Most find databases—especially dedicated fundraising software—more helpful. Usually, a campaign support staff person maintains the records and generates the reports. Every organization finds its own way to assure that accurate information is funneled to the support person. But suffice to say, someone should be responsible for taking notes at each meeting and getting that information to the data entry person. Moreover, volunteers and staff members are urged to report results of contacts to the campaign staff or volunteer leaders who assure that the information is also entered into the records. These latter "call reports" are frequently summarized and entered into the Comments field of the database.

Minutes that stress who is going to do what by when are more helpful than meeting notes that describe general discussions. "The committee then discussed solicitor assignments and follow-up steps" is not very useful information. Information that really makes capital campaigns work sounds more like this: "Zelda Goodoffices agreed to arrange a meeting with John and Mary Greatprospect to discuss their commitment. Zelda will go with our CEO and request a $150,000 commitment to name the boardroom. She will report the results of her contact at the next capital campaign meeting."

Minutes are just one way of presenting information. Computer-generated reports are also helpful. Lists can be sorted by request amounts. Early meetings are devoted to top prospects—those rated with the highest capacity. Lists can also be alphabetized. This helps campaign leaders quickly check on the status of any prospect. Alphabetized lists also help the campaign team know who is included in the universe of prospects. If the data entry routine includes next steps and to-do dates, lists can also be segmented on these dates. Thus, a campaign leader could have a printout of everything scheduled to be done during the next several weeks and could use this report to call all campaign workers and remind them to complete their tasks.

Suffice to say, every capital campaign professional has his or her favorite reports and method of monitoring campaign progress. All find it helpful to summarize campaign activities using a master prospect list, as illustrated in Exhibit 10.3. Equally important is the solicitor report (see Exhibit 10.4, "Sample Solicitor Report"). This report is printed with a page break after each solicitor's list of prospects. At least two sets of solicitor reports are generated. Each solicitor gets a copy of his or her individual report, showing who to contact and the status of each prospect. The other set is kept by a campaign leader, who calls each solicitor to discuss the assignments and to urge the campaign worker to complete the assigned tasks.

In addition to the solicitor assignment and prospect tracking information that commands most of the campaign workers' attention, other issues come up at meetings. From time to time—especially early in the campaign—committee members might discuss refinements to campaign materials. Policy clarifications might be needed. Orientation and training sessions need to be planned and scheduled. And during many meetings, some time is devoted to cultivation events. Common concerns are:

- Who was invited to each cultivation gathering?
- Who came?
- How did the presentation go? What can we do to make the presentation stronger?
- When and where is the next relationship-nurturing gathering?
- What steps can we take to increase attendance at this next social and informative happening? Can we arrange "warm and personal" invitation follow-up phone calls?
- Which of our prime prospects have not been invited to a cultivation event? Which intermediate phase or second-tier prospects should be invited to cultivation gatherings now? Who will be on the next invitation list?
- What will the invitation look like? When do the invitations have to go out?
- Who is responsible for food and other arrangements for the gathering? Who is responsible for planning and executing the presentation?

EXHIBIT 10.3   SAMPLE ANNOTATED MASTER PROSPECT LIST

INTERNATIONAL INSTITUTE OF ASIAN ARTS
ANNOTATED MASTER PROSPECT LIST

NAME/ COMMENTS	REQUEST AMOUNT	SOLICITOR	PLEDGE TOTAL
Greg Abler Comments: Greg is away from Santa Barbara until September, 2004. M. Bevins will contact him then and ask Greg to consider one of the $30K gift opps.	$30,000	M. Bevins	
Mr. & Mrs. Kevin Adams	Unrated	Unassigned	
Mr. & Mrs. David Albin Comments: A. Fieldhouse spoke to David and Lisa. They seem very interested in the new computer room for the visiting scholars ($150K). Follow-up visit scheduled 06/03/04.	$150,000	A. Fieldhouse	
Mr. & Mrs. George Barton	$3,000	D. Mumford	
Barbara Beason		C. Downey	$75,000
Mr. & Mrs. Arthur Camden Comments: Arthur and Mary attended the cultivation gathering at Jan and Stanley's house. They seemed very enthusiastic. Cleta should schedule an initial personal visit ASAP.	$15,000	C. Downey	
Carter Industries Comments: A. Fieldhouse met with Carter's CEO, Larry Waxman. He said that the corporation would make a commitment in October. Fieldhouse will call Larry in September and encourage him to be as generous as possible. Request $30K.	$30,000	A. Fieldhouse	
Dr. & Mrs. Edward Dees Comments: Aaron will talk to Ed and Susan about their choice of named gift opps.		A. Fieldhouse	$300,000
NOTE: In most capital campaigns, the nonprofit organization will have 300 to several thousand capital campaign prospects. The database also includes addresses, phone numbers, and other data.			
Mr. & Mrs. David Subia		D. Mumford	$15,000
Webster Corporation		F. Fine	$25,000
Xavier Foundation Comments: Application due November 1, 2004.	$500,000	(Staff)	
Mr. & Mrs. Andrew Young	$3,000	Unassigned	
Mr. & Mrs. Darrell Zachary	$1,500	Unassigned	

EXHIBIT 10.4   SAMPLE SOLICITOR REPORT

INTERNATIONAL INSTITUTE OF ASIAN ARTS
SAMPLE SOLICITOR ASSIGNMENTS REPORT

Solicitor: A. Fieldhouse

Prospects   **Pledge Amount**

Mr. and Mrs. David Albin 1946 Washington St. Santa Barbara, CA 93105 H: (805) 665-4394	PREVIOUS GIVING HISTORY: Total Previous Giving: $37,500 Most Recent Amount: $5,000 Most Recent Date: 03/27/03

Comments: A. Fieldhouse spoke to David and Lisa. They seem very interested in the new computer room for the visiting scholars ($150K). Follow-up visit scheduled 06/03/04.

Carter Industries 3009 Spruce St. Santa Barbara, CA 93106 W: (805) 798-5014	PREVIOUS GIVING HISTORY: Total Previous Giving: $17,500 Most Recent Amount: $2,500 Most Recent Date: 12/15/03

Comments: A. Fieldhouse met with Carter's CEO, Larry Waxman. He said that the corporation would make a commitment in October. Fieldhouse will call Larry in September and encourage him to be as generous as possible. Request $30K.

Dr. and Mrs. Edward Dees $300,000 1497 Madison St. Santa Barbara, CA 93104 H: (805) 837-4738 W: (805) 837-2938	PREVIOUS GIVING HISTORY: Total Previous Giving: $43,220 Most Recent Amount: $23,220 Most Recent Date: 11/15/2003

Comments: Aaron will talk to Ed and Susan about their choice of named gift opps.

Paul Gardner 5731 Main St. Santa Barbara, CA 93105 H: (805) 834-7234	PREVIOUS GIVING HISTORY: Total Previous Giving: Most Recent Amount: Most Recent Date:

Comments: Personal friend of A. Fieldhouse. Aaron will request $30K.

All of this is to say that capital campaign meetings are devoted to volunteer and prospect management, campaign policies and strategy, communications, and cultivation activities. Lots of talk gets the organization nowhere. Decision-making conversations concerning who does what by when make all the difference—especially when leaders decide who is going to ask which prospect for what financial commitment before our next meeting!

After all, the number-one reason people don't give is because they were not asked. Make sure that your meetings and reports keep campaign workers focused on their most essential tasks: getting appointments and urging prospects to make generous multiyear commitments.

THE INTERMEDIATE PHASE

Some overlap may occur with each campaign phase. At times the campaign's top prospects may still be considering their commitments when campaign workers move into the intermediate phase. All or most of the *initial* quiet phase contacts should have been made. However, campaign leaders need not wait until all commitments have been finalized before contacting the campaign's intermediate phase prospects. That said, all board members should have made their commitments.

Following the completion of the board campaign and initial contacts with prospective pacesetting contributors, volunteers (who now include generous supporters recruited during the advancement phase) may approach the organization's second tier of contributors. These prospects should have been invited to participate in cultivation activities during the advancement phase. So they know something about the capital and endowment campaign. In all probability, they are expecting a visit.

During this intermediate phase, the organization focuses on the following tasks:

- Develop more elaborate printed campaign materials.
- Intensify prospect identification and research activities.
- Recruit a broader base of volunteers. Provide orientation and training.
- Solicit what Kent Dove, in his book, *Conducting a Successful Capital Campaign, 2nd Edition* (Jossey-Bass Publishers, 2000), refers to as "special gifts," that is, the campaign's very generous second-tier prospects.
- Prepare grant applications. Staff members monitor deadlines and work to maximize application effectiveness based on timing and percentage of goal attained. This is especially important for challenge grants, such as The Kresge Foundation.
- Secure at least 50 percent of the capital and endowment campaign goal.
- To transition to the public phase, plan to stage a public announcement event. Consider going public with a kick-off extravaganza. Garner the maximum amount of publicity possible as the organization transitions into the public phase and the solicitation of the broadest base of prospects.
- Continue cultivation activities.

Be sure that the volunteers are well oriented and have received enough role-playing and training opportunities. At the same time, keep in mind the advice offered in Chapter 8: Don't overtrain. Help volunteers increase their comfort levels; don't overwhelm them.

By not going public prior to securing at least 50 percent of the goal, campaign leaders can adjust the goal based upon their ability to attract pacesetting commitments. Waiting until 50 percent of the goal is secured also inspires confidence. Momentum is established. Everyone feels like a winner. With such an approach, no one can doubt that the campaign will succeed.

THE PUBLIC PHASE

The public phase, or general phase as it is also called, is the capital campaign's most broad-based appeal. This is also the most visible part of the campaign. Publicity and communications are maintained at their maximum intensity. Campaign leaders give every potential supporter an opportunity to participate. Public phase tasks include:

- Recruit and activate a large pool of volunteers. Train and motivate volunteer solicitors.
- Continue and intensify the number of social and informative cultivation gatherings. Host numerous receptions for potential donors.
- Stage a public kick-off extravaganza early in the public phase if one has not already been held.
- Assure that training sessions have a social atmosphere. Maintain enthusiasm. Have fun. Keep everyone focused on face-to-face contact.
- Have regular reporting meetings to help assure that everyone completes their tasks.
- Mail and phone capital campaign prospects who could not be contacted in person.
- Plan and stage a victory celebration.

Note that the *only* time during the campaign that *might* include mail, phone solicitations, or "name-a-brick" campaigns is late in the public phase. Moreover, recognize this as a staff function. Volunteers should be encouraged to continue making personal contacts. Late in the campaign they might also wish to conduct group solicitations. In this latter case, volunteers invite groups of general phase prospects to gatherings at upscale homes or in motivational settings. Commitment forms and campaign materials are available. And presenters urge attendees to be as generous as possible and make their commitments at these gatherings.

Throughout the entire campaign, the chair and other leaders urge team members to stay focused on personal contacts. Their mantra is, "Take a rich person to lunch." Staff and volunteer leaders keep good records and continue to track assignments. They urge campaign workers to complete the follow-up visits generated by earlier contacts.

The steps just described lead the campaign inexorably toward its goal. When the goal is in sight, plan a victory celebration. At this most uplifting event, acknowledge and thank volunteers and supporters as generously as possible. Seek balance. Major donors should feel as important as the campaign workers. All should leave knowing that they played a major role in making a visionary project a reality!

PLEDGE FULFILLMENT AND FOLLOW-UP

Throughout the campaign, staff and volunteers stress the importance of multi-year pledges. At the conclusion of the campaign, the organization will have adequate cash and a healthy pledge balance. Some of the early supporters may have completed their pledge payments; others will continue making capital campaign pledge payments for an additional number of years.

With this in mind, campaign organizers must design activities that foster continuing positive relationships with campaign supporters and a thoughtful pledge fulfillment routine. People who sign commitment forms rarely renege on their commitments. Resource development professionals estimate that, on average, not more than 3 percent or 4 percent of the capital campaign pledge total is lost due to the donor's failure to make the pledged contributions. However, conservative accounting might suggest that the organization establish an account for unfulfilled pledges equaling 5 percent of the pledge balance.

Some attrition is unavoidable. Circumstances change. Supporters move and lose interest. Some might experience career setbacks. Backers become seriously ill. Donors die.

To minimize the expected pledge balance shrinkage, stay in touch with pledgers. Continue to make them feel important and appreciated. Begin by inviting all supporters to acknowledgment events. Celebrate the capital campaign victory soon after the campaign is completed. Later, be sure to include everyone with a pledge balance to a building opening or new facilities dedication ceremony.

The organization's business or development office has a responsibility to maintain accurate and up-to-date pledge payment information. Quality record-keeping begins by recording each supporter's pledge total, contributions to date, pledge balance, and expected payment schedule. Record the donor's preference for annual, semiannual, quarterly, or monthly pledge payments. Occasionally in church campaigns, some members of the congregation will make weekly pledge payments.

Send gracious reminders and return envelopes on a schedule determined by each supporter's preferences. Dedicated fundraising software makes this task easier. An alternative for small nonprofits is to send quarterly reminders to folks with a pledge balance. In any case, the reminder should note the pledge total, contributions to date, the resulting pledge balance, and the contribution amount that is due.

Professionals with fundraising responsibilities are careful not to neglect overdue pledge payments. They monitor reports of missed contributions. They respond in a timely fashion. At times, they might send a gracious second reminder. Experienced staff might personally contact the donor. In some cases, a personal visit might be in order. Resource development professionals know that if they wait too long, some donors will get further behind and not be able to fulfill their pledges. Given the opportunity to adjust the payment plan, most donors will fulfill their commitments.

In all cases, nonprofit leaders remain sensitive to the donor's unique circumstances. By remaining empathetic, nonprofit leaders enhance the institution's reputation in the community. Such an attitude is in the organization's long-term best interests. Every capital campaigner knows that the organization will have pressing facility needs in the future. As important, people working in the nonprofit sector want to respond to their supporters' concerns with compassion and understanding.

The nonprofit's pledge tracking system should also accommodate new or increased pledges. The intention is not to conduct a never-ending campaign. Well-designed capital campaigns have a beginning, middle, and conclusion. However, savvy capital campaigners know that new prospects who might emerge may be interested in any remaining gift opportunities. As important, campaign leaders can also approach their best and closest donors for increased or extended pledges. These selective and gracious requests result in the funds needed to cover any unforeseen expenses—and every capital project has some.

Also, print a list of all donors who made a single gift or a single-year commitment. Decide which donors to approach for additional capital campaign contributions. Some people are reluctant to make multiyear pledges. However, many respond positively to a gracious solicitation in the second and third years of the pledge payment period. Stress the importance of additional capital campaign contributions to meet the goal or for unanticipated expenses and enhancements to the facilities plan.

Use the pledge fulfillment period to strengthen the organization's ties to campaign supporters—especially new donors who previously had not fallen under the organization's sphere of influence. All capital campaign contributors and pledgers should receive timely news about the project, building progress, programs, and the people the campaign has helped. Personal contact will help cement these most important relationships. New capital campaign donors can be converted to long-term supporters.

BUILDING ENDOWMENTS

There are six ways of building an organization's endowment funds:

1. Establish an endowment and promote planned gifts for the fund.
2. Solicit current gifts on an ongoing basis for the endowment fund.
3. Include endowment fundraising as part of the capital campaign.
4. Conduct a strictly endowment campaign following the same principles used in a capital campaign.
5. Designate a portion of the organization's surplus to serve as "quasi" endowment funds. (Recognize that these undesignated funds are not accounted for as permanent endowment funds. What the board can do, the board can undo.)
6. Any combination of the five preceding techniques.

A simple way of getting started with the first strategy is to remind constituents to remember the organization in their wills and estate plans. Consistent reminders in newsletters and ongoing communications produce excellent results. Well-established organizations can further enhance their outcomes by investing in a more comprehensive charitable gift planning program.

To implement the second strategy—soliciting current gifts for the endowment fund—just ask. Consider special mailings. Or, better yet, take the organization's most generous supporters to lunch. Ask them to consider additional contributions to the endowment fund. Some might make a current gift. Others might consider a planned gift. Some might do both.

During the luncheon get-togethers, organization representatives thank donors for their generous support. When the subject turns to endowment, donors are surprised to realize that a contribution equaling 20 times the amount of their annual support can perpetuate their annual contributions. For example, a donor who contributes $1,000 annually may donate $20,000 to the endowment fund. Assuming a modest 5 percent yield, the endowment would produce $1,000 annually. If the yield is somewhat greater, the endowment will grow and help the organization respond to inflation.

The third strategy—the combined capital and endowment drive—is very common and is favored by thoughtful planners. Supporters of visionary building projects want to know that the nonprofit institution can maintain the facilities. As important, capital and endowment campaign contributors view their support as an investment. They know that endowment funds provide the long-term stability the institution needs to support its vital programs and services. In some institutions, endowment funds also serve other important purposes. Some endowments provide scholarships. Some subsidize services for low-income people. And many endowment funds augment the organization's general operating funds. All of these needs can easily be wrapped into a comprehensive capital and endowment campaign.

The fourth strategy—the purely endowment campaign—is somewhat less common. At times, foundations established to support a specific not-for-profit institution conduct endowment campaigns. By augmenting their endowment funds, these support foundations can help their mother institutions thrive and flourish. University foundations, hospital foundations, foundations in support of a specific religious denomination, and other support foundations more frequently conduct ongoing comprehensive fundraising activities. However, there are times when the need for endowment funds dominate the organization's thinking. At such times, the organization's closest supporters may respond favorably to an intensive endowment campaign.

One way endowment campaigns differ somewhat from capital campaigns is in the mix of current and deferred giving. In a purely capital campaign, the funds are needed within the three- to five-year pledge period to pay for construction, renovations, facilities, equipment, and furnishings. Architects and builders must be paid. Thus, the emphasis is on current multiyear pledges. Similarly, in a capital and endowment campaign, the organization must first secure the funds needed for the capital project. The endowment funds can be acquired in a mix of current and deferred giving. This is true for combined campaigns or for strictly endowment drives.

For example, a combined capital and endowment campaign might have a total goal of $30,000,000. Of this amount, $20 million could be dedicated to new and renovated facilities and furnishings. Of the remaining $10 million endowment goal, $5 million might be donated during the three- to five-year pledge period; the remaining $5 million would be committed in the form of "expectancies," that is, commitments made in the donors' wills and estate plans.

In the combined capital and endowment drive, several campaign management issues arise, including the following:

- Training sessions will need to cover the case for endowment funds as well as the need for capital funds. Some campaign workers will need specialized knowledge concerning charitable gift planning.
- The organization will need to pay special attention to deferred gifts record-keeping, for accounting purposes and for reporting campaign totals. More-

over, the organization must ensure that it has a system for monitoring long-term relationships with people who have remembered the institution in their estate plans.

- During the campaign, organizers will need to intensify prospect research and focus on each prospect's interests and level of involvement. Some might be offered an opportunity to make a capital and endowment gift. Others might be more interested in one or the other. Campaign visitors will need to be flexible in their approach. Careful research will help the organization narrow in on the gift opportunity likely to inspire the most generous commitment possible.

CAMPAIGN ORGANIZATION AND STRUCTURE

To succeed, capital campaigns need people—board members, fundraising staff, community volunteers, campaign consultants, and the organization's executive team. These campaign workers need to be organized and focused on the campaign. They zero in on identifying prospects, nurturing strong relationships, meeting in person with potential supporters, and offering them an opportunity to make generous commitments in support of the organization's visionary plans.

The organization pays special attention to prospects capable of making major gifts and pacesetting lead gifts. The organization assures that all potential major and special gift prospects are visited.

One general rule holds that nonprofits need one volunteer for every five prospects. Some volunteers can handle more; but five appears to be the ideal number. Volunteers who assume responsibility for too many prospects often don't make any appointments at all. They view the task of calling on numerous prospective supporters as onerous. This becomes a psychological block that cannot be overcome. With this in mind, some professionals recommend as few as three prospects for each volunteer. To be sure, if every volunteer secured three to five appointments, most campaigns would do very well indeed.

Another maxim holds that campaigns need at least three prospects for every gift the organization must secure. So if the gift pyramid indicates that the campaign requires 120 gifts to reach its goal, campaign workers must approach 360 prospective donors. Dividing 360 by 5, we soon conclude that we need at least 72 volunteers to complete the assignments. In a larger campaign requiring 1,000 capital campaign contributions, the organization would need to identify 3,000 prospects and would, in theory, also need to recruit and organize 600 volunteers.

To accomplish this Herculean task, the classic organization calls for a campaign chair, a capital campaign cabinet, an advance gift committee, a special gift committee, several division chairs, many team captains, and numerous volunteer solicitors (see Exhibit 10.5).

EXHIBIT 10.5   CLASSIC LARGE CAPITAL
CAMPAIGN STRUCTURE

Campaign Chairperson

Executive Director Consultant ———┐
and Development Staff ——————————┘   ├———————— Treasurer, Support, and Records
Campaign Cabinet: Advance Gift and Division Chairs
and Other Key Liaisons

Division 1	Division 2 Major Corporations	Division 3	Division 4 Major Individuals	Division 5	Division 6 Other Special Constituencies
Advance		General		Business	
Team Captains 1 2 3 4	Team Captains 1 2 3 4	Team Captains 1 2 3 4	Team Captains 1 2 3 4	Team Captains 1 2 3 4	Team Captains 1 2 3 4
Vols × 4	Vols × 4	Vols × 4	Vols × 4	Vols × 4	Vols × 4
1____	1____	1____	1____	1____	1____
2____	2____	2____	2____	2____	2____
3____	3____	3____	3____	3____	3____
4____	4____	4____	4____	4____	4____
5____	5____	5____	5____	5____	5____
6____	6____	6____	6____	6____	6____
7____	7____	7____	7____	7____	7____

The organization may be expanded regionally, by schools, or departments.

Each division chair helps recruit and solicit 4 to 5 team captains.

Assign 7 to 10 volunteers to each team captain. (The team captain should help recruit and solicit at least 5 of these volunteers.)

Have each volunteer select 4 to 5 prospective donors. The volunteers should be comfortable approaching their prospects.

Campaigns may be organized by regions, around major departments of the institution, or by donor type—affluent individuals, major corporate prospects, banking and financial institutions, and foundations. Alternatively, aspects of the campaign can be organized around the prospect's relationship to the institution— trustees, administration, staff, faculty, alumni, vendors, and so on. Without regard to the structure recommended, many campaign organizers begin with concern for the daunting task of recruiting a great number of campaign leaders and volunteers.

So much for theory. Let's get practical.

Campaign organizers should recruit as many volunteers as possible. They should also maintain their perspective. Most capital and endowment funds come from leadership gifts. The top 10 capital campaign commitments should account for one-third, one-half, or even more of the campaign total. Therefore, experienced capital campaigners concentrate their efforts on recruiting and organizing the top leadership for the campaign.

A number of factors reduce the need to recruit large numbers of volunteers for the intermediate and public phases.

- Although volunteers might help in nurturing relationships with family foundations, development staff assumes most of the responsibility for foundation relationships and grant applications.
- In many cases, the nonprofit CEO has the peer relationships needed to call on many of the prospects.
- One or more retired volunteers might accompany staff on numerous visits to prospects.
- During the public phase of the campaign, it is possible to solicit 10, 15, 20, or more prospective supporters at group gatherings.

This is not to say that your organization should not make every effort to recruit and organize the maximum number of volunteers possible. But do take comfort in the knowledge that in many campaigns a few key volunteers and staff raise the vast majority of the dollars pledged. If your organization cannot mount a classic campaign with numerous volunteers and hundreds or thousands of prospects, but can identify 50 to 100 leadership prospects capable of making six- and seven-figure contributions, by all means organize your campaign around thoughtful approaches to these few angels. Adopt a simple structure similar to the one illustrated in Exhibit 10.6.

VOLUNTEER RECRUITMENT

Chapter 3 provides advice concerning the recruitment of board members. The suggestions in that chapter also work well when recruiting capital campaign volunteers. The approach must be gracious. It is best to have a volunteer with a peer relationship make the approach. Teaming a volunteer with a key staff member works well. And the language suggested ("Adopt us," "I.M. Respected thought you would enjoy an opportunity to serve," "Help us put together the ideal team to accomplish this vision," etc.) is as helpful for recruiting capital campaign volunteers as it is for recruiting board members.

Recall the recommendation to consider recruiting people suggested during the precampaign planning study. People expanding the capital campaign volunteer pool do well to consider the names of potential leaders suggested by the interviewees. Of course, interviewees who expressed a willingness to serve are natural choices to help with the capital campaign.

Perhaps the most important sources of names to consider as campaign volun-

EXHIBIT 10.6   SIMPLE CAMPAIGN VOLUNTEER
STRUCTURE

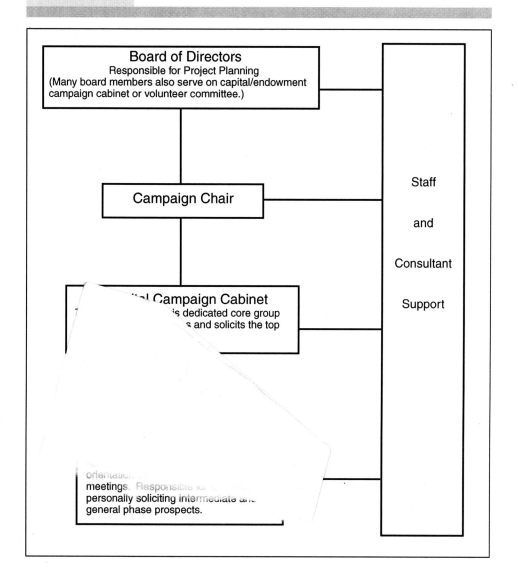

Board of Directors
Responsible for Project Planning
(Many board members also serve on capital/endowment
campaign cabinet or volunteer committee.)

Campaign Chair

Campaign Cabinet
's dedicated core group
s and solicits the top

orientation
meetings. Responsible to
personally soliciting intermediate and
general phase prospects.

Staff

and

Consultant

Support

teers are the organization's current list of top donors and the organization's top prospect list. These people are, by definition, generous people who have peer relationships with the community's philanthropic leaders. Look to these names first. Get them involved. Recruit them.

Often, relationship-nurturing activities precede the recruitment. And because volunteers are expected to donate prior to soliciting others, campaign leaders must clarify responsibilities during the recruitment—including the expectation of a generous campaign contribution.

CAMPAIGN TIMING

In every case, the campaign plan and volunteer structure reflects the sequential nature of the solicitations. The closest prospects with the greatest resources are solicited first. When the top prospects have been approached, and several pacesetting gifts have been secured, campaign leaders can begin to solicit the second-tier special gifts. Finally, the organization conducts the general or public phase of the campaign. An effective campaign is structured so that each subsequent gift level is solicited at the appropriate time by people with peer relationships to the prospects at each gift level.

Campaigns are prospect-driven. The volunteer structure and campaign timeline are determined by each organization's relationship to its pool of prospects.

Organizations that have long-term relationships with generous supporters have a good chance to secure one or more lead gifts—even before the campaign begins. It is not unusual to know of a $1 million or more lead gift at the time of the planning study. Such organizations begin with a significant portion of the

EXHIBIT 10.7 CAPITAL CAMPAIGN WITH A STRONG START (LEAD GIFTS COMMITTED PRIOR TO STUDY OR VERY SHORTLY THEREAFTER)

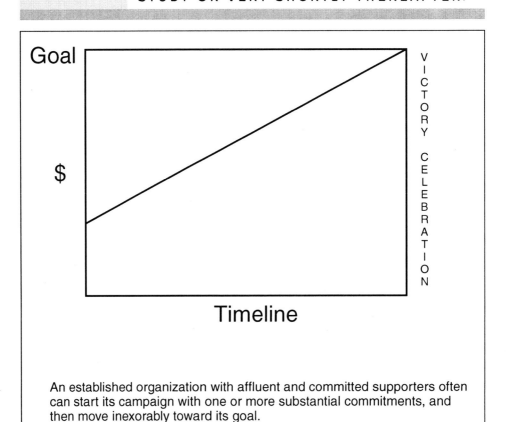

An established organization with affluent and committed supporters often can start its campaign with one or more substantial commitments, and then move inexorably toward its goal.

goal in place and then move steadily toward their goal. A graphic representation of such a campaign would look like Exhibit 10.7.

In contrast, some organizations *must* have a campaign, but have not yet formed close relationships with affluent prospects. In response, campaign leaders plan sufficient time for prospect identification and intensive cultivation activities prior to implementing the study. These relationship-nurturing activities continue during the quiet phase of the campaign. In such cases, leadership gifts might not be readily available. Campaign organizers can begin with the most generous commitments possible. Such a campaign will build slowly. After some time, a pacesetting commitment might be secured. Alternatively, a challenge grant might give the campaign its needed boost. A graphic representation of this model is shown in Exhibit 10.8. Note that campaign workers need to be patient

EXHIBIT 10.8   ALTERNATIVE TIMELINE

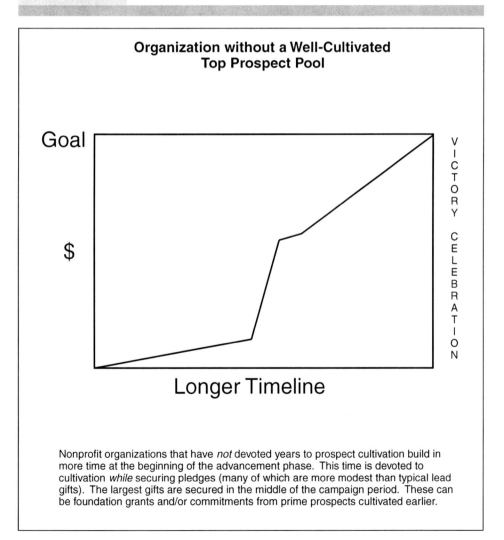

Organization without a Well-Cultivated Top Prospect Pool

Goal

$

Longer Timeline

VICTORY CELEBRATION

Nonprofit organizations that have *not* devoted years to prospect cultivation build in more time at the beginning of the advancement phase. This time is devoted to cultivation *while* securing pledges (many of which are more modest than typical lead gifts). The largest gifts are secured in the middle of the campaign period. These can be foundation grants and/or commitments from prime prospects cultivated earlier.

during the slow beginning. Momentum is easier after the lead gift has been secured.

In all cases, it is helpful to allow time for cultivation activities and for the prospects to come to their decisions. Remember that, on average, it takes 18 months from the time a major gift prospect first hears about a capital project to the time the prospective donor actually contributes.

With this sobering thought in mind, successful capital campaign organizers intensify prospect identification and targeted awareness programs as soon as the need for a capital campaign becomes known. Organizers uncover their top prospects early on and immediately begin to nurture positive relationships with each prospect. Early cultivation is the critical success factor in all campaign timing decisions.

CHAPTER 11

Grants and Government Funding

When volunteer campaign leaders first contemplate the need for pacesetting leadership gifts, they often turn their attention to corporate contributions, foundation grants, and public funding. In response, some campaign consultants are quick to remind volunteer campaign leaders that approximately 84 percent of all philanthropy comes from *individuals.*

There is some right and wrong in both the volunteer and consultant responses to the need for large gifts. Volunteers frequently underestimate the generosity of individuals. Some can't imagine that many individuals can and will gladly donate $100,000, $1 million, or more to a capital campaign. And while most consultants are realistic concerning corporate and foundation giving, they often are not experienced in garnering public support. Because public support is not considered part of philanthropic fundraising, this possibility may be neglected.

Moreover, many volunteers overestimate the importance of corporate and foundation gifts. They imagine *numerous* six- and seven-figure commitments from corporations and foundations that rarely consider capital campaign contributions in excess of $25,000 or $50,000.

This is not to say that some corporations and foundations won't consider contributions of $100,000, $1 million, or more for a capital campaign. Some do. But campaign organizers need to be realistic. The corporate or foundation decision makers must have a strong interest in the project. And to be considered a true prospect for a pacesetting gift, the corporation or foundation should have a history of making capital campaign commitments at the required levels. As always, research is the key to thoughtful assessments.

CORPORATE SUPPORT

Support for capital campaigns and comprehensive campaigns that include capital, annual, and endowment components can take many forms. Corporations can be encouraged to consider the following: annual support through donor recognition programs, equipment underwriting, capital and/or endowment contributions, sponsorships of special events or performances, purchase of tickets for special-event fundraisers, underwriting of seminars or special projects, in-kind donations, and volunteer support.

Corporate support can come from pretax corporate income (outright gifts), the corporate advertising and marketing budget (sponsorships), corporate matching gift funds, and from corporate foundations.

A comprehensive approach can encompass all these sources of funding. The overriding principle, however, can be summed up in that old fundraising axiom, "Successful fundraising is the right prospect being asked for the right amount for the right project by the right solicitor at the right time in the right way."

The nonprofit organization's approach should be prospect-oriented. Staff research and volunteer input will help determine the following:

- The appropriate amount to request from the corporation's decision makers
- The project or gift opportunity most likely to appeal to the prospective donor
- The volunteer solicitor most likely to elicit a positive response

Volunteers with peer relationships in the business community are central to the nonprofit organization's success. Such volunteers can help the nonprofit organization get business leaders involved with the capital campaign.

To garner ongoing operating support, many nonprofit organizations establish corporate "gift clubs" with appropriate donor benefits. A comprehensive approach will make use of these gift clubs *and* highly targeted solicitations for capital and endowment gifts. At all times, the nonprofit organization's representatives listen carefully to the corporate leaders to determine which sponsorship or gift opportunities most appeal to each corporation.

In simple form, here is how the program might work: Volunteers and staff working together help determine a challenging, yet feasible, request amount for each corporate prospect. Following this determination, campaign organizers can match the request amount with an appropriate named gift opportunity. The staff then personalizes presentation materials geared to that specific request. Staff working with volunteers visit the corporate decision makers and conduct the solicitation interview. Pledges are graciously acknowledged and staff helps assure that all donor benefits are delivered as promised.

Many of the requests for funds will require more than one visit. During the preliminary visit, the campaign team can discuss a range of potential projects. Volunteers and staff can help keep these initial contacts focused on named gift opportunities or gift clubs in the corporation's capacity range. Another important early message to regular contributors is that the nonprofit organization needs and appreciates the corporation's continued ongoing support. As always, capital campaign contributions are *in addition to* annual support.

Moreover, nonprofit representatives can use the initial meeting to discuss the possibility of using corporate marketing or advertising funds for a sponsorship. In cases where the corporation makes grants through a foundation, the initial visit with the local executive can be used to elicit support and advice concerning the corporate foundation.

If the corporation has a foundation, obtain and carefully read all available guidelines. Also keep the local managers informed about your proposal and application. Don't be intimidated by the process. Compared to many foundation processes and government grants, most corporate foundation proposals are relatively short and simple. The keys to success are support from the highest local corporate executive and clearly stated objectives that benefit the community.

Cultivation of Corporate Decision Makers

Every nonprofit organization can develop a simple-to-administer cultivation and leadership awareness program geared to its local and regional business community. Cultivation activities described in Chapter 6 make as much sense for corporate leaders as they do for individuals.

Too frequently, relationship-nurturing strategies are an afterthought to the development effort. Nonprofit organizations planning capital campaigns can strengthen their ties to the business community by proactively scheduling cultivation activities geared to business leaders. Volunteers and staff should track information concerning who has been invited to which gatherings, who came, and their reactions to the proposed capital campaign.

The most effective way to assure continued support from the organization's corporate donors is to promptly and appropriately express gratitude for the corporation's investment in the organization. All prospective corporate donors should also be thanked for the time they took to meet with the nonprofit's volunteers and staff. This should be done whether the solicitation resulted in a pledge or not. Of course, pledges and contributions should be thanked within 48 hours of the date of the commitment.

The nonprofit organization's aim is to design and administer an acknowledgment program with consistent, yet flexible, donor benefits. In order to appeal to each corporation's interests and giving capacity, campaign organizers can create a wide range of gift opportunities. When designing named gift opportunities, look closely at all the main architectural features of the project. Also consider attractive donor acknowledgment walls and prominent displays in busy public spaces, such as lobbies and main corridors.

Of course, the ultimate achievement in prospect cultivation is to recruit the decision maker for a leadership role in the capital campaign. Campaign leaders who are also corporate executives frequently use their influence within their companies to motivate large commitments. They also have the peer relationships needed to garner additional generous support from other companies.

FOUNDATION SUPPORT

Information about foundations can be obtained from the Foundation Center and its cooperating collections in each state. (Note: To find the closest cooperating collection, visit the Foundation Center's Web site, www.fdncenter.org.) A number of fee-based foundation databases are also available.

The aim of the research is to uncover foundations that provide capital campaign support. To be a viable prospect, the foundation must also make grants in your nonprofit's geographic area and for its purpose. A foundation that supports capital projects for education institutions in Pennsylvania is not necessarily a prospect for a medical facility in Alabama.

To remain realistic, you must read the guidelines and examine the foundation's giving history. Some foundations provide grants on a regional basis. For example, the J.E. & L.E. Mabee Foundation in Tulsa, Oklahoma, provides capital funding for nonprofit institutions in Arkansas, Kansas, Missouri, Oklahoma, New Mexico, and Texas. Many foundations support only local projects. Some limit themselves to one or two categories of nonprofit organizations. And many exclude capital and endowment projects.

When researchers gain access to the Foundation Center database, they can download information, including: guidelines, grant history, contacts, foundation priorities, and application instructions. Carefully note the range of grants that the foundation has made. Note both the purpose of the grant and the dollar amount committed. Know the low, high, and middle ranges for capital campaign contributions. Common sense tells us that the organization is most likely to succeed when it applies for grants in the foundation's middle to high range. Organizations with visionary projects may consider applying for grants slightly above the foundation's usual range.

In some cases, foundation program officers provide advice concerning the amount to apply for and the application process. In other situations, the foundation may be small and understaffed. Such foundations often state that calls and inquiries are not welcome. Again, it pays to read the application guidelines carefully.

Some people seem to think that there is a secret language that only grant writers know. Not true. The reality is that grant reviewers are looking for straightforward and clear answers to their questions. Foundations may require answers to any or all of the following:

- What is your organization's history and record of accomplishments?
- Describe your organization's mission.
- What need do you serve?
- What other organizations are working on this problem and how are you collaborating with them?
- What populations do you serve?
- What challenges or problems must your organization overcome?
- What are your facility and endowment needs?
- How will the institution's facility plans support the organization's goals?
- What grant amount is the organization requesting?
- What other support has the organization garnered?
- How will the foundation grant be used?
- How will you evaluate the success of this project?

People who can write clear answers to those questions and put together realistic budget projections can do well in the foundation arena. But it is prudent to keep in mind that all foundations receive far more requests for funding than they can accommodate.

THE KRESGE FOUNDATION

Tax-exempt, nonprofit organizations—including higher-education institutions, healthcare institutions, human service agencies, science and environmental organizations, arts and humanities institutions, and public affairs organizations—may apply to The Kresge Foundation for capital campaign challenge grants. The Kresge Foundation funds projects across the entire United States and, at times, internationally. According to the foundation's guidelines, "Religious organizations, elementary and secondary schools, community colleges, private foundations, and individuals are not eligible to apply." There are a few exceptions to the eligibility requirements, so potential applicants should carefully read the material provided by The Kresge Foundation and call or write for clarification if any questions arise.

Complete contact information can be found on The Kresge Foundation Web site, www.kresge.org. The information there is very detailed. So for up-to-date, complete, and accurate information, you are strongly advised to visit the site and read the contents carefully. Here are a few of the highlights:

- The Kresge Foundation challenge grants can be used for construction, renovation, purchase of major equipment, and purchase of real estate.
- The Kresge Foundation is motivated by strong projects that also increase the organization's fundraising capacity. The challenge grants are designed to

stimulate new gifts and increased giving from previous donors. In short, The Kresge Foundation believes that a successful capital program "leaves in its wake a stronger board and a giving capacity that is broader and deeper."

- The applicant organization proposes a deadline for raising all of the funds needed to complete the project and meet the challenge. The challenge period is typically at least 6 months but not more than 18 months from the date of the foundation's decision.

- The Kresge Foundation tends to favor visionary projects with total fundraising goals *greater* than $750,000.

- The Kresge Foundation expects strong board giving.

- In general terms, "at least 20 percent and sometimes as much as 50 percent of your project fundraising goal should be raised before applying to the foundation." More recently, The Kresge Foundation has stressed the 50 percent requirement.

- Competitive proposals to The Kresge Foundation request grants ranging from one-fifth to one-third of the balance that must be raised. Many recent grants have ranged between $150,000 and $600,000.

- The review process takes four to six months.

- The Kresge Foundation is pleased to meet or speak with applicants prior to the proposal submission. However, appointments should be made weeks in advance.

- The project planning should be fairly far along. Schematic drawings would be a minimal requirement. Design work or construction documents lead to more accurate project cost estimates.

- The application includes a cover letter, fact sheet (available on the Web site), and a narrative statement containing organizational information, project information, and fundraising information.

The Kresge Foundation challenge grants are important components of many capital campaigns. Frequently, the final dollars raised from the organization's broad base of supporters are the most difficult funds to raise. To overcome this obstacle, The Kresge Foundation challenge grants are designed to inspire a large number of modest and generous gifts from the organization's expanding cadre of supporters.

GOVERNMENT FUNDING

Grants from city, state, and federal government sources are not typically included in capital campaign goals. However, such funding is often an important part of the total capital budget. Government funding may be a component in meeting project costs for The Kresge Foundation grant process. In such cases, "significant government grants should be committed prior to making an application . . ."

Capital campaigns focus on philanthropic fundraising. Government funding is often classified as "contract income" because, despite some political rhetoric, government agencies *don't give away money*. They *purchase services* for the common good.

Without regard to how the organization classifies its income, government funding can, at times, contribute to the overall capital project. City, county, and state agencies may provide funds for the capital project—especially if the nonprofit agency is a regular recipient of government funding and provides ongoing community services. However, laws and customs vary greatly. Still, it pays to stay close to the community's political leaders, elected officials, and government employees. They can be invited to annual dinners and other cultivation gatherings. The nonprofit organization's executives and program officers also should meet frequently with them to seek advice and to update them on the organization's progress.

In general, elected officials and government employees should not be recruited to serve on the capital campaign volunteer committee. Elected officials tend to use their relationships to raise political campaign contributions. And ethical government employees work to avoid even the appearance of an impropriety in their granting processes. Consequently, service on the nonprofit organization's board or capital campaign committee can be awkward if the organization wants to receive government funding.

In addition to local funding, nonprofit organizations should investigate the possibility of federal funding. The federal government of the United States of America is the largest source of grant funds in the world, and some of those grants can be used for capital projects.

The federal budget is immense and complex. Members of the congressional delegation from each state can help nonprofit institutions uncover possible sources of capital funds. At times, an influential United States senator or representative can even help the organization get support for a specific capital project.

Nonprofit agencies that have been awarded past grants from the government agency often receive requests for proposals (RFPs) directly from the agency. Similarly, nonprofit organizations can request to be placed on the government agency's list of RFP recipients. Information about federal government grants can also be found by exploring the "Catalog of Federal Domestic Assistance." To get a sense of the range of grants and capital funding possible, nonprofit leaders can explore this invaluable resource at the General Services Administration (GSA) Web site, www.gsa.gov. Click on Catalog of Federal Domestic Assistance and the world of federal grants will open up to you. The Web site even has helpful information about identifying funding resources and developing grant proposals.

Many federal programs are administered through state and local government agencies or departments. This is another reason that nonprofit leaders should maintain positive and professional relationships with local officials and program administrators. These officials can help identify funding sources, and might also help assure the success of the application. It never hurts to have a champion within the agency.

LOBBYING

At times, nonprofit leaders manage to lobby successfully for appropriations for their organization's capital projects. Again, laws vary from city to city, county to county, and state to state. Moreover, the possibility of federal appropriations (as opposed to competitive grant applications) varies greatly depending upon the nature of the nonprofit organization and the clout of its congressional delegation.

Despite all the obstacles, persistence and patience can produce positive results. While whole books have been written on this subject, a few general principles might serve as a guide. These include:

- *Bring something to the table.* Nonprofit organizations have something that almost every political leader wants: access to the community's opinion leaders and power structure. Introduce state legislators and other political leaders to the nonprofit organization's board of directors and affluent contributors. Invite the legislators to small gatherings where they will meet *their* potential future backers. Be generous in acknowledging the political support the organization does receive.

- *Make a strong case.* Be brief. Be able to tell any political leader you meet your organization's strongest points in the shortest amount of time. Tip O'Neill popularized the phrase, "All politics is local." Let political leaders know how your capital project will benefit their constituents.

- *Recognize that all legislative bodies have relatively few key decision makers.* As with capital fundraising, political lobbying should be highly targeted. The nonprofit organization need not work to influence each and every legislator. Learn who chairs the key committees that will review your appropriation. Find influential people from their districts to go with the nonprofit representatives when calling on these legislative leaders.

- *Ask questions.* Seek advice from the political leaders closest to your organization. Ask: What funding sources might be possible? What should we do to help guarantee success? Whose support is needed? Should we try to gain bipartisan support? When is the best time to move forward with this project? What advice do you have to offer?

- *Be reliable.* Politicians have long memories. Always be truthful in your claims. Convey accurate information. Keep all your promises and commitments. Be a person of your word.
- *Seek firm commitments.* Some political leaders find it easy to remain generally supportive but uncommitted. Many make vaguely helpful affirmations and tell constituents that they like their programs. However, nonprofit leaders need to know if the person they are talking to will really champion their cause. Can they be counted on to vote for an appropriation? Will they use their clout to muster support for the project? You can be gracious and still get answers to these most important questions.

In conclusion, nonprofit leaders should show the same care in all of their dealings with political leaders, elected officials, and program administrators as they do with the capital campaign's top prospects. At times, government funding might exceed private sector donations. The cautionary note is to be sure to get a realistic appraisal of the nonprofit organization's odds of receiving such funding.

Another source of public funding is the dedicated *mill levy.* In the following section, Dale Dekker and Patricia Branda describe the key success factors in a mill levy campaign. Note the close relationship to the prerequisites for a successful capital campaign. Also note that while this discussion deals specifically with a school fund, others can employ the same principles in garnering support for their nonprofit organization—especially when the organization is a governmental or publicly funded institution.

SIDEBAR   DALE R. DEKKER, AIA, AICP, ASID, AND PATRICIA BRANDA, MPA

ROAD TO A SUCCESSFUL MILL LEVY CAMPAIGN

Capital improvement funding for public education is at a critical stage. Pick up an educational newspaper or journal or talk with school board members or administrators from most school districts and you are likely to read or hear about lack of money for schools. It is becoming more difficult to maintain educational and programmatic budgets. There is a trend nationwide to reduce maintenance and operation budgets in an effort to save instructional programs. In many school districts, facilities and equipment are aging, and today's deferred maintenance items will be tomorrow's capital improvements.

Not only are school facilities "wearing out," but these facilities must be changed to accommodate the restructuring of curriculum and instruction. The schools built for the baby boomers in the late '50s and '60s were designed around a curriculum and pupil-teacher ratio (PTR) that physically shaped school design. Today, with new technologies, new curricula standards, lower pupil-teacher ratio requirements, enhanced special education programs, and new teaching methodologies, school facilities are in need of being "restructured" to support the educational goals of the school district, instead of "structuring" the educational program around a district's existing facilities.

In recent years, greater collaboration with other organizations has resulted in schools taking on a more important role within a community. Schools are expanding to include before- and after-school programs for children, and activity centers for adults and neighborhoods. Schools are also joining with other private and public human service providers to address specific community social needs. Joint-use opportunities with other public/ private entities could impact (and ultimately help fund) the types of spaces and programs offered by our public schools.

Even with this potential help from other groups, it is likely capital improvement needs will always be greater than the available financial resources, with equity being an important issue. In the past, capital improvement funding has been a major political football in many school districts. Some individual schools within a school district have strong, vocal parent constituents who can put tremendous pressure on both school boards and on administrations. This can influence capital funding priorities.

There is no doubt that, beyond local constituencies, public education exists in a political environment. Public school districts have to respond to and conform to both national and state mandates. Usually, mandates which lower PTR's and increase the need for more classrooms are not supported with additional capital funding; this places the school district in the position of having to do more with less.

Combine all of the preceding factors in an uncertain economic climate and a conservative "taxing" environment and then try to sell an increase in property taxes to the voters!

Several years ago, Albuquerque Public Schools (APS) did try to sell an increase in property tax to the voters. We asked voters for additional money for school facilities and, for the first time, they said no. "Business as usual" was no longer an effective way to get things done. We needed to develop a new strategy.

STRATEGY FOR SUCCESS

We realized a comprehensive and broad-based approach is necessary to effectively gain support for capital improvement needs. An important tool in articulating these needs is a Facilities Master Plan—the road map defining the capital improvement's direction, needs, and opportunities within the district. For this plan to be successful and to be able to gather support for necessary elections, it must have support of people who trust the plan, the way it will be conducted. To establish this trust, critical elements must be recognized in preparing a successful facilities plan and ultimately presenting a Capital Improvement Plan (CIP) "package" to the voters.

1. *Facts.* Develop a sound base of information relative to existing facilities' conditions and relative to the history of utilization, construction, and maintenance of school facilities.

2. *Goals and objectives.* Clearly define what the instructional and curriculum goals are for the district and what impact these goals and objectives will have on each individual school.

3. *Growth.* Provide short-range and long-range enrollment projections for each school.

4. *Establish funding priorities.* Develop a process that most adequately addresses the health/safety, physical condition, and educational/instructional facility needs of each individual school within a district.

5. *Involvement and communication.* Involve and provide the framework for active participation of parents, teachers, staff, students, board members, and other key individuals in the planning process. Promote an open, collaborative, participatory planning environment in developing the district's broad goals and objectives as they relate to facilities.

6. *Resources.* Effectively utilize the human and professional resources already available within the school district, particularly in the facilities and curriculum department. These individuals are the key to creating the vision, promoting the need, and informing the voters.

7. *Accountability.* Within the planning framework, document and be prepared to substantiate all proposed capital improvements in relationship to cost/benefit from a facility point of view and cost/benefit from an educational/instructional point of view.

This planning effort describes a process that ultimately provides the foundation for a school system's capital program.

Selling Your Needs to the Voters

So a plan has been developed. Now what? The Facilities Master Plan outlines facility needs. It is the foundation for the package that must receive voter approval. But how are taxpayers convinced? For our Mill Levy Extension—just two years after the defeated proposed levy—which would generate $125 million over a five-year period, we developed a successful campaign strategy utilizing some key elements.

1. *Facilities plan.* The document and plan that identifies the needs, establishes the cost, and provides for community participation and involvement in the planning process. The plan must be judged as having thoroughly, equitably, and objectively analyzed the needs of the district.

2. *Equity.* From a funding and a constituency point of view, the facilities plan must be viewed today, as well as in the future, as a plan and a process that equitably and consistently applies the same criteria to all schools. It must also be viewed as accomplishing this using the available resources in the best way possible.

3. *Polling.* The polling of voters and a clear understanding of how the voters are thinking become essential in developing a successful campaigning strategy.

4. *Authority.* It is important to vest in one key individual within the district the responsibility for disseminating information to the community regarding the needs of the district.

5. *Funding options.* The exploration of all available funding options, or combinations of options (bond issues, state funds, emergency capital outlays, etc.), is necessary to develop the best package for the available anticipated revenues.

6. *Business/community involvement.* Developing broad-based support and awareness of the facts and issues from within the business community and the school communities is critical to a campaign's success.

7. *Focus on children.* Efforts and taxes will benefit children through enhanced learning environments, current technologies, and curriculum opportunities; therefore, the focus of the campaign must be kept on the children.

8. *Campaign.* Asking for taxpayer resources in support of a district's needs is a political campaign; therefore, organize, communicate effectively to the voter, and, above all, develop a strategy that wins!

Through our involvement and participation in a Capital Improvement Plan for the Albuquerque Public Schools, and through our experience with a successful mill levy extension, following a failure two years before, we learned a comprehensive and broad-based approach is absolutely necessary to effectively gain support for the needs of our students.

Printed with permission from Dale R. Dekker, Dekker/Perich/Sabatini, and Patricia Branda.

The preceding section dealt with ways of assuring a broad base of support for a mill levy election. Campaign organizers also work to garner support from as many donors as possible during the public phase of the capital campaign. Remember, however, that success in capital projects requires focus. Leaders of nonprofit organizations should adopt a rifle fire rather than a shotgun approach. Target your most intense efforts and personal communications toward the individuals, corporate executives, foundation officers, decision-makers, and opinion leaders who will assure the success of the campaign. Genuine and warm relationships precede major commitments.

CHAPTER 12

Churches and Faith-Based Institutions

In the first section in this chapter, Robert Habiger describes the six elements required for a successful building planning process for church congregations. This discussion was originally written for the *Environment and Art Letter*, a publication of the Archdiocese of Chicago. And though it was directed to a Catholic audience, and especially for people interested in a liturgical point of view, the process described contains lessons for people of all faiths. As important, his advice concerning "fostering ownership" holds true for all projects. People involved in secular projects can interpret Mr. Habiger's remarks about "spiritual formation" as a call for rededication to the organization's mission.

SIDEBAR

ROBERT D. HABIGER, AIA

FOSTERING OWNERSHIP OF THE BUILDING PROJECT

When a building committee is formed to lead a congregation in the construction or renovation of a place for worship, it is asked to make many critical decisions rapidly. While it is often necessary to proceed quickly, doing so increases the likelihood of discord among parishioners. R.D. Habiger & Associates has found that for a process to be successful, six elements are needed. If any one element is missing, the potential exists for conflict and a struggle for control to the detriment of churchwide ownership of the project. The six elements are a sense of purpose, spiritual formation, training, organization, a planned design process, and measurable results.

A SENSE OF PURPOSE

Just as a person asks, "What is my purpose and what guides me?" so must every project. Obviously, the purpose of a church renovation or construction project is to create a new place for worship. But the process is as important as the product. Successful church projects are grounded in and guided by Christian values. Everyone involved needs to value and practice commitment, integrity, honesty, trust, openness, confidence, and community. The practice of these values helps the parish and the professionals develop a partnership around the design table.

SPIRITUAL FORMATION

The process of building or renovating a place of worship is first and foremost a spiritual opportunity. Not only does a building or a room take shape, but a community of people also is formed. Exploration of the demands that liturgy makes on architecture—the questions of how and why we worship—allows us to reflect on God's presence in our life as a community and our lives as individuals. The nature of church construction or a renovation project requires more than simply starting and ending each meeting with a prayer. It requires that the entire process be conducted as a ritual that acknowledges the sacramental character of the world, the goodness of historical change, and the richness of God's gifts to us. Making the decision to embrace the bricks-and-mortar task as an opportunity for spiritual growth allows new and deeper relationships to flourish among participants.

TRAINING

It is unrealistic to expect that the people who serve on a parish building or renovation committee will know everything necessary for the process. In addition, as the committee is required to work together over a long period of time, it is critical that committee members understand each other's gifts and way of thinking. Internal training is necessary. Often the best approach is to utilize the liturgical design consultant as a facilitator in developing the knowledge of the committee and its working relationship.

ORGANIZATION

The buzzwords now popularly used to describe an appropriate process for church construction or renovation are *collaboration* and *consensus*. Collaboration is sharing of information so as to identify the single best solution for a current problem. Consensus is achieving an understanding that everyone can live with and determining whether anyone is uncomfortable or in disagreement with the proposed issue before moving forward. Without the right organizational structure, however, all the talk of collaboration and consensus will be for naught.

A construction or renovation process that is organized to facilitate open communications is a must. Three important groups are necessary. First is the building committee. It is directly responsible to the parish pastoral council and the diocese. Along with the liturgical design consultant, architect, contractor, and pastor, the building committee forms the design team. It makes the decisions that lead to the completion of the project.

Next, specific task forces focus on particular areas of concern for the project. For example, if a new organ is part of the plan, the organ task force would do the research and make recommendations to the building committee concerning the type of organ and purchase options. The task force stays in existence for a predetermined time span, long enough to research properly a question or issue.

To represent the church community, groups convened as advisors may be invited to participate in a selected number of sessions to review and comment on each major step in the process. The advisors meet to clarify and affirm what is being proposed by the design team. They should represent all ages, experiences, and groups of the church. For a 2000-household church, we would recommend a goal of involving 125 advisors.

The flow of information is from task force to design team to advisors for review and then back to building committee for final decisions. We recommend that the pastor be part of the design team. However, we encourage using the building committee as the final forum for consensus. It destroys the action of collaboration if the final word comes from the pastor. He is most appropriately one party to a team decision.

PLANNING THE DESIGN

The places in which we gather to give praise and glory to God have a profound effect on our lives. Some places of worship give us a greater sense of wonder, awe, and reverence than others. Understanding how a place of worship can reveal meaning or cause disappointment is critical in the planning and design of any place of worship.

Planning and design must focus on why certain places give a more powerful experience of the sacred than other places: What is it about scale and proportion, the use of light and shadow, the use of height and depth, the use of natural materials, and human technology and artistry that evokes the presence of the holy and invites sacred action? Not asking such questions has led to the multiplicity of places for worship that disrespect architectural symbolism and the bodily senses, and give disheartened meanings to worship. Three basic points can be made about design.

First, the environment must be appropriate to the *ritual actions* in houses. The environment for worship is first and foremost a place for corporate action. It is a place for a community to be "gathered together in one place," as the second chapter of the Acts of the Apostles emphasizes. The place for worship must have integrity and unity so as to feel complete when the assembly gathers. It should be inviting, comfortable, and hospitable.

How we place the seating, other furniture, and works of art is critical, not coincidental.

Second, the space must be designed to promote a specific kind of action: *encounter*. An encounter between persons involves the whole person. The space must help delight the senses of sight, touch, smell, taste, and hearing. The use of materials and a seating organization that encourages congregational singing is but one example of how vital the notion of encounter is to Christian worship. Lighting is equally important, not only for visibility, but also for atmosphere and beauty. Genuine encounter— between God and individual persons, between God and a community, and among the members of the community—stimulates participation in worship.

Third, a place for worship must exude the *mystery* of divine-human and human-human encounter. The design must strive to express God's presence in our lives and in the wider creation. A sense of the sacred is expressed best through a sensitive use of symbol. While we cannot accurately image God, we can embody in symbol and in sign the divine love, mercy, and goodness in our lives. A place that reflects a living tradition, that embodies the contemporary understanding of church and that provides a vision of our future in God is the goal. . . . This is how places of worship are said to be "timeless"—not unchanging and unchanged, but transcending all fads and trends and touching something genuine.

MEASURABLE RESULTS

For a successful construction or renovation project—pastorally, architecturally, even financially—measurable results are invaluable. While it is easy to say the result will be the renovated interior or new construction itself, it is wrong to assume that the product is less important than each intermediate step in the process. Having smaller goals within the process minimizes the pressure placed on attaining the larger goal. And advancing through a process step by step helps overcome the natural tendency to resist change.

Such measurable results include the completion of a renovation plan or master plan showing the steps to be taken over the next few years. It can include the completion of fundraising for this project, an educational program, the completion of schematic designs, the bidding phase, the construction phase, and the rite of dedication, or commissioning of new artwork. It is important to put together a set of milestones and articulate steps to be taken toward the completion of each one. Not only does this give substance to the ongoing process, it also diminishes the opportunity for dissent because you can show that you are on track to the final goal: completion of the renovation or new construction.

Like ingredients in a recipe, these six key elements are necessary for a successful pastoral building or renovation process. And similar to the way gourmet cooks deviate from a published recipe, following their intuitions and relying on their skills and materials to enrich the flavor, so too we find that each church community will require different proportions of these essential elements. As you move toward implementing your renovation or construct plan, don't forget to have the building committee "taste the mix" in its current state, adjusting the original recipe to correct the flavor. For what is at stake here is a process that will sweeten the church's life or sour it, and a product—the place for worship—that will nourish or starve this generation and generations to come.

Printed with permission from Robert D. Habiger and the *Environment and Art Letter,* a publication of the Archdiocese of Chicago.

NOTE

In his remarks Mr. Habiger spoke eloquently about fostering ownership for the church project. Robert's ideas are central to building project success. In the following sections, I offer some advice concerning capital fundraising for faith-based institutions. In developing my approach to church campaigns over the years, I consulted several authorities. Foremost among these is my dear friend, W. D. Broadway, a Baptist minister who helped raise the funds needed to build more than 70 churches, representing many denominations. Many of the ideas that follow can be directly attributed to him.

CAPITAL CAMPAIGNS FOR FAITH-BASED INSTITUTIONS

Fundraisers working with a broad spectrum of faith-based institutions recognize that each religion and denomination has its own theology and its own language. In many cases, successful faith-based capital campaigns are based upon prayer. Members of the congregation or parish are asked to "Pray for the success of the campaign and for discernment as to how much to pledge." Again, the language will vary. In some churches, members of the congregation are asked to "Pray for discernment as to what the Lord would have you do for this campaign." In other churches, members might simply be asked to "Give prayerful consideration to your campaign commitment." In all cases, members of the congregation are reminded that their pledges are important to the church, synagogue, or mosque.

This latter point is as important to secular campaigns as it is to faith-based organizations. Campaign leaders want potential donors to elevate the campaign to a high level of personal commitment. Capital campaigns require potential donors to give serious consideration to their pledge levels. A church leader might ask for "prayerful consideration." A spokesperson for a secular campaign might ask a prospective donor to recognize the project's importance to the community and to give "thoughtful and deliberate consideration" to his or her pledge.

As with all capital campaigns, prospects are reminded of the importance of multiyear commitments. Three- to five-year pledge periods are common.

CHURCH CAMPAIGN THEMES

Capital campaign themes for faith-based institutions should reflect the spiritual basis of the campaign. Members of the congregation expect all of their relationships with the religious organization to be uplifting. Exhibit 12.1 lists some ideas for church campaign themes. Members of the campaign cabinet sometimes choose to combine two of the ideas into their campaign theme. This works well with themes such as "Rooted in Tradition . . . Building for the Future," or "A Spiritual Journey . . . Arise and Build," or "Vision for Tomorrow . . . Education, Service, and Fellowship." The latter theme was used in a campaign for renovations to a multipurpose ancillary building.

DETERMINING GOALS

The church's first step is to understand its total capital and endowment needs. Early on, the members of the congregation should be encouraged to "dream big." Visionary plans inspire. After outlining or describing all of the potential capital projects, church leaders can get preliminary estimates of the cost of each component of the plan.

The next step is to estimate fundraising potential. A very preliminary estimate can be made based on a multiple of the total amount contributed each year to the church. Total all contributed income, including weekly offerings and special collections. Most churches find they can raise three to five times this amount for a capital campaign. Of course, the annual contributions can be expected to remain at the same level or slightly higher during the capital campaign and pledge payment period.

A more conservative estimate of capital campaign fundraising potential can be made by excluding special collections. In *The Lost Art of Church Fund Raising* (Precept Press, Inc., 1993), Ashley Hale states that, "A professionally managed building fund campaign should raise at least three times the budget." Mr. Hale further states that "the budget" is not an accurate phrase but is used to describe the undesignated contributions to the annual operating budget. His book also has a more detailed description of ways to refine the estimation of giving potential.

If the church has active members who are particularly affluent, and the economy is strong, the estimates can be on the higher side. If the economy is weak

EXHIBIT 12.1   POTENTIAL CHURCH CAMPAIGN THEMES

A Faith Journey	Faith and Excellence
A Journey Together	Faith in Action
A People . . . Together	Forward Together
A Spiritual Journey	For Such a Time as This
A Time to Build	Foundations for the Future
A Time to Grow	Keeping Faith
Advancing through Faith	Many Gifts, One Spirit
Arise and Build	Now and Forever
Adventure in Faith	Opportunities Unlimited
Adventure in Faith, the Second Mile	Rise Up and Build
Because We Care	Rooted in Tradition: Building for the Future
Breakthrough	Saints Alive
Breakthrough to Our Dream	Sharing the Vision
Bridge to the Future	The Future is Now
Building in Faith	The Second Mile
Building to Serve	Together We Grow
By Faith We Build	Together We Share
Commissioned . . . To Grow	Touch the Future
Continue the Dream	United We Build
Cornerstone	Upon This Rock
Daring to Believe	Vision for the New Millennium
Face to Face toward the Future	Vision to Victory
Facing the Future	Vision Unlimited

and the church has few affluent members, the estimate is closer to the three times the annual contributions figure.

Another factor that influences the goal is the number of donating households relative to the total giving. A church with a large number of donors raising less money than comparable churches can often achieve capital campaign goals that are disproportionate to current annual giving. Their solution is to treat stewardship as a ministry. Members of the congregation can be educated as to the benefits of generosity. With such an approach—and a project that is well accepted by the congregation—the capital campaign goal based on a multiple of annual giving can, at times, exceed the five-times figure.

Do not confuse the number of donors with the number of "members" or "registered families." Getting nondonors to contribute is a serious concern. However, capital campaign goal estimates are best based on current giving levels and numbers of participating households. Many churches have "registered families" that have not participated in years—if ever. Also, "members" who never give ongoing support rarely respond with generosity during the capital campaign.

Perhaps the most important factor affecting the goal is the nature of the project. Based on personal experience and conversations with members of numerous congregations, the following list—in descending order of importance—represents the priority church members place on a range of projects.

- New sanctuaries, churches, and worship spaces
- New family centers and multipurpose buildings
- Renovations and expansions of existing worship spaces
- Renovations of multipurpose buildings

Church leaders can more safely use optimistic goals for capital campaigns to build a new church. Organizers are wise to be more cautious in setting high goals for renovation projects, especially those for ancillary buildings.

With the large number of factors that influence the fundraising potential, setting goals is as much an art as it is a science. Campaign leaders would do well to consult an experienced capital campaign consultant concerning the appropriateness of any goal.

Consultants will sometimes recommend a range of goals. It is common practice for church campaigns to have what might be called a *victory goal, challenge goal,* and *hallelujah goal.* The victory goal is a somewhat conservative estimate of giving potential and is also an amount sufficient to pay for the project's highest priorities. The challenge goal is a somewhat optimistic projection of potential and covers more of the total project expenses. The hallelujah goal is a very optimistic estimate and is sufficient to cover every aspect of the church's most visionary plans.

ADJUSTMENTS TO THE GOAL

If the church, synagogue, or mosque has funds available for the building project in its building fund or operating surplus, the amount available can be considered when setting the goal. For example, if the total project costs equal $3 million, and the organization has the capacity to raise only $2.5 million, but $500,000 is available, the $2.5 million goal is entirely appropriate. By raising that amount and using it in combination with the accrued funds, the organization can fulfill its aspirations.

Religious institutions might also consider raising as much as they can and borrowing the remainder. As with all borrowing, the organization should always project cash flow and be conservative in estimating which mortgages or loans can be sustained. For example, planners might set out to raise at least 65 percent of the total project costs. Many religious institutions can sustain the payments and interest on the remaining 35 percent. Organizations that raise more than 65 percent of the project costs have less interest to pay and more money available for ongoing ministries. Organizations that raise the entire project costs free up future contributions for the church's evolving priorities.

DEFINED CONSTITUENCY CAMPAIGN

Fundraisers refer to campaigns for churches, synagogues, and mosques as "defined constituency" campaigns. Some organizations, such as the American Lung Association, the American Heart Association, Muscular Dystrophy Association, and others can expect contributions from large numbers of mail-responsive donors. Their constituency encompasses charitable people throughout the general public. But spiritual organizations must look to their internal constituency for support. Some church leaders seem to think, "It's not you. It's not me. It's the other fellow behind the tree." But when it comes to church contributions, there are no "other fellows behind the tree."

So church leaders begin their campaigns with a clear sense of who the prospects are. These include members of the congregation. In some campaigns, the prospect pool can be expanded slightly to include past members of the congregation who still have close ties to the church, and a few—and highly selected—friends of the pastor and church leaders.

Because the constituents are easily identifiable and already bonded with the institution, faith-based campaigns can be shorter than secular campaigns. A church with several hundred active members can complete its capital campaign in a two- to six-month period. Of course, the pledge payment period would still be three to five years. And the amount of time spent planning the project can vary greatly. It is most important to assure that all members of the congregation have an opportunity to have input during the planning process. This helps assure the greatest buy-in and maximum financial support.

Religious institutions with more complex projects run campaigns that are comparable in length to secular institutions. For example, a church planning renovations to its worship space, expansions to its school, and enhancements to its community center might plan an 18-month to two-year campaign. This would allow time to organize the church campaign, school campaign, and even an external effort for the community center.

A MODEL CHURCH CAMPAIGN

The following six-month schedule outlines an approach that works well for congregations with at least several hundred active members. Some churches, especially those with small congregations, can manage much shorter campaigns.

Again, the campaign is based on prayer. Members of the congregation are always asked to pray or give thoughtful consideration to their commitments. As important, they are allowed time to consider their multiyear pledges. The building campaign, with its seven components, is designed to build momentum.

Months 1 and 2: Campaign Preparation

During this phase, leaders finalize the capital improvement budget and agree to the campaign goal. The campaign's consultant may conduct confidential interviews to help refine the plan. The campaign cabinet and volunteer leadership is recruited. The campaign materials are developed, including the campaign brochure, a capital campaign prayer, a "prayer pledge," and commitment cards. Organizers review the church's donor lists and identify the "advance gift" prospects—the church's most generous supporters. Campaign leaders develop gracious ways of rating congregation members' capacity to support the campaign. The campaign calendar and schedule of cultivation gatherings are established. The gift handling, accounting and record-keeping systems, and acknowledgment policies and practices are established.

Months 3 and 4: The Advance Gift Phase

During this phase, the pastor and campaign leaders personally and quietly visit with the congregation's most generous and affluent members. The visits can be one-on-one meetings, quiet lunches, or intimate gatherings of several couples. Campaign leaders keep careful records of campaign assignments and the results of each get-together.

The advance gift prospects are informed that the campaign will be based upon prayer. They are asked to pray for the success of the campaign and to consider making a generous multiyear commitment. Most important, advance gift prospects are encouraged to make their multiyear pledges early. They are told that their gifts will inspire others and help assure the success of the campaign. During the advance gift phase, members of the campaign cabinet are also encouraged to make their early and generous pledges.

One important message is, "Not equal giving, but equal sacrifice." Campaigns fail when they seek the same amount from everybody. Campaign leaders are encouraged to discern the levels at which they choose to participate.

During the advance gift months, the committee finishes up any work left from the preparation phase and also prepares for a volunteer leadership supper. This preparation includes gathering lists of every person who volunteers in any capacity for the church, printing and mailing the invitation, and making arrangements for the supper. Prior to this important gathering, campaign leaders add up the amount committed by the advance gift prospects.

During the Fourth Month: The Volunteer Leadership Supper

Every church volunteer receives a written invitation and is encouraged to attend this informal gathering. Some churches use regularly scheduled volunteer appreciation gatherings to present a special capital campaign program. Others plan relatively inexpensive buffet menus. The food need not be elaborate, but the program should be lively, uplifting, and inspiring.

The reason this event is so important is that it contributes to the campaign's momentum. Advance gift folks give the campaign a jump-start with their most generous early pledges. The volunteers may not be the church's most affluent members, but they tend to give generously relative to their means. People who consistently share their time and talent are the same people who are generous with their treasure.

During the program, the pastor, campaign chair, and a few others speak briefly. The campaign team reviews the importance of the capital projects. A well-respected member of the congregation also reports that a few generous people have already quietly pledged a relatively high percentage of the total goal. Perhaps 1 to 5 percent of the congregation's households have committed 25 percent of the goal during the advance gift phase. The program concludes by asking all the volunteers to begin to pray for the success of the campaign and to begin to consider what they might pledge. The volunteers attending the supper receive the campaign materials and are asked to make their commitments prior to the building banquet. Campaign leaders explain that these early commitments, when totaled, will inspire the remainder of the congregation.

Months 4 and 5: Intermediate Phase

A small number of campaign workers follow up with the church's pool of volunteers, especially those who attended the volunteer leadership supper. The campaign representatives personally visit, call, or write to the volunteers and remind them to pray and return the commitment cards to the church office. To the extent possible, campaign leaders speak to members of the church's larger pool of volunteers on a one-to-one basis. During this stage, campaign leaders continue to keep careful records concerning who is expected to call on whom.

The campaign leadership also prepares for the next steps. Recruiting a large number of campaign visitors, sometimes called *visiting stewards,* is one of the most important tasks to plan and execute as early as possible. Making arrangements for the building banquet also requires early preparation.

Prior to the building banquet, the campaign communications intensify. Early communications, in the form of sermons, testimonials, and newsletters, encourage people to plan to attend the building banquet. People are also asked to begin to pray for the campaign. The prayer card is read at every Mass or service.

Shortly before the building banquet, the large number of campaign workers—called volunteer visitors or visiting stewards—gather for a training session. The early training makes it possible for rapid follow-up immediately following the building banquet. And volunteers who make their commitments prior to the banquet help boost the campaign total.

Late in Month 5: Building Banquet

Every member of the congregation is invited to the building banquet. Congregations with sufficient volunteers might even plan an accompanying children's "pizza party." This "baby-sitting service" makes it possible for parents to attend the building banquet without the distraction of young children.

This event is promoted as "one of the most important gatherings in the church's history." In addition to the written invitations, members of the congregation receive calls from trained volunteers. The volunteer callers extend warm and personal invitations. They let the church member know that the pastor would appreciate their attendance. The volunteers are also trained to carefully count attendees and to overcome the most common objections to attendance.

The event, which may include music during the dinner portion of the gathering, is somewhat more elaborate than the volunteer leadership supper. However, the program is similar. Members of the congregation receive all the campaign materials. The capital campaign project is reviewed. If possible, a representative of the architectural firm speaks. The pastor delivers an inspiring message. And a highlight of the evening occurs when the amount raised to date is revealed. Often, 15 percent or fewer of the households have made commitments equaling 50 percent or more of the campaign goal. When this is revealed with a large and attractive sign, one often hears a gasp from the attendees.

Presenters review the campaign materials and repeat the main messages of the campaign. Attendees are encouraged to begin to consider their multiyear commitments. They are also asked to pray for unity of the congregation, pray for the pastor, pray for the architect and builders, pray for the success of the campaign, and, finally, to pray for discernment as to their level of participation in the campaign. The attendees are also told to welcome the volunteer visitors who will call on them.

Month 6: Congregationwide Campaign

Volunteer visitors call on members of the congregation who attended the building banquet. This is their first priority because attendees know more about the project than those who did not attend.

People who could not or did not choose to attend the building banquet receive a letter from the pastor or campaign chair. The letter summarizes the good news conveyed at the banquet. The letter also may contain the campaign materials and commitment card. To save postage, some congregations distribute the campaign materials during in-pew presentations after the building banquet.

Campaign workers visit as many people as possible in their homes. They also visit church members after Mass or the weekly services. Some congregations set up tables for volunteers to meet with members of the congregation. This works well if the church has a large welcome area.

Volunteers phone and mail people they cannot meet in person. Communications are very intense. The pastor gives two or three sermons on stewardship and the importance of the capital campaign. There is a two- or three-minute presentation at every Mass or service designed to encourage people to bring in their commitment cards or mail them to the church office. Volunteers also offer to pick up their commitment cards in their sealed envelopes.

Late in Month 6 or 7: Victory Celebration

A victory celebration can be as simple as a coffee and donut affair with banners and balloons, scheduled after each Mass or service. If the schedule and budget permits, a larger gathering for the entire congregation can be planned to take place on the church property. In either case, donors and volunteers should be thanked. Everyone should be thanked for their prayers and good wishes. Campaign leaders can announce that the campaign met or exceeded its goal.

After the seven major steps and phases of the campaign, the church's volunteers and staff need to assure that the postcampaign activities are well administered. Commitment reminders can be mailed monthly or quarterly. Members of the congregation should receive capital campaign envelopes in which to send their pledge payments. As with all campaigns, donors should continue to be thanked. Invitations to groundbreakings and other celebrations work well for this purpose. And there is no substitute for personal expressions of gratitude from the pastor.

KEY VOLUNTEER ROLES

The model campaign just described places a great deal of importance on the role of volunteers. Here are some of the key volunteer campaign positions and their related responsibilities:

Honorary Chair(s)

- Serve as a symbol and advocate for the campaign.
- Attend meetings of the campaign cabinet or steering committee, if wished.

- Consider a prayerful commitment to the capital campaign.
- Attend selected key campaign gatherings.
- Help in any special way the honorary chair's time, talent, and interest permit.

Capital Campaign Chair or Co-Chairs

- Chair approximately 7 to 10 meetings over a six- to seven-month period.
- Work closely with the pastor and consultant to formulate and refine plans.
- Help recruit volunteers.
- Urge volunteers to complete their tasks.
- Work with advance gift chair to help secure advance gifts.
- Make a self-satisfying financial contribution to the building campaign.
- Write or refine the "Letter from the Campaign Chair" contained in the campaign brochure. Approve capital campaign letters sent to the members of the congregation that are signed by the campaign chair.
- Speak at major gatherings such as the building banquet.

Advance Gift Chair or Co-Chairs

- Work with pastor, campaign chair, and consultant to recruit a small team of advance gift visitors.
- Personally visit five advance gift prospect households and encourage the congregation members to give prayerful consideration to a generous leadership gift.
- Attend a small number of intimate dinners with the pastor and advance gift prospects.
- Make a self-satisfying financial contribution to the building campaign.
- Make a follow-up visit or call to households.
- Encourage other advance gift team members to make their visits.
- Call each team member to find out how their visits progressed.
- Attend campaign cabinet meetings.
- Devote sufficient time to the preceding tasks. The busiest time for the advance gift chair is the brief period prior to the leadership supper.

Volunteer Visitors Chair

- Recruit 7 to 10 team captains who will then recruit 7 to 10 visiting stewards for each team. (These numbers can be adjusted for each church.)

- Attend and help facilitate two visiting steward orientation sessions.
- Call team captains and encourage them to stay in touch with their team members.
- Help coordinate the prayer visits with congregation members.
- Make a self-satisfying financial contribution to the building campaign.
- Attend campaign cabinet meetings.

Arrangements Co-Chairs

- Help make arrangements for two special gatherings:

The leadership supper (for volunteers)

The building banquet (for all)

Arrangements include invitations, food, location, and decorations for both events. The building banquet might also require music. (Speaker and presentation issues are the responsibility of the campaign cabinet.)

- Help recruit building banquet volunteer callers and hostesses. The callers phone each household to encourage attendance and to count the number of people who say they are coming. The hostesses welcome people to the building banquet, help distribute campaign materials, and collect attendance sheets at each table.
- Make a self-satisfying financial contribution to the building campaign.
- Attend campaign cabinet meetings.

Communications Co-Chairs

- Work with consultant to produce at least six campaign newsletters or simple bulletins.
- Produce signs and banners for in-pew presentations.
- Produce signs and banners promoting the campaign.
- Secure testimonial speakers for church services and for the leadership supper and in-pew presentations. Other campaign cabinet members can also provide help in this area.
- Work with the consultant to produce campaign brochure and other printed material.
- Develop creative communication vehicles that promote the campaign.
- Make a self-satisfying financial contribution to the building campaign.
- Attend campaign cabinet meetings.

Campaigns for faith-based organizations are among the most satisfying projects in the nonprofit sector. Prospective supporters are already close to and committed to the organization. They know that they are involved in a cause that is bigger than themselves. These are the attributes of successful campaigns that *all* nonprofit institutions should strive to establish.

It comes as no surprise that 42 percent of all philanthropy is directed to religious organizations. The depth of the involvement and dedication that accompanies spiritual experience is a conversion process that *is* available to secular organizations that care about their donors and that focus on the most pressing societal needs.

CHAPTER 13

Historic Preservation Projects*

MARK THALER, AIA

Whereas nonprofits may often decide to build new buildings to suit their needs, many will decide to renovate historic buildings in their communities. Some will make this decision with great enthusiasm; others will make it more reluctantly.

Over the past 20 years, as an architect specializing in the restoration and adaptive reuse of historic buildings, I have heard the reasons behind these decisions repeated again and again. People who are enthusiastic about renovation often say that the building has charm, that it is part of the history of the community, that "they simply don't build 'em like that anymore," and more recently that it is a wise use of resources. Those who are reluctant are often concerned that it will be too expensive, that they would prefer to have a "state-of-the-art" facility, that the restrictions preservationists might place on them are too onerous, that the buildings don't meet current life safety or accessibility requirements, or that they are just too cramped. Whether these concerns are insurmountable can be best determined when the organizational goals are clearly defined.

As with any type of building project, it is important for an organization to define its goals as the first step in the renovation process. These goals should be a logical outgrowth of the organization's strategic planning. Every organization should periodically ask itself questions like: Where does the organization want to be in the next decade or beyond? Will its primary mission change; or, will the way in which that mission is fulfilled change? Is there a secondary mission that the organization might have? Once the organization's goals are clearly identified, the project can become one means of reaching those goals.

For example, maintaining or restoring a community landmark is a valuable secondary mission for many nonprofits. They are acting as stewards of their community's civic and cultural legacy. Beyond pure altruism, such a secondary mis-

*Printed with permission from Mark Thaler, AIA and Einhorn Yaffe Prescott Architecture & Engineering, P.C.

sion offers practical benefits. When communicating an improved or expanded program for the community and the preservation of a historic building, the non-profit can have a powerful message for a capital campaign and one that greatly increases the potential pool of donors. On the other side of the coin, a nonprofit that decides to abandon a historic building may face criticism and find itself in a public battle at the very time that it needs community support. To make such a decision wisely, it is important to thoroughly evaluate the options available. This should be done with a qualified architect.

SELECTING YOUR ARCHITECT

Much like physicians and attorneys specialize in various branches of medicine and law, architects tend to specialize in specific project and building types. An architect specializing in both historic preservation and the type of facility in question will be an invaluable partner in defining project goals, assessing pros and cons, and developing a program for the project. Referrals from peer institutions that have completed similar historic preservation projects, or from your State Historic Preservation Office (SHPO), are a good place to begin your search.

If you have not already done so, you should designate a building committee that is empowered to act on the organization's behalf. The committee should understand what it wants in an architect. Experience in projects similar to the one that you are undertaking is important, but so is the level of service that you might expect, both in the early design phases and during construction.

Many organizations will prepare a request for qualifications (RFQ) and send it to a pool of architects to solicit their interest and ask for their firms' qualifications. The nonprofit may be able to get assistance in preparing this document from peer institutions that have previously solicited for architects or from a local architect in the community who may not be interested in pursuing the project.

After reviewing the qualifications, the three to five firms that appear to be the best candidates are typically invited for an interview. Determine exactly who your organization will be dealing with, because, ultimately, it is individuals who will carry out your project and it is important that you have a good rapport with the people with whom you will be working.

After selecting the most qualified architect for your project, a fee can be negotiated based upon the project's complexity. If the project remains ill-defined at this early stage, the architect may suggest a separate fee to do preplanning services with some range defined for the later phases.

At this point, you should provide the architect with any drawings, specifications, or reports that exist for the building, as well as historic documentation such as old photographs, newspaper descriptions, or information from your local historical society.

Once your architect has been selected, a thorough evaluation of options can begin.

PREPLANNING AND EVALUATION OF OPTIONS

The evaluation of a historic building can be carried out on several levels of detail, depending on the situation. If there is no question that the nonprofit will remain in the building, the architect might conduct a survey and identify specific deficiencies that need to be addressed in the project. These can then be incorporated into the contract documents (drawings and specifications) that the architect prepares. This approach might also be warranted if the project schedule is very tight, the building is not complicated or already has good documentation, and there is reasonable certainty that the architect will immediately move into the preparation of contract documents. If measured drawings of the building do not exist, it is likely that they will need to be prepared at this time.

Many potential donors will require that a thorough written analysis be prepared. The most common types are: an *existing conditions report, historic structure report (HSR),* and *feasibility study.* As there is a wide range of issues that may or may not be covered in such a report, it is best to have the architect provide examples of studies he or she has done and be explicit about what will be provided. It is important to understand what potential donors require and to establish exactly what the architect will include in his or her study.

An existing conditions report will usually include an analysis of the building's systems; foundations and structure; floors; walls; ceilings; doors; windows; roof; mechanical, electrical, plumbing, and fire suppression systems, as well as other significant systems that may be present in the building. Life safety, code, and accessibility issues may also be addressed in such a study. An existing conditions report is often used as a benchmark to determine which aspects of a building may need to be addressed as part of a building renovation project.

A historic structure report would normally contain all the elements of the existing conditions report, plus incorporate archival information that documents the original construction of the building, changes that have taken place over time, and significant events that have taken place in the building. Architects that are experienced in historic preservation can often figure out how a building may have been modified over time by physical clues as well as archival information. Paint analysis is often done in conjunction with such a study to identify original colors and decoration that have long been lost to history. The restoration of the original decorative treatment of a building can be a spectacular transformation that excites great public interest. Most historic structure reports will also contain recommendations for repair and restoration. Many will identify *preservation zones* in the building, identifying the most important areas that should be restored while identifying other areas that can be readily modified to accommodate program changes and building support spaces. A historic structure report can provide exciting information about the building's history and the changes that have taken place over time. This information can be used to guide the planning effort and excite the imagination of potential donors and the public alike.

Feasibility studies typically include a test fit of the proposed program against space in the building to determine whether an addition is required and to assess whether the building can accommodate other program requirements, such as heavier structural loads, advanced heating and cooling systems, data and telecommunications systems, and code and accessibility requirements. Site issues may also be addressed, including zoning, parking, landscaping, and even traffic concerns. Feasibility studies can also address issues of budget, schedule, phasing, and market analysis.

An experienced historic preservation architect will be able to integrate the information gathered during the preplanning process with his or her experience and creativity to reveal the potential of your historic building. While it is not always possible to renovate a particular building for a particular use, most historic buildings can be successfully renovated to provide twenty-first century amenities, while maintaining the legacy of past generations.

COMMON ISSUES IN HISTORIC PRESERVATION PROJECTS

Controlling Costs and Preparing for the Unknown

Many people worry that construction costs will skyrocket during renovation projects because of "unforeseen conditions." This is a valid concern that is best addressed by hiring an architect who has experience dealing with historic buildings, and to use contractors who have similar experience. They will know what to look for and will be able to anticipate certain hidden conditions. For example, a white powdery residue found on masonry, called efflorescence, is a telltale sign of moisture within the wall. It points to the need for masonry pointing or perhaps roof repairs. If there was a leaking roof, rot may have occurred in the wood framing over time. One important unknown that is often excluded from the architect's scope is investigating the presence of hazardous materials. These surveys are more often done by specialized environmental consultants.

Because the architect prepares the contract documents upon which the contractors base their price, it is important that the architect address these issues as fully as possible before construction. The nonprofit representatives should ask their architect what types of issues they may encounter during construction and what they can do to minimize uncertainties ahead of time. When it is practical and cost-effective, probes or nondestructive testing can be used determine whether a hidden condition exists. However, expecting to anticipate every unforeseen condition before construction is unreasonable. *Allowances* can be included in the construction contract to address the repair of certain hidden elements. These dollar amounts are simply contingencies that are carried in the contract for work that will probably take place, though the actual scope is difficult to determine. *Unit prices,* included in the construction contract, can then be used to compensate the contractor based upon a predetermined cost per square foot, or per brick, or whatever was previously agreed upon. If the work exceeds the allowance amount, the contractor may be entitled to a *change order* for additional compensation. If the cost of the work is less than the allowance, the result would be project savings.

When a project is put out for bidding, contractors are much more likely to bid on specifically what is included in the contract documents without accounting for unforeseen conditions that they are not contractually obligated to address. If they were to do so, they would be placing themselves at a competitive disadvantage. As discussed in earlier chapters, however, contractors or construction managers can be brought on board early in the design process, when they can provide valuable insights from their own experience and suggest reasonable contingencies as well.

Several years ago, an Episcopal church in upstate New York required repair of its slate and metal roof and conservation of the bluestone and brownstone façades and 180-foot tower of their 1850's vintage church. Much of the original brownstone carvings and small pieces of bluestone were flaking off. Church leaders were very concerned that an accurate estimate of the work be done and that the construction amount stay within the estimate. They also wanted to ensure competition by bidding the work to several contractors.

The first step was to conduct a complete investigation of the stonework on the entire building. An 80-foot boom truck provided access to the lower areas of the building, while professional rappellers, with video and camera equipment, provided documentation of the tower. This information was used to prepare a scope of work and was incorporated to the contract documents.

Next, several prequalified contractors were engaged to repair a single bay (see Exhibit 13.1). While they gauged the difficulty of the work, the church saw an example of their craftsmanship. When all subsequently bid the project, they understood what was expected and were very competitive. When the project was complete two years later, there had not been a single change order requested by the contractor.

Costs were controlled by conducting a thorough analysis of the building, getting input from qualified restoration contractors before bidding, and thoroughly documenting the scope of work to be bid. Although this process was not a guar-

EXHIBIT 13.1   SMALL TEST, MORE ACCURATE OVERALL PRICE ESTIMATES

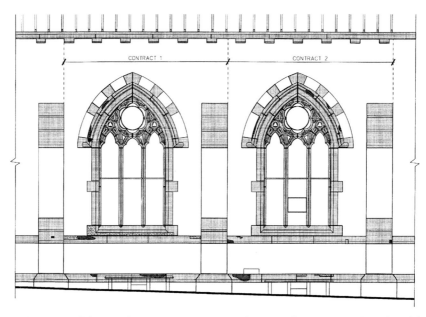

By providing prequalified restoration contractors an opportunity to actually restore a small portion of the entire project, contractors were able to provide more accurate pricing and the church was able to assess their level of craftsmanship. Drawing by Einhorn Yaffee Prescott Architecture & Engineering, P.C. Printed with permission.

antee against unforeseen conditions, it helped lessen the probability. It is wise for all owners to have funding in place to cover contingencies that might arise.

Finding Space

One difficulty that many preservation projects encounter is that the building can't accommodate the existing program, let alone have space for enlarging the program.

Options for dealing with this dilemma include: constructing an addition or acquiring adjacent buildings that can be incorporated into the complex; removing part of the program to a satellite location; creating a more efficient design within the building; or finding additional space within the building envelope.

The solution must take into account many factors, including: whether the building will need to stay occupied during construction; construction phasing; whether it is possible to build an addition or acquire new space; and the budget, to name a few.

The option that is most often overlooked by owners is finding additional space within their own building. It is sometimes possible to redesign existing basement or attic spaces to provide much needed program space (see Exhibit 13.2). Grades can be changed and new windows added to bring daylight into an underutilized basement. Attics may be able to be turned into valuable office space with the introduction of skylights or dormers. These changes may require that mechanical systems be rethought and perhaps relocated. Providing an underground mechanical vault outside of the building can free up valuable square footage in an otherwise cramped building.

When evaluating such change in use, it is necessary to consider all of the ramifications. A thorough understanding of building codes as they apply to historic buildings is vital. Providing adequate means of egress, environmental controls, and accessibility are some of the issues that must be addressed.

As part of a recent library renovation, we were required to upgrade all systems within the historic building while it remained fully occupied. Our solution was to utilize two large light wells as swing space. Large skylights were constructed above the light wells. This allowed construction of new centralized mechanical spaces at the lower levels with new skylit reading rooms above.

EXHIBIT 13.2   USING EXISTING SPACE
FOR EXPANDED PROGRAMS

Floors were inserted into the lower levels of existing light wells to provide mechanical space below, and reading rooms above, providing crucial swing space so the building could remain occupied during the renovation. Photographs by Einhorn Yaffee Prescott Architecture & Engineering, P.C. and Peter Van der Walker Photography. Printed with permission.

In another case, the existing basement floor elevation was excavated by 18 inches to provide enough headroom to make the space usable (see Exhibit 13.3). After determining the depth of the existing foundation walls, we found that this could be accomplished without expensive underpinning of the foundations, yielding an additional 18,000 square feet of building to be fully utilized.

Integrating Technology and Modern Engineering Systems to Historic Buildings

The insensitive design of modern engineering systems has compromised countless historic buildings. Ceilings are routinely boxed out around windows so that large ducts can be installed above dropped ceilings; sprinkler piping is suspended like spider webs; and surface-mounted electrical conduits are attached to decorative moldings.

Equally as important as guaranteeing that your architect has experience in historic preservation is ensuring that the engineers he or she works with are equally experienced. The working relationship between the architect and structural, mechanical, electrical, plumbing, fire protection, and telecommunications engineers is crucial to your project's success. Integration of those systems to a cohesive design that respects the building, meets the needs of the maintenance staff and user, is energy-efficient, and allows for flexibility is a complex part of the design process that many owners never see.

A thorough understanding of the historic aspects of the building is necessary for the engineers to design their systems without needlessly compromising the building (see Exhibit 13.4). There are often existing chases and shafts in the building. These voids can be identified through historic drawings, discussions

EXHIBIT 13.3   BASEMENT SPACE CONVERTED
TO PROGRAM SPACE

Underutilized basement space can often be transformed into vibrant program space. Photographs by Einhorn Yaffee Prescott Architecture & Engineering, P.C. and Chun Y. Lai Photography. Printed with permission.

with maintenance personnel, cameras, or even ultrasonic techniques. Inactive fireplace flues may be able to accommodate return airshafts; old electrical conduits may be reused; and old piping that is embedded in the construction could be lined with epoxy to extend its life another 50 years at a fraction of the cost of replacement.

Engineers experienced in historic preservation projects are more likely to be able to discuss options with your maintenance staff. Radio-controlled alarm systems, high-speed air distribution systems, and mist-type fire protection systems can potentially minimize impact on historic buildings, but it is necessary that you understand the advantages and disadvantages that each offers.

Providing Accessibility

Providing accessibility to the disabled can be difficult in a historic building. If your facility is not currently accessible, it is important to do what you can to make it so. Understand the law. The Americans with Disabilities Act (ADA) is a federal law that has ramifications for every public place in America. Additionally, many states have accessibility guidelines that must be met, especially when undertaking a substantial renovation project.

Many of these codes and laws waive certain requirements for buildings that are certified as historic. The certification generally means that a building has been listed in the National Register of Historic Places, is considered a contributing building within a National Register Historic District, or is in some way designated as historic by a state or municipality. When a building is so des-

EXHIBIT 13.4   INSTALLING NEW SYSTEMS WHILE
                         PRESERVING HISTORIC CHARACTER

Careful coordination and sensitivity to the historic character of the building are crucial in inserting new engineering systems to historic buildings. Installation of a new sprinkler system for the first-floor lobby at right was accomplished by removal of the flooring above to minimize disruption to an important historic space. Photographs by Einhorn Yaffee Prescott Architecture & Engineering, P.C. and Chun Y. Lai Photography. Printed with permission.

ignated, the owner may be able to work with the local building official or State Historic Preservation Office to obtain a waiver.

There are many ways that accessibility can be incorporated into a historic preservation project. The intent of the law is to provide access to all Americans when it can be reasonably accomplished, and to do so in a respectful manner. Sometimes it may not be possible to meet all of the requirements within an existing building.

In a recent project in New Mexico, a former railroad resort hotel that had been abandoned for more than 30 years was being transformed into a multipurpose building that included housing, dining, classroom, and administrative spaces. The grand but derelict building was never designed to be accessible. Despite this fact, all of the options that could provide accessibility were analyzed. Historic photographs showed a large covered carriage entry once located at the building's entrance. By restoring this element, a ramp could be incorporated along the steps, providing a gracious entrance that reinforced the historic character of the building (see Exhibit 13.5). The original veranda level was

EXHIBIT 13.5   RESTORED FEATURE ALLOWS ACCESSIBLE RAMP

The opportunity to restore the long-missing covered carriage entrance also provided an opportunity to design an accessible ramp at the main entrance that blended harmoniously into the historic character of the building.
Photographs by Einhorn Yaffee Prescott Architecture & Engineering, P.C. Printed with permission.

raised to meet the first-floor level of the building to eliminate another obstacle, and a two-sided elevator provided access to the four main levels and two intermediate levels of the building.

By being proactive and working with code officials, the State Historic Preservation Office, and the state advocate for the disabled, it was possible to meet the needs of all these constituencies while maintaining the budget and enhancing the historic character of the building.

Life Safety

Historic or not, no one wants to utilize an unsafe building. Fortunately, building codes and fire codes have been developed to safeguard building inhabitants. However, many codes were written specifically for new construction and were prescriptive in their approach. Existing buildings often received a cursory chapter that required the building to be brought completely up to modern code requirements if substantial renovation or a change of use was planned.

Realizing that the cost of bringing existing buildings up to meet all modern requirements was leaving many buildings vacant within its older cities, New Jersey became one of the first states to implement a rehabilitation code. In essence, this code adopted the philosophy that all buildings must meet minimum criteria and that any renovations to a building must make that building safer than it was prior to renovation. This code has sparked significant redevelopment and many states are considering similar legislation.

Most codes do have some leniency for historic buildings; however, the underlying premise remains: No one wants to utilize an unsafe building. That said, architects who deal with historic preservation projects extensively do come across prescriptive code requirements that do not necessarily make buildings safer. It is at this point that architects talk about the "spirit of the code" versus the "letter of the code" with local building officials. It is also at this point that the architect may apply for a variance.

Specialized life safety consultants can provide detailed computer modeling of buildings that show how quickly fire and smoke will spread and how quickly inhabitants could exit the building. These studies are invaluable in understanding whether code requirements are warranted or are even safe.

In a recent study of a state capitol building with long corridors that open onto a central rotunda, the life safety consultant proved that the building was far safer as originally designed than with fire doors separating the corridors from the rotunda, as the building code would have required. The reason was that smoke in any of the corridors could empty out into the rotunda dome without reaching toxic levels before the inhabitants could escape. With the doors enclosing the corridor, the smoke would build up too quickly. Though this is a unique situation, the point is, many historic buildings have unique characteristics and such analyses can potentially save tens of thousands of dollars.

Dead-end corridors and single means of egress issues are often encountered in historic preservation projects. Redesigning certain areas is sometimes required (see the side-by-side drawings in Exhibit 13.6). Adding sprinkler protection and early fire and smoke detection systems beyond what would otherwise be required may be an acceptable alternative to the building code official—if the occupancy of those areas is limited.

When the installation of sprinkler and fire detection systems is required, or new fire stairs or exit ways must be built, they should be done in a way that is as sympathetic as possible to the historic building.

Preservation Restrictions or Covenants

Many times, owners of historic buildings are afraid to have their buildings designated as historic in any way. The reason generally comes down to the fear that their ability to modify, or even eventually demolish the building, might be compromised. This reasoning is fundamentally flawed.

The National Historic Preservation Act of 1966 established the National Register of Historic Places, State Historic Preservation Offices (SHPO) in each state, and guidelines for the treatment of designated historic properties. (Note: The SHPO has a different name in each state; however, it is the agency that has been so designated to handle these issues for their state.) These guidelines have evolved into *The Secretary of the Interior's Standards for Rehabilitation.*

Although local restrictions may prevent a historic building, or any other building for that matter, from being altered or demolished without proper

EXHIBIT 13.6   PROVIDING ADDITIONAL SAFETY

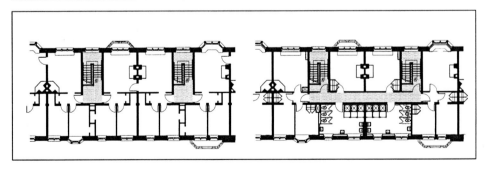

The second-floor plan at left shows four student room suites in a historic dormitory building. By enclosing the stairways and providing a through corridor, as shown on the right, it was possible to provide two distinct means of egress with minimum disruption to the building. Drawings by Einhorn Yaffee Prescott Architecture & Engineering, P.C. Printed with permission.

authorization, there is nothing in the national legislation that would prevent an owner of a building listed on the National Register of Historic Places from demolishing or inappropriately altering the building unless federal funding was involved. Many states have similar restrictions on the use of state funding for these purposes. The only time that such a restriction might take effect is when the owner has accepted federal or state funding for the project, or if he or she has previously accepted such funds that provided for a deed covenant on the property for some specified period of time.

If a building is not officially designated as historic, the State Historic Preservation Office is still required to review projects receiving federal funding if the property is over 50 years old. If the building is deemed "eligible for listing," the same restrictions apply. These restrictions require that the project is carried out in accordance with *The Secretary of the Interior's Standards for Rehabilitation.* Any architect with real historic preservation experience should be aware of the standards.

The advantages of having a building listed on the National Register of Historic Places are significant. Many grants are available only to buildings that are so designated, and building code and accessibility requirements may be lessened or waived for designated historic buildings.

ADDITIONAL RESOURCES

Nonprofits that decide to renovate a historic building should enlist the aid of the many historic preservation advocacy groups that exist. The National Trust for Historic Preservation in Washington, DC can provide contact information for similar statewide organizations. These groups can suggest where to look for resources, provide sound advice, and put you in touch with similar nonprofits that have undertaken successful projects.

Your State Historic Preservation Office can also provide advice and information on potential funding sources. Many states now have grants for historic preservation projects that are undertaken by nonprofit organizations.

Some nonprofits look to developers who are eligible to receive federal historic preservation tax credits of 20 percent of the construction costs. These can be in addition to other tax credits such as those for creating low-income housing. The properties can then be leased back to the nonprofit organizations. These regulations are, however, quite complex and require expert counsel. Your State Historic Preservation Office should be able to identify people to assist you if this arrangement might be of interest.

CHAPTER 14

Parting Thoughts

Several main themes have permeated this book. Among these are:

- To think seriously about acquiring new or renovated facilities, nonprofit leaders should study all their options, select a plan of action, begin estimating total costs, and continually refine these estimates.

- Early on, the organization should begin nurturing positive relationships with potential donors with the capacity to support the capital campaign at the levels required.

- The precampaign planning study (feasibility study, philanthropic planning study, campaign advancement assessment, philanthropic assessment, or what have you) is vital to the cultivation process and is integral to the campaign.

- The choice of project delivery strategy is an important one. To choose wisely, nonprofit leaders should speak to several architects and contractors to fully explore these options.

- The design process can be interrupted. Nonprofit organizations can view the development of schematic drawings as a logical pause point for the precampaign planning study and capital campaign. This minimizes the early expenditures but provides enough information to estimate expenses and explain the case for support to potential donors.

- Alternatively, the organization may go a bit further in design. If the organization pauses after 30 percent to 35 percent of the design work has been done, the cost estimates will be even more accurate, and the construction manager can have greater input into the design process. This can increase practicality and allow for "value engineering." Moreover, many donors expect to see as much planning and design work as possible early in the campaign.

- The Kresge Foundation can be an important prospective supporter of many capital campaigns. Evaluators at The Kresge Foundation value detailed design and careful planning. (Schematic drawings are a *minimum* requirement.)

- Capital campaigns should not reduce annual giving. Ongoing annual support can be integrated to a comprehensive campaign. At a minimum, campaign leaders monitor their top prospects and tell them that, "Your capital campaign support is *in addition to* your annual contributions." Also, special-event fundraisers and direct mail for ongoing support continue throughout the campaign and pledge payment period.

- Endowments are an integral part of many campaigns. New facilities and programs require sustained support. Endowment funds help fill that need. Endowment contributions may be in the form of one-time gifts, multi-year contributions, and/or deferred gifts. Charitable gift planning helps donors better provide for family and loved ones, as well as for the non-profit institution.

- All communications related to the project and the capital/endowment campaign should focus on the needs of the people served.

- Strong, well-trained boards and volunteer campaign teams are essential to success. Strong staff and consultant support are also crucial.

ANOTHER LOOK AT PROJECT DELIVERY

Howard Mock, chairman of Jaynes Corporation and a past president of the Associated General Contractors of America (AGC), also served as a campaign chair and volunteer for a number of capital campaigns. His perspective is instructive. In a recent conversation, Mr. Mock emphasized the importance of a strong case and a well-defined plan. He said:

> Nonprofit leaders might want to examine a plan like CM at risk or CM/GC. With this approach, when the construction manager/general contractor comes on board, design is 30 percent to 35 percent complete. That's a bit beyond schematics. Programming is more complete, systems are defined, some finishes are selected, and some specs are also developed.
>
> This gets the construction people involved a bit earlier than the traditional process. Architects and construction managers agree that value engineering is best accomplished early in the design process. Value engineering assures the best value for the investment. In some cases, the nonprofit organization may be encouraged to spend a bit more initially for a system that will save tens or hundreds of thousands of dollars over the life of the system. At other times, perfectly suitable alternative materials or systems might be available for far less initial expenses. That's what value engineering is—getting the most value for the nonprofit organization's limited resources.
>
> Perhaps the greatest advantage to this approach of getting 30 percent of the design work done is the impact on fundraising. As a volunteer and a donor, I

know that people want to know what their funds will be used for. With this approach, there is a well-developed plan, good cost estimates, and *a clear understanding of how the nonprofit organization's facilities will be used to provide enhanced services.* It's sure easier to get people committed when plans are that clear and well developed.

In Chapter 4, Dale Dekker recommends the AIA Form B141 contract. Mr. Mock also noted that the AGC developed model contracts that can be very useful to the nonprofit organization. Information concerning the AGC contracts is available at the Associated General Contractors of America Web site, www.agc.org.

INSTITUTIONAL DIFFERENCES

It is natural when writing a book such as this to provide general advice. Let me take this opportunity to state that there are a few "universal truths" in capital campaigns. Among these are:

- Organizations that seek the average gift are mathematically assured to *fail* to meet their full potential.
- Those that seek many small gifts get many small gifts, but fail to reach their goal.
- Capital campaigns need generous leadership level gifts to succeed.

That said, it would be unwise to move forward with your campaign without knowing some of the differences that are common among various segments of the nonprofit sector. Let's look at the unique qualities some bring to the capital and endowment campaign. (Note: Some of this material was originally included in the "Capital Campaign" chapter of *The Complete Guide to Fundraising Management,* but these updated thoughts are worth including here.)

Churches and Synagogues

Church and synagogue capital campaigns are generally much shorter than other campaigns. However, a significant amount of time and thought should be devoted to project planning. Project organizers must work to assure that members of the congregation have ample participation and buy-in for the planning process. But the actual campaign can be accomplished in a two-, three-, or four-month period. A six- to eight-month campaign may allow more time for prayer and the development of leadership level commitments. If the campaign is complex and includes a church school or a community center with external constituents, the campaign can become as long as other secular campaigns.

In church and synagogue campaigns, the distribution of gifts tends to be flatter than in other capital campaigns—but not necessarily. If the congregation has several extremely affluent members, they can be encouraged to make large leadership gifts during the advancement phase. In such a case, 50 percent of the contributions may come from 7 percent to 10 percent of the participating households. More commonly, approximately 15 percent of the households can be expected to contribute 50 percent of the campaign total.

Make note that in church campaigns we are talking about 10 or 15 *percent* of the donors contributing 50 percent of the contributions. In other campaigns, we speak about the *top 10 donors* contributing one-third to one-half of the campaign. In a church with 500 contributing households, 50 to 75 donations will account for 50 percent of the capital campaign total. In secular campaigns, 10 contributions may be expected to result in 33 percent to 50 percent of the campaign total.

Churches and synagogues are essentially *closed constituencies.* The contributions come from congregation members, relatives of congregation members, friends of the pastor or rabbi, former members of the congregation, and a very few other people with some connection to the congregation. There is no possible broad base of support other than the congregation. The leaders for the campaign are already members or leaders of the congregation. Those who have been generous in the past may very well be expected to be generous in the future.

The most successful congregational campaigns are based upon prayer and stewardship. The campaign is structured so that each member of the congregation is offered an opportunity to give prayerful consideration to his or her commitment.

Hospitals

With a rapidly changing healthcare environment, hospitals and other healthcare institutions must build flexibility into their plans. The case for support must be relevant to the community, patients, the board, and to all stakeholders, especially the staff. Above all, the plan must make economic sense.

In hospital campaigns, approximately 15 percent of the donations come from the board of directors. Another 15 percent may be obtained from the staff. Of course, this percentage is higher than in campaigns for other types of nonprofit institutions where the staff is not composed of physicians, specialists, and relatively well-paid administrators. Moreover, healthcare institutions are staffed by workers of modest means who are dedicated to the care and well-being of the institution's patients. These people are often generous relative to their means.

Universities

The trustee campaign is especially important in universities. Approximately 20 percent of the goal can be expected to be achieved from the trustees. Alumni might be expected to contribute at least another 20 percent of the campaign. In younger institutions, this may not be possible; however, in older, established universities with numerous affluent alums, the percentage donated might be much higher.

Foundation funding can be expected to play a larger role in university campaigns. After all, university campaigns often encompass a broader array of projects and grant opportunities than any other type of institution might be in a position to offer.

Universities have a greater likelihood of recruiting large numbers of capital campaign volunteers than any other type of institution. However, professional staff plays a major role in cultivating and soliciting prospects. Finally, universities often conduct comprehensive campaigns that include multiple institutions within the university family. These campaigns often include and count: all special facility needs, all annual support contributed to each school of the university during the multiyear campaign and pledge period, and a comprehensive endowment campaign.

Community Colleges

Community colleges have not traditionally invested in alumni relations. Development professionals at community colleges point to the fact that many alums go on to get a four-year degree at a state or private university, and invariably, the former community college student forms a stronger relationship with the university.

But we don't know if this lament is unavoidable. Too few community colleges have made a concerted and consistent effort to create a sense of pride in their graduates and former students. Even the terms "alumnus" and "graduate" may miss the mark. Many students at community colleges attend to acquire an education they can use immediately. Some get associate degrees. Some take courses in subjects that interest them. Some take practical courses such as accounting, drafting, or culinary arts. Some get an affordable liberal arts education. Others receive technical or vocational training that leads to immediate employment.

Suffice to say that community colleges must begin to strengthen their relationships with former students.

Community colleges differ greatly from each other. Some are in rural settings; others are in large cities. Some are funded by the state; others are not. Some have established private support foundations; others have not. Some have a focus on liberal arts. Some have a focus on technical and vocational training. Some seek a balance. For these and many other reasons, each community college campaign is quite unique. Most often the campaigns succeed when corporate or financial institutions in the region form partnerships with the community college. Corporations need well-trained employees. Community colleges have the capability to custom-tailor training programs to the needs of the corporate partner.

Regional leaders responsible for economic development often view the community college as the key to economic growth. Again, each institution must find its natural constituencies and mold the case for support to respond to the aspirations of those who might be expected to support the campaign.

Private Schools

If the school is old enough, alums might play a significant role in the campaign. Otherwise, the board of directors, founders, current parents, and grandparents form the heart of the campaign. Occasionally, it's possible to garner support from local corporations and financial institutions. Some view strong private schools as important to their ability to attract and retain top management. Other decision makers view private schools as important sources of quality education for our nation.

Arts Institutions

Great cities have strong arts and cultural institutions. The season subscribers, the museum members, and the arts constituents form the heart of each organization's support. Arts organizations frequently also have the ability to attract "movers and shakers" to serve on their boards of directors.

So, in any capital or endowment campaign, we would expect at least 15 percent of the funds to come from the board. A more challenging, yet achievable goal, might be 20 percent of the campaign. The board of directors should be composed of people who can solicit the vast majority of the funds needed for a successful capital and endowment campaign. They can approach affluent individuals and corporations that might be expected to support the endeavor.

A charismatic conductor and music director can play a role. A suave museum director can work miracles. Development staff might form strong relationships with community leaders. But, when it's all said and done, for the campaign to succeed, the movers and shakers have to move and shake.

Social Service and Youth Groups

As with most campaigns, the board of directors might be expected to contribute 15 percent of the goal. If the board is obligated under its bylaws to include "clients" and representatives of the constituencies served, the board contributions may not equal 15 percent, but still must be generous relative to the board members' means. Of course, the staff may be encouraged to participate, but the salaries paid to employees of such agencies are generally more modest. Similarly, the constituents cannot be expected to play a significant role. Therefore, the funds must come from affluent individuals living in the community, church groups, corporations with local headquarters, corporations with significant operations in the area, financial institutions, foundations, and others.

If the organization has a long history of service in the area and a well-developed list of supporters, those who have been generous in the past may be expected to play a leadership role in the capital campaign.

As with all capital campaigns, the case for support should avoid "institutional needs" and focus on the people being served. When framing the case for support, also be aware of "compassion fatigue." Some donors are burned out when they hear of chronic social problems. Homelessness, poverty, hunger, the challenges faced by immigrants, and so many other social ills don't always resonate with donors. These supporters and former supporters view the problems as intractable.

Our job is to demonstrate that the organizations we serve are addressing the root causes of these problems, not just the symptoms. We are giving people a hand up, not a handout. The metaphor of teaching a person to fish, rather than giving the person a fish, is well received by donors. Invest in the time needed to refine your institution's plans. Also invest in the time needed to develop a well-crafted case for support.

FINAL REPORTS

If you and your nonprofit organization follow the advice in this book, the campaign will have a victorious conclusion. If, conversely, things do not go as smoothly as expected, you might still expect considerable progress to be made. In either case, it behooves organization leaders to prepare a report outlining the successes and/or challenges. The volunteers and staff members expect no less. Those who read it will share in a sense of accomplishment.

Dennis Stefanacci, ACFRE, one of our nation's leading and most successful fundraisers, contributed the following report. While it was not prepared as a final report to staff and volunteers, it nonetheless contains much of the uplifting language you might expect from such a document. Please pay particular attention to the importance of leadership gifts and the especially well-executed communications plan.

SIDEBAR   DENNIS STEFANACCI, ACFRE

LIFELINES: THE CAMPAIGN
FOR GOOD SAMARITAN AND
ST. MARY'S MEDICAL CENTER

As Intracoastal, the health system's parent organization, prepared to respond to the ever-changing healthcare environment, its goals remained fairly simple: to carry out its stated mission of providing new, innovative programs and services that would immeasurably improve the health of the Palm Beach community from year to year in a friendly responsive way, and above all else, to have as its sole responsibility serving with skill, care, and compassion those in need of its services.

But meeting the challenge was not going to be easy. It would require not only sound fiscal management by the institution, but also an extraordinary philanthropic commitment by the community to help ensure the same quality of care that the community had come to expect from Good Samaritan and St. Mary's Medical Centers.

The resolution? A communitywide major fundraising effort called LIFE-LINES, which represented the theme "for the care of your life" and had as its logo the palm of a hand indicating one's lifeline.

This $27.5 million capital campaign had five major components:

- $12 million to construct a new Cancer Institute at Good Sam

- $10 million to add a wing to St. Mary's to house the Children's Hospital

- $3.5 million to expand both hospitals' heart and stroke programs

- $1 million to develop a trauma pavilion at St. Mary's

- $1 million to underwrite the costs of the campaign, including "carrying costs"—the cost of interest during the pledge payment period—while construction and equipment acquisition was underway

Eight months after the beginning of the quiet phase of the campaign, the campaign was announced at a major donor event at Good Sam with more than 40 percent of the goal committed. Fourteen months later, at Intracoastal's annual Renaissance Ball, guests were surprised with the announcement that the campaign had reached completion with more than $34 million raised, $6.5 million over goal. An extraordinary feat, especially considering the fact that the campaign had taken less than two years to complete.

What made this a successful campaign? Many things contributed, but the following demonstrate what can be accomplished with the right volunteer leadership, an exceptional team, and the cooperation of several architectural firms working together to create a vision for the future that made sense to the community.

SOLID CAMPAIGN PLAN

Although outside campaign counsel was not used in this campaign—a function I served—a solid and well-thought-out campaign plan, including a communications plan, was developed in-house that became this endeavor's blueprint for success.

STAFF

Simultaneously with the development of the campaign plan, the Intracoastal Health Foundation staffed up by adding two individuals to help manage the research/gift recording for the project and to assume some of the responsibilities for the annual fundraising programs so that I, as senior vice president for Institutional Advancement, and the foundation's lead major gifts officer could spend a significant amount of our time on the campaign.

COLLATERALS

While the vision for LIFELINES was based on the demonstrated interests of the community, it became clear early in the planning of the campaign that first-rate collaterals would be required that not only told a compelling story about this effort, but that also were first-rate. While these pieces were expensive, they set the tone for the importance for this endeavor, as well as its impact on the community now and into the future.

COMPREHENSIVE COMMUNICATIONS PLAN

The Palm Beach community is one that thrives on public recognition of significant philanthropic support and social status. Therefore, it was critical for the success of the campaign that all major gifts—that is, gifts of $500,000-plus—be recognized in both the Palm Beach *Daily News* (called the "Shiny Sheet" because the paper used ensures that the ink does not rub off; it is the newspaper exclusively for the residents of Palm Beach), and the *Palm Beach Post,* West Palm Beach's newspaper. Additionally, the two local social magazines—*Palm Beach Illustrated* and *Palm Beach Society*—as well as other social magazines in southeast Florida—*Florida Trends, Boca Raton Magazine,* and *Ocean Drive,* for example—carried ongoing success stories about the campaign.

During the 14 months of the public phase of the campaign, more than 50 stories appeared in these publications, orchestrated by the foundation staff in line with the communications plan, with the purpose of ensuring that gifts were announced on an ongoing basis to keep the excitement and interest in

the successes of the campaign at its highest level. And, finally, as also articulated in the plan, these announcements generated additional gifts that, in
turn, generated future stories.

It is clear that one of the major keys to the extraordinary success of the
LIFELINES campaign was the team's ability to keep the campaign in front of
the public, while setting the kind of philanthropic examples that others
wanted to follow. Had that not been possible the chances are great that the
campaign would have taken much longer to complete.

Number of Gifts Received

There were only about 200 gifts of $10,000 or more for this project. The
largest was $5 million, followed by two at $3 million, and seven at $1 mil-
lion or more; additionally, there were 35 gifts of $100,000 or more. Most
importantly, though, all gifts to the campaign were outright gifts, received
over as long as a five-year period. Clearly, the size of these gifts is an excep-
tion to most campaign gift projections, yet in a place like Palm Beach, the
standard for success.

So what made this campaign different? Why were there so many high-end
gifts to this project? The answer is relatively simple: Snowbirds!

A phenomenon in south Florida is the influx of individuals from the North-
east—primarily New York, Boston, and Philadelphia—who have made the
decision to spend the winter months in south Florida (called the "season"),
particularly in Palm Beach. For the most part, these are people of great
wealth (during season, Palm Beach is considered to have the largest con-
centration of wealth of any city in the nation) who are sophisticated donors.
They are actively involved in their northern communities as major donors,
and are well acquainted with estate planning and capital campaigns. Most
have teams composed of trust officers, accountants, brokers, and tax attorneys who advise them on their gift-giving, and who understand the tax benefits of such philanthropy.

Additionally, these individuals are interested in having the same high
quality of healthcare that they receive in the north, and are willing to support local institutions—like Good Sam and St. Mary's—to ensure that it is
available to them when they need it.

Not surprisingly, then, most of the major gifts to the LIFELINES campaign
came from this segment of the community.

Volunteer Leadership

The key in this campaign was in selecting the campaign leadership. It
became clear early on that it was important to select influential individuals
who were highly respected by the Palm Beach community, who had strong
ties to either Good Sam and/or St. Mary's, and who had never led a major
capital campaign in the community. Careful research resulted in the identifi-

cation of two such individuals—each committed to one of the hospitals—who became the co-chairs of the campaign.

Their appointment brought with it the creation of an extraordinary steering committee, whose members assumed active leadership of the campaign. It was because of this leadership that access was made available to those members of the Palm Beach and West Palm Beach communities who were both interested in, and capable of, making major gifts to the campaign.

PARTICIPATION OF ARCHITECTURAL FIRMS IN THE CAMPAIGN

One of the most unique aspects of LIFELINES was the integration of several architectural firms into the development of the campaign plan that were not only versed in the special construction requirements of any hospital facility, but also understood the fundraising process. Each played a vital role on the team in both designing facilities that "fit" within the financial goals set for the individual projects within the campaign and in designing facilities with named gift opportunities in mind.

They understood that the issues and funding opportunities associated with the Cancer Institute were different from those associated with the Children's Hospital. Those that were integral to the Trauma Pavilion were very different from those that were critical to the expansion of the heart/stroke program, and yet similar because they were directly related to the completion of either/or both of the Cancer Institute and Children's Hospital projects.

These firms provided renderings, illustrations, detailed plans, and budgets to the campaign leadership and staff, which enabled the team to present very comprehensive proposals to potential donors, including the incremental operational costs of such additions. Without their active participation, the campaign would most likely not have been as successful or, at a minimum, would have taken a longer time to complete.

CONCLUSION

In sum, the lesson to be learned in this project, I think, is that every campaign is different, and yet all contain the major components of any campaign. I have been privileged to lead many such campaigns and have learned that nothing replaces solid planning and the development of a team of volunteers, staff, and other interested partners who immediately internalize the project, and as a result, are invested in its success.

In a nutshell, it's a process that takes great patience and perseverance, but as with any process, is designed to garner success. Developing the correct process and fully implementing it can only lead to success. Because, after all, that's what processes are for.

Printed with permission from Dennis Stefanacci, ACFRE.

NEXT STEPS

It has been said before but is worth repeating: *Keep your donors and volunteers involved*. The effort needed to help prospective donors appreciate the value of their investments in your institution is considerable. Once the commitment has been made, value it. Appreciate your donors. Keep them involved.

Consider rereading Chapter 2; consider adopting the "Partnership Model." Drive out the "we/them" mentality. Welcome the "us" and "win/win" attitudes needed to bond with your institution's volunteers and financial supporters. They will be with you with increased annual support. Many will provide generous support for the next capital campaign. And many will remember your nonprofit institution in their wills and estate plans.

Of equal importance is to continue to invest in staff development. Capital campaigns are growth experiences. "What fire doesn't destroy, it hardens." Build on your staff's new-found strength and knowledge. Continue training. Encourage growth. Serve your institution. Serve the profession. And reap the rewards.

Above all, work to assure that your institution remains worthy of support. Board and staff members can become experts in organization behavior. They can learn what makes a nonprofit organization strong. They can build strong institutions with the first-rate facilities needed to address our society's most pressing concerns.

To paraphrase David L. Bradford and Allan R. Cohen in *Managing for Excellence* (John Wiley & Sons, Inc., 1997), by reading this book, you are among an increasing number of leaders who have "dedicated themselves to mastering the new mind-set and skills required to achieve extraordinary performance."

Index

for religious institution campaigns, 241–245
short, 216
Tippng Point, The (Gladwell), 32
top ten gifts, 7, 9, 113, 200
tours of facilities, 107
traditional process of construction, 81, 82, 84, 86–87
training. *See* orientation (training)

unit-price contracts, 86, 253
universities, 267

values, organizational, 7, 59
vendors, 85, 97
victory celebrations, 19–20, 208, 245
videos, 139–141
vision, 31–32, 47, 59
visits, solicitation, 173–184
volunteers, 21–22
    leadership supper for, 243
    numbers needed, 212, 214

place in organizational structure of, 215
as prospective donors, 96
recruitment of, 193–194, 197–198, 214–215
roles of, 245–247
solicitation by, 19, 103, 106, 171–190

warranty inspection, eleven-month, 76
warranty inspections, 76
wayfinding, 60
wealth
    of board of directors, 40
    of church members, 238
    of prospective donors, 97
Weinstein, Stanley, 24, 98, 112, 265
wills and estates, 210, 212

youth organizations, 2, 176, 268–269

CPSIA information can be obtained at www.ICGtesting.com

262790BV00007BB/1/P